F. Scott, Ernest and Me

F. SCOTT, ERNEST AND ME

Tony Davis

BANTAM
SYDNEY AUCKLAND TORONTO NEW YORK LONDON

To Carolyn

F. SCOTT, ERNEST AND ME
A BANTAM BOOK

First published in Australia and New Zealand in 2007
by Bantam

National Library of Australia
Cataloguing-in-Publication Entry

Davis, Tony.
F. Scott, Ernest and me.

ISBN 978 186325 554 7.

1. Davis, Tony. 2. Authors, Australian – France – Paris – Biography.
I. Title.

A823.3

Transworld Publishers,
a division of Random House Australia Pty Ltd
20 Alfred Street, Milsons Point, NSW 2061
www.randomhouse.com.au

Random House New Zealand Limited
18 Poland Road, Glenfield, Auckland

Transworld Publishers,
a division of The Random House Group Ltd
61–63 Uxbridge Road, Ealing, London W5 5SA

Random House Inc
1745 Broadway, New York, New York 10036

Cover and internal design by saso content & design
Cover photograph courtesy Lonely Planet Images
Typeset in 11/15 pt Palatino Light by Post Pre-press Group, Australia
Printed and bound by Griffin Press, South Australia

10 9 8 7 6 5 4 3 2 1

Contents

It was a colossal tome and faulty from start to finish . . .
Everybody I showed it to said it was terrible . . .
I was attempting at the start what a man of genius
would have undertaken only at the end.
I wanted to say the last word at the beginning.

Henry Miller describes his first book
in *Tropic of Capricorn* (1939)

PROLOGUE

THE GREAT WORK

THE UNPUBLISHED NOVELIST ARRIVED in Paris in April 1995, fully aware that if he was going to be one of the giants of twentieth-century literature, he didn't have much time.

Fortunately, he wasn't approaching it from a standing start. He'd had a poem published in an anthology only a decade or so earlier and, more recently, a children's book rejected by a major publisher with a personally written note rather than a form letter.

Yet somehow it wasn't enough. He needed to write a novel. Not just a novel, but a magnum opus. He needed to soar high above the clouds. So after years of procrastination, he sold the business that was keeping him from his real ambition and nervously awarded himself an arts grant.

In the service of an outrageous cliché, he moved to the world's premier city of art and literature to look for a down-and-out garret (ideally with a view of several towers, arches, domes and flying buttresses) in the city where Ernest Hemingway found his true voice, F. Scott Fitzgerald worked on Tender is the Night, *Eric Blair transformed into George Orwell and Henry Miller starved while creating the first of his stunning* Tropic *novels.*

There, inspired by the city and its history, and with a monumental, success-guaranteed literary idea already swelling inside his head, this would-be man of letters began the task of producing something that would outlive himself, the garret, the arches, the domes, the flying buttresses and maybe the entire city itself. It was going to be a tour de force, a pièce de résistance, *a work of greatness. A Great Work.*

Simple, really.

✣✣✣

Yes, I admit it. I should have arrived ill, broke and with a dodgy visa, having jumped the train to Dover and stowed away on the Calais ferry. I should have spent my last few banknotes on a whore and a bottle of low-grade alcohol, comfortable in the knowledge I could sleep under the massive durmast oaks of Paris's Bois de Boulogne parklands until I met a fiery Latin girl who looked like Beatrice Dalle and never wore a stitch inside her chaotic, bay-windowed apartment located among the strip joints and bordellos of Pigalle. As a true artist I would have known instinctively that, when not flinging plates or making passionate *amour*, such a girl would leave me in peace to bash away on the beaten-up Remington portable which, apart from the harmonica salvaged from my previous drug-and-alcohol-fuelled relationship, was the only thing I hadn't hocked.

Alas, it was not the case. I had flown into Paris with a tightly packed suitcase, a cash-card, a near-new laptop computer and no harmonica. I was going to stay at a friend's flat, and an entirely comfortable one at that. With flowers in window boxes, polished wooden floors, and one of those ornate lifts modelled on a wickerwork picnic basket. Near Place de la Bastille, in fact, in the increasingly trendy eastern part of the city.

Still, mine wasn't entirely a trip to the moon on gossamer wings. I'd arrived via America, Russia and Britain, still suffering the effects of what was supposed to be a minor operation. After years of pretending my four wisdom teeth were not severely impacted, I'd had them removed *en bloc* during that tiny gap between finishing work and leaving for overseas. My swollen, infected, smashed-up mouth wouldn't open more than a centimetre for the first month and it was to be three long months before it stopped aching. Okay, I couldn't boast starvation, syphilis or a dependency on a dangerous and illegal substance. But I had a sore mouth, a burning desire to write and I was determined to produce great art in the greatest city in the world.

It wasn't my first trip to Paris, nor the first time I had stayed with Sandrine. I had known her since she had flatted with a friend of mine in Sydney many years earlier.

'Even the French laugh about how much the French complain when they go to other countries,' Sandrine once told me. 'They like France, and fear that anywhere else will be less like France than France is.' Despite this national tendency, Sandrine had maintained a sight-unseen obsession with Australia since her teenage years, and had been determined to spend at least a year there when she finished her engineering degree. On arrival she'd completed the big lap of the country then settled in Tempe, south of Sydney's centre. Sandrine hung out with our circle, introducing us to *foie gras* and French pop music, both courtesy of her sister Fabienne, who would regularly send packages stuffed with tins of incomparable goose liver paté and CDs of very comparable French songs.

When I arrived in Paris to write my novel there was much air kissing for old time's sake (one kiss on each side in the capital, but down south it can be as many as four kisses when you meet a friend or close acquaintance).

'*Bonjour* Tony, *ça va*?'

'*Ça va*!' I replied, expressing my delight to have finally arrived and pretty well exhausting my stock of French conversation. With talk switching straight back into English, there was more *foie gras* (the standard extravagance for special occasions), a glass of Champagne – real Champagne – and the relaying of lists of dinners and social encounters that had been organised in my honour.

'*Santé*,' Sandrine said, lifting her glass as her parents arrived to join in the welcoming party. On cue, the afternoon sun streamed into the large third-floor apartment. 'It is wonderful to see you here and – *oh-la-la* – there are so many exciting things happening in Paris at the moment.'

I'd forgotten how Sandrine said *oh-la-la* when she became excited. Until I met her, I'd assumed the expression was used only by second-rate English actors playing Frenchmen in BBC television comedies of the 1970s. I had also forgotten how tall and thin Sandrine was, despite her love of rich food, how penetrating her green eyes were and how cheerful and unflustered she always seemed to be. It wasn't just her light-coloured hair that made Sandrine the antithesis of the popular image of a fiery, passionate Latin. I had never seen her lose her temper, speak ill of anyone, fail to avoid an argument or take anything other than a positive outlook on any situation. I had often thought that Sandrine could, with a clear conscience, cast the first stone.

Now she was to be my translator, cultural interpreter and real estate advisor. It was a huge head start.

✣ ✣ ✣

SO THERE I WAS, within a day of arrival, sitting in a large apartment with two French balconies (which is to say two balconies too small to walk onto), looking down at the bustle and commotion of the Avenue Parmentier as the traffic raced toward République and Place Léon Bloom. I fired up my laptop, I smiled, I munched on my baguette, procured from the magnificent *boulangerie* on the corner. I read some more of the notes I had scrawled in the past few weeks of travelling. I banged some words into the laptop and made another cup of coffee.

Sandrine was at work. She was a manager in an insurance office. She wore clothes around the house and was as sensible and well-balanced as anyone who is the subject of a French arthouse film isn't. In my defence, George Orwell had a favourite aunt living in Paris who would slip him a handful of francs whenever the going was too tough, something the Brit pointedly failed to mention in *Down and Out in Paris and London*. And Hemingway might have thumped on about extreme poverty in his Paris memoir *A Moveable Feast*, but even by his own account he did most of his writing while sipping red wine in fashionable Left Bank cafés.

Nobody, it seemed, went to Paris to tell the truth, but I was going to change that.

The horns honked outside, the motorcycles roared, the cars squealed their tyres. People on the street yelled *blehr blehr blehr* and produced deep guttural Rs straight from the Edith Piaf songbook. A gentle breeze blew in through the open shutters. I was living out the lyrics of the song 'The Last Time I Saw Paris'. I heard laughter in every street café. My heart was warm and gay. Well, happy. The last time I saw Paris . . . was the last time I looked up from my screen. All I had to do to complete the picture was to create a work of genius, and that was already underway with all the ease and optimism that rushes in at the start of any new project.

✣✣✣

WITH MY BUSINESS sold and the madness of commerce receding, I wasn't only going to write a grand-scale novel, I was going to slowly and thoroughly read one. *The* one. After all, getting my wisdom teeth out wasn't the only scary thing I'd been putting off since my late teens. I had also avoided James Joyce's *Ulysses*.

Ulysses was the book so many had said was the greatest ever written. Joyce had spent the best part of eight years working on it, all the time battling iritis and other horrendously painful eye problems and the knowledge that his book's frankness would likely render it unpublishable. The least I could do in return was to spend a few weeks, or a few months if necessary, digesting it. I had carried the 933-page Paladin edition halfway around the world and hadn't yet quite got so far as opening it, but the moment was nigh.

As for my own book, I already knew what it was to be called and what it would be about. The opening chapter had almost fully formed in my head during my travels. I also had a pile of foolscap pages, napkins, bus tickets and hotel notepads covered with sentences, ideas, chapter titles, snatches of conversation and other things I had built up over the previous year. I was possessed of a fearsome resolve not to write just any novel. I was going to capture the warmth and distinctive Australianness of the two families that Tim Winton so beautifully portrayed in *Cloudstreet,* the descriptive powers Peter Carey achieved with the relationship between the stern father and wayward son in *Oscar and Lucinda* and the emotional intensity of George Johnston's *Clean Straw For Nothing,* where a gifted, lucky couple are parachuted into paradise but still manage to tear themselves to pieces. I was also going to inject the clarity, reason and honesty of the essays of George Orwell (hidden aunt notwithstanding), the sharpness and acidity of Joseph Heller's *Catch-22,* and the grandeur and profundity of, well, *Ulysses* I supposed, though I'd have to get back to you on that one.

It couldn't be too hard. I was sure I knew what I wanted to say, I had plenty of experience putting words together and, for the first time ever, I had sufficient time and funds set aside. I needed just 1000 words a day and, in my years as a journalist, I had regularly written a great deal more than that. This would give me a book in three or four months. Even allowing for a few problems and diversions, I could beat Joyce by seven and a half years, then have a few months up my sleeve to absorb every morsel of the French capital before my money ran out.

I also had to master the French language, of course, but that would take only three months. I knew because it said so on my box of self-instruction tapes.

1

A Place Doubly Blessed

The Old Court House, long since judged too small for its original function, had always been much more than a standard issue, single-storey government building. Its imposing form was realised in richly hued, locally quarried sandstone, the roof tiles were from Marseilles, the marble highlights from Florence, the portico copied from the Four Courts building in Dublin.

It was in the paved courtyard of the Old Court House, at the centre of today's forest of Coca-Cola umbrellas and small-talking lunchers, that the first shooting took place. It was once said that every resident remembered where he or she was when the news rang out. But that was a very long time ago.

What of today's lip-studded, notch-haired youngsters who hang around the noisy mouth of High Street Megazone? Do they realise that this was once among the richest and most progressive places on earth? That the remnants of grandeur that surround them are only an insinuation of former glories, because the soldiers dismantled many of the most significant buildings and took them away, brick by brick?

Do they know or care that the inhabitants once

proudly identified themselves as Undermanners or Baymen and never Australians? That thirty kilometres from the Town Hall, an ornate glass and iron-lace customs building once carried the legend: 'You are now entering the Independent City-State of Undermoon Bay'? That today's grating town slogans could be rightfully replaced with 'Site of the Great Experiment'?

The answer is a resounding no. Yet there are reasons no-one shouts too loudly about those mad, hectic, exciting, extraordinary and impossibly wealthy times. Fascinating reasons . . .

❖❖❖

THERE WAS A BOISTEROUSNESS in the Paris air as I typed the last few paragraphs of my scene-setting introduction to *Undermoon Bay*. It concerned a forthcoming election to choose the fifth president of France's Fifth Republic. In the left corner was the Socialiste candidate Lionel Jospin, who looked and sounded like a retired primary school teacher nominating himself as treasurer for the parish tennis association. In the right corner was Jacques Chirac. He was regal-looking, booming and arrogant, though he was also a de Gaullist so it's very possible that some or all of these adjectives are redundant.

Chirac, the clear favourite, was determined to end fourteen years of Socialiste government. He was playing up to *la Grandeur de France*, the long-held Gallic belief that France has a unique destiny, that it sits at the very pinnacle of civilisation and has a right to lead. Chirac talked of a renewed, more powerful military. His party was even refusing to rule out a return to nuclear testing in the Pacific

Ocean. 'This is a decision I will leave to the experts in the armed forces,' Monsieur Chirac said in the apparent belief that people within the armed forces, when given the choice between blowing up something and not blowing up something, would engage in deep contemplation and reach a rational decision.

Being France, the election had included Trotskyites and other leftist throwbacks, plus Jean-Marie Le Pen, whose Front National party had garnered 4.6 million votes in the earlier round of the election by playing to fears about black immigration and waving around a banner depicting Joan of Arc. Now it was just down to two: Jospin and Chirac would fight a winner-take-all presidential finale after May Day.

'May Day?' I said to Sandrine. 'Didn't that go out with communism?'

'Not in France,' she replied with a mixture of amusement and mild national shame. 'May Day is still big and so are the communists.'

She said you needed a licence to hold a demonstration, or *manifestation*, but everybody seemed to be issued with one. And thanks to May Day, it took just a few days for me to see my first big Paris *manif*.

I walked down rue Oberkampf, its footpath stuffed with pots of flowers and trestles covered with cheeses, its air filled with the aroma of freshly baked bread and car fumes and tobacco smoke and more tobacco smoke and more car fumes and freshly cooked turkey and seafood on huge trays being wheeled out of open-fronted shops. And I stood alone at the side of Boulevard Voltaire near the large, Gothic-looking Saint-Ambroise church, barraged by chants I couldn't understand, banners I couldn't read (despite some of them being three lanes wide) and extremist red impulses that I couldn't quite fathom. I watched the unionists, the homosexual lobbies, the feminists, the unemployed, *les sans papiers* (foreigners without visas or residency) and leftists of every splinter chanting as they walked down the tree-lined boulevard between the huge monuments at Place de la République and Place de la Nation.

Everybody from ferals to well-dressed professionals and hard-hatted construction workers flowed past in the moving sea of balloons, drums, placards, badges, painted hammers and sickles, and flags in a hundred shades of *rouge*. I was surrounded by the magnificent rows of apartment buildings with long balconies and wrought iron balustrades that line Boulevard Voltaire, and I was happily reflecting that it wasn't my job to agree or disagree with what anyone had to say, or fight to the death to defend their right to say it.

My eyes followed a pretty young woman with dark and expensively coiffured hair as she walked with one fist in the air. '*Blehr, blehr, blehr,*' she chanted forcefully between more restrained snippets of conversation into the mobile phone she was pushing into her ear with the other hand. Perhaps she considered that smashing the system and launching class war is something you should advocate at least one day a year, as long as you continue to look good and don't miss any office gossip.

The surrounding architecture was classic *Belle Époque*, from the much romanticised 'beautiful period' before a couple of world wars knocked the stuffing out of France. And even the buildings' sandy grey colouring looked magnificent in the early spring sun. Paris was again revealing itself as a world of soft, almost dirty colours, where every awning, shop window, dress, park, flower, bus or news-stand looked so much brighter and more interesting by contrast. While the rest of the world was working with straight Fujicolor, the Parisians were using a much softer and more sophisticated palette. And nothing stood out against these muted tones like several hundred bright red hammer-and-sickle flags.

Sandrine had assured me any rightist protesters would be kept separate from the main throng by the endless rows of *flics* (standard police) and *CRS* (riot police). But the huge presence of authority across the city didn't stop some of Jean-Marie Le Pen's skinhead supporters celebrating May Day by throwing a twenty-nine-year-old Moroccan man into the Seine.

'It is unfortunate that he drowned,' Le Pen said the next day. 'But in a city of ten million, random acts happen.'

There was an election in six days. It was depressing, it was thrilling, it was mystifying but it was merely a background rumble. After all, I was there to write a book, and I needed to get properly underway.

✣✣✣

THE INTRODUCTION TO *UNDERMOON Bay* was a modern perspective on a washed-up town with a past that was impressive and shameful in equal measure. The story would then jump back a little over 200 years to the time the fourteen ships in Australia's First Fleet unexpectedly broke into two groups and formed rival colonies at Sydney Cove, New South Wales, and Foundation Point, Undermoon Bay.

My introduction explained how Undermoon Bay and its

hinterland – the city-state that refused to federate with the six other Australian states in 1901 – was graced with such an abundance of natural riches and astonishing beauty that it was popularly known as 'a place doubly blessed'. According to my plan, the text would concern greed and corruption, politics, false idols, architectural hubris, the evils of marketing, the perils of parenthood, the failure of relationships, international trade, the hijacking of sport by big business, hypocrisy, revenge, the use of foreign aid for self-enrichment and the role of class in a classless society. And with all that covered, I could think about chapter two.

But nothing much more was going to happen unless I found a place of my own. If I couldn't crash with Betty Blue or her identical twin in a state of permanent, airborne-plate-charged creative tension, I had to at least move beyond the reach of a kind, gentle, sensible friend who couldn't understand why I wasn't putting up my feet and enjoying her extraordinary cooking, limitless hospitality and the delights of the finest city that earthlings have devised.

'I have worked out an itinerary,' Sandrine had said. 'This is your first proper stay in Paris and there is so much you must do before you become too involved with your book. And of course it is spring and it is the nicest time. Every park is filled with flowers in bloom and everything is, we say, *en fête*.'

Sandrine didn't understand that Paris could wait. My literary mission could not. I needed a place of my own. And quickly.

Apartment hunting wasn't helped by my impatience to start writing something beyond the introduction to

Undermoon Bay, nor by the fact the Australian dollar was falling like it had just been shot. Nor, indeed, by the realisation, after a visit to an *agence immobilière* or two, that even when located in an office in a huge, turreted seventeenth-century building and possessed of an accent that would very likely make women melt, a real estate agent is still a real estate agent. The third agent I saw was a man named Stéphane. He was *un ami* of *un ami* of Sandrine's and his special selling technique was to sit you in his office – seventeenth-century, *avec* turrets – and play videos of the apartments he was letting.

'This *appartement* you will find very interesting,' Stéphane said, in English, when each one came on the screen. I quickly learned that 'very interesting' didn't mean 'filled with things that will ignite your curiosity'. It meant cheap, except the French are so coy about discussing money they have no word or phrase for cheap. The closest they get is *pas cher*, which means 'not expensive'. Or *bon marché*, which is even less precise. Or *tres intéressant*, which is vaguer still. Talking turkey is not something the French generally like doing.

Sandrine's father, the softly spoken, grey-haired Gilbert, kindly offered to drive me to what seemed the best of Stéphane's apartments. He did so with all the wild, horn-honking, tyre-squealing enthusiasm even the meekest Parisian puts into motoring. In the 14th *arrondissement*, only a few hundred metres from the Montparnasse cemetery, which houses the tombs of Jean-Paul Sartre and Simone de Beauvoir, I sat in the back of a much-dented Renault trying to work why Sandrine's father was hopping out of the car at a set of traffic lights while the vehicle behind beeped furiously. The French call it parking. Sandrine also leapt out and I followed.

Having driven so fast to get there, it was apparently important that we slowly stroll to a café for a leisurely coffee before knocking on the door of the first apartment. The façade and streetscape had featured strongly on the videotape, and they were impressive. A well-dressed man answered a suitably formidable door to what appeared to be a beautiful building. There was an exchange in French, after which he led us down a long hallway that wended around storage bays to what was itself no more than a modified storage bay.

'It is a very nice part of Paris,' Sandrine said to me, quietly. 'But you wouldn't want a fire here.'

'It is on the ground floor. It is not a problem,' the man responded in fractured English, replicating Sandrine's stage whisper. 'This is very central. The *métro* is just over zer.'

Sandrine took photos. Gilbert, who had not spoken, took one slow look around the tiny, dark room with its peeling paint and threadbare, bug-infested carpet. He then produced that magnificent Gallic expression that involves concertinaing the nose, pouting the lips and forcing the air out so that it makes a farting noise.

The use of videos, Stéphane had boasted, was 'at ze leading edge'. But it took just a few apartments to show it was actually the *mis*leading edge. On the television screen you could never see the leaking plumbing or home-made electrical arrangements, nor could you sense the dampness or dreariness, or guess that the apartment's one frosted-glass window didn't open. And if it did, you wouldn't want to see or smell what was on the other side.

It was hard to believe that such an affluent city had so much substandard accommodation – and that it was all being offered to me. Furthermore, Stéphane's apartments were *very interesting* only in a Parisian context. The price of a pleasant, even luxurious, freestanding house in Sydney seemed to equal one small room filled with junk furniture in the roof cavity of a large building in Paris. If I wanted two rooms, and didn't mind being in the basement and looking up onto a garbage bin storage area, Stéphane could secure me a place smack-bang in the centre of the Les Halles red-light district (the terms *smack* and *bang* being entirely appropriate).

'I'm not feeling good about this,' I whispered to Sandrine as we arrived at another run-down building in a narrow, charmless street.

'Don't worry,' she replied, green eyes flashing. 'The right apartment is here in this city somewhere. The front doesn't matter, it is inside that counts.'

What was inside this time was a small, cold, one-bedroom dwelling with the open shower recess in the kitchen, next to the sink. '*Oh-la-la*,' said Sandrine. I practised concertinaing the nose, pouting the lips and forcing the air out to make a farting sound. I had no wish to cook while showering, or shower while cooking. What I wanted was simple: *un pigeonnier*, a small but comfortable attic with ventilation and a view. But after visiting another two agents on my own, I was no closer to finding it. I was also thoroughly depressed, though at least a little wiser.

Paris real estate is all about two things: the square metres and the *arrondissement*. Square metres are those, you guessed it, 100-centimetre-long, four-sided things that provide an endless opportunity for fudging by agents. I became convinced some agents measured the square metres from the outside of the walls or, like a television screen, from the bottom left-hand corner to the top right.

The *arrondissement* is the district. There are twenty of them curling around Paris from the 1st, taking in the Jardin des Tuileries and Place Vendôme, to the 20th, on the eastern edge of the city with the massive Père Lachaise cemetery almost dividing it in two. Each *arrondissement* is its own little self-contained world, with a unique flavour, but unmistakably Paris. And telling someone which *arrondissement* you live in immediately identifies you, much as an accent does – or once did – in London. There are thousands of subtle nuances connected with each *arrondissement* but, in broad terms, west and south were posh, the north and east were generally not.

The outer rim of this snail shell of *arrondissements* is the huge ring-road known as the Boulevard Périphérique. The land beyond the Périphérique may be as close as 2.5 kilometres from the Eiffel Tower or Montmartre's Basilica of the Sacré-Coeur, and for the most part it is vastly cheaper to rent. But it simply isn't Paris. It's the *banlieue*, or suburban belt. No-one could be expected to produce art there.

The weather was supposed to be warming but spring soon turned windy and cold. Still, climbing out of bed every morning had an air of unreality about it. I wanted to soak up every bit of Paris: every smell, sound and view. A few days after arriving I was walking down the street to buy some milk and a baguette. The background music was a thousand car tyres rolling, a million horns being beeped, cranes hoisting skips into the air outside scaffolded buildings and letting them come crashing down, trucks reversing, the whole city hissing and buzzing with energy.

It all simply filled me with awe. I felt I should be in a striped T-shirt and beret, humming Maurice Chevalier. I had left my old world behind. I didn't have to go in to work, there would be no petty rivalries or distractions or office politics, I had the rest of the year to do exactly what I wanted to do. I jumped onto a *métro* carriage to find a jazz trio – saxophone, double bass and drums – playing Dixieland and Hollywood film songs. On another day, one end of the carriage was screened off with black crepe. To the accompaniment of a ghettoblaster, a busking puppeteer brought to life a diva flamboyantly waving a handkerchief as she sang the big aria from *Carmen*.

For the rest of the year, at the very least, the city would be all mine. I couldn't help but write long lists of the things I adored or, at the very least, found intriguing or compelling. Just in case, perhaps, I ever wrote about Paris. Not that I was ever going to write about Paris. Unbending fate required me to record the far more interesting and important happenings in Undermoon Bay. Anyway, what more needed to be written about Paris? Writing a book about Paris is almost as big a cliché as writing a book *in* Paris.

✣✣✣

The election posters that competed for attention offered a simple choice: vote RPR (Chirac) or Socialiste (Jospin). I realised something about living in a foreign country, shameful though it might be. When you own no property, earn no wage, pay no income tax and have no investment in the immediate local future, the lack of moral responsibility is a delight. If a car alarm sounded out on the street, or I heard glass shatter, I knew it had nothing to do with me. If the police were taking bribes or beating up those they had arrested, that was a dreadful thing, but it was an issue for the people around me. It was no responsibility of mine. And if the French decided to elect as their next president Jacques Chirac, with his ridiculous statements about nuclear tests, or the head of the parish tennis association, Lionel Jospin . . . well, why was that a concern of mine?

I felt only bemusement when Jean-Marie Le Pen said the French were misguided to be proud of their soccer team because it was largely made up of blacks and Arabs. I didn't need to be angry. An artist is above that mundane plane of existence.

Through a combination of television news I could scarcely understand and the *International Herald Tribune* that I bought once every few days, I learned that the latest huge *manif* was because the outgoing president, François Mitterrand, had visited the site near Pont du Carrousel where skinheads had thrown the unfortunate Moroccan into the Seine. Thousands turned up in a display of support. A small number also turned up to jeer.

On election evening I was eating pasta and talking to Sandrine. The windows were wide open. 'Les Guignols', the political puppet show that nearly everyone in France watched, was on the television.

'Who the French choose for president will be a mystery until the final moment,' Sandrine explained, as she filled our wineglasses. 'It is not like America where you are allowed to have exit polling or progress reports. We don't know anything until everything is added up. Then, on the dot of 8 p.m. each time, all the television and radio stations announce the result.'

We looked up at one minute to the hour and waited. A jack-in-the-box filled the screen. Sixty seconds later it sprang open and a rubber caricature of Jacques Chirac's Easter Island face burst out. A massive noise erupted from almost every building around us. It was more cheer than sigh, but there was a bit of both.

'Ah, Chirac,' said Sandrine. She was inscrutable. It may have been a good thing, it may have been bad. Either way, Chirac, a long-time mayor of Paris, was the new president of France on his third attempt. Chirac had been nicknamed Chameleon Bonaparte for his ability to fluidly change his opinions to meet the popular tide – and to be just as bombastic and dogmatic about his reversed view. The television soon showed what looked like hundreds of thousands of people cramming the bottom end of the Avenue des Champs Elysées and Place de la Concorde, adjacent to the Tuileries. They were screaming Chirac's name and partying like there was no tomorrow.

In fact, there was a tomorrow, a very big tomorrow. It was May 8, the fiftieth anniversary of the defeat of Germany in World War II. There would be marching and pageantry, more dancing in the streets and one last official appearance of the outgoing president.

I watched the parade on the television. François Mitterrand slowly and painfully descended from a French military vehicle, saluted the troops, received a folded flag and watched a rather bizarre display of military men riding motorcycles in intricate patterns.

Mitterrand, I had read, was a youth with far-right

leanings. He worked for the collaborationalist Vichy government during World War II but eventually joined the Resistance. He reinvented himself as a socialist, made it to the top, nationalised everything, placed punitive taxes on the rich, handed the ensuing bounty to the poor and then decided France couldn't afford it. Mitterrand then became a champion of the free market. Through all this, he and his supporters were able to pretend it was *socialisme* as normal. It worked too, as Mitterrand's two full terms of seven years added up to the longest presidency in French history. In contrast, Charles de Gaulle's double term ended early; in 1969 the General had threatened to tender his resignation after eleven years as president if voters didn't approve his constitutional referendum. The people called his bluff and de Gaulle had to go through with it, no doubt mumbling 'bug*geur*', as he walked out the door of the Elysée Palace for the last time.

Now Mitterrand looked horribly pale and frail – he had lied to the French people about his health (and various other things) for years, it later emerged – and he clearly wasn't long for this world. There was respectful cheering and clapping for the wounded political soldier, mixed with the shouting, cheering and celebrating of several hundred thousand deliriously happy Frenchmen and women. I wondered when these people did any work. But of far more concern was my book. Or to be more accurate, my books: *Undermoon Bay* and *Ulysses*.

2

Washing in the Shadow of Greatness

The first call today is a small printing works. It operates from a rented shack – premises would be too grand a word – on the unnamed road running south from Black's Point. The owner is Kingsley M. Baker, a bloated man in his late forties whose single tool of trade is a relatively modern but extremely battered 'one-strike' French printing press. This two-metre-tall wood-and-steel contraption found its way out of revolutionary Paris in the 1790s, ending up in the northern English city of Liverpool. It was badly damaged in a fire in 1808 and the only solution was to repaint it and ship it to the new prison colony. Junk for the colonials. Stealing from thieves.

Baker will often reword your sentences because he doesn't possess a sufficient stock of metal letterblocks to make up a long and complicated page. He has only one font – pica – and some customers receive a mixture of italic and roman lettering. Several of Mr Baker's vowel blocks have accents or little dots sitting above. But what can you expect so far from the real world?

The appearance of Kingsley M. Baker is marked by the most elaborate patterns of facial hair. His eccentric habits go beyond noisily chewing tobacco and – at the oddest moments – polishing a large silver fob watch on his bushy sidelevers. They include walking up to gum trees, putting a hand on each side and slowly caressing the trunk. This forms part of his earnest attempt to come to terms with this harsh place, this prison that seems worse than any other, even for free settlers.

❖❖❖

Commencing a novel is exciting. I should know, I've started many. The first may have lacked even a title. It concerned a wealthy businessman who learned he was going to die and went on a wild spending spree. He divested himself of all his money just in time to learn – and maybe you're way ahead of me here – that he had been misdiagnosed and was in perfect health the whole time.

Okay, nobody was going to accuse me of flying too close to the sun. I took the idea from a television show someone had told me about. So the novel was unoriginal as well as unfinished and quite a few other uns too. But I was only nine. I don't remember much else but I do remember the opening scene in which the main character (and perhaps the only character) was standing in his office looking at a graph and working out the latest movements in the price, or perhaps production, of coal. I remember thinking at the time how sophisticated this was; examining a coal chart was exactly the sort of thing a successful businessman would do in the hours before being told he had a dicky ticker.

If and when I was diagnosed with a fatal disease, the nine-year-old version of me had already worked out what he would do. He intended to set a new world record by jumping a motorcycle over a row of parked cars. The mark was eighteen (the buses came later) and was held by a man with the unlikely name of Evel Knievel. Even more unlikely, perhaps, was that this feat was considered important in my life, and indeed in the Western world, at that time. And with a fatal illness and nothing to lose, why wouldn't you try to jump nineteen or twenty cars on a motorcycle?

The fascination with all things two-wheeled inspired my one other primary school novel. It was about a motorcycle racer who was on the cusp of world-circuit domination. There were many improvements in this later work. Firstly, the clever plot twist: the book's hero didn't win the world championship, which was the only obvious denouement when I had started writing. Instead, I used my god-like authorial powers to smash him up in a spectacularly diabolical accident. Resigned to never being champion, the rider went on to run a race team in the hope he could pass on to others the success that had eluded him. Grown-up plot or what?

This book had realism born of research. The engine specifications of the motorcycles were included along with accurate top speeds, and on a separate piece of paper I had assembled an extensive list of human bones, so their subsequent breaking could be recorded within the narrative. But the real highlight, as I remember it, was the cover. I drew it with Texta colours and laminated it with clear contact, perhaps hoping to create the sort of bookshop appeal that would see it in a display bin at the front of the store. But the readership proved disappointing. It was just my father and one classmate, Peter.

'It's quite good,' I remember Peter saying, 'for a book

about motorcycle racing.' It was better than 'rubbish' but it wasn't exactly Cyril Connolly on Hemingway's *The Old Man and the Sea*: 'No page . . . could have been done better or differently.'

My father was his usual encouraging self but added, as always, 'You must try to write as clearly as you can. No-one should ever have to read a sentence twice to know what it means.' Neither of my brothers was sufficiently captured by the book's shiny cover to show any interest in the contents. This was a career-defining failure; indeed it led to a complete change of direction. I decided I should be a philosopher instead, basing this on the notion that books were very long and hard (my motorcycle novel was upwards of fifteen handwritten pages). Philosophers, however, had to write only short sentences to fill the bottom line of each page of those flip-over desk calendars.

I started to write deep and meaningful self-contained sentences, but realised that even these became pretty difficult after you'd done six or seven. 'The rarest thing is common sense' is one that comes to mind. It was inspired by Sister Clare, the 180-year-old nun who taught me in Fourth Class and was continually telling me I didn't have any. She also told me I was a 'bold, brazen article' and 'would never be a scholar'. The latter remark didn't fill me with dread, since I didn't know what a scholar was, other than someone who, presumably, wasn't bold, brazen and article-like. Common sense told Sister Clare that I deserved to be regularly hit across the legs with a leather strap in front of the whole class. I can't remember any of my other philosophical musings, but they could well have been along the lines of 'The eighteenth car is always the most difficult to clear.'

Now there would be nothing so banal. I had maturity on my side and Paris to inspire me. Surrounded by excellence – everything I saw screamed it – I couldn't help but strive for it. Nothing second-rate could possibly be produced in Paris. Surely. But what was the over-arching theme this time? Childhood is the usual place to go for first novel inspiration and, certainly, my strongest memory of that time is of constant hunger. In keeping with romantic artistic notions, I'd love to say that this was because my family was desperately poor, the war was grinding on and plague had already consumed most of the village. But I was hungry simply because no matter how much I jammed in my mouth, it never quite filled me. I was a kid who loved eating and had a metabolism that ate breakfast, lunch and dinner for breakfast. No quantity of calories would add bulk to my skeletal frame.

When I wasn't eating or building fanciful mechanical creations in the shed (then tearing the skin off my arms and legs by smashing them), I had a pen in my hand. I never questioned it, it seemed the thing to do. My father was a journalist. My father's father was a journalist and his father in turn was . . . a Welsh coalminer. But if he'd had the money to buy a typewriter, things might have been different. And from the very first, doing things on paper – stringing words together and illustrating them – seemed effortless. Or if not effortless, then certainly less effort*ful* than most other things considered by grown-ups to be worthwhile. Like maths homework.

✣✣✣

'WHAT ABOUT TRYING THE *FUSAC*,' Sandrine brightly suggested when I trudged back to Avenue Parmentier after another depressing round of apartment inspections.

'Sounds like some sort of explosive,' I replied. 'What a good idea.'

FUSAC, it turned out, was an acronym for *France–USA Contact*. It was an English-language magazine that mixed Parisian property classifieds with advertisements where communists, Christian fundamentalists and Scientologists piled on incentives for lonely people to come on board, 'artistic' photographers offered part-time work to young females (no experience necessary), and handsome vegetarian masochists sought non-smoking dominatrixes for conversation and possibly more.

There it was, in the first copy of *FUSAC* I picked up: a *chambre de bonne*, or maid's quarters, in the roof of a small block tucked behind the Arc de Triomphe. Available immediately.

'The price includes parking,' explained Alberto, the Italian-born landlord who lived in the same building in one of the large non-maid's quarters downstairs.

'Where?' I asked, purely out of academic interest.

'On the street outside.'

The apartment at number 20 rue le Sueur was forty-five square metres, made up of two small rooms. It was, I later learned, opposite the most notorious serial-killing site in France. The parking was of course impossible, the street madly crowded with cars, delivery vans, mopeds and those strange black French bicycles with the little petrol engines hanging over the front wheel. As I didn't have a car, it was hardly a problem. Most importantly, the apartment was sunny and clean and cheerful. I signed up immediately and turned up with my bags at the nearby *métro* Argentine a few hours later.

Despite a monthly rent that was comparatively *pas cher* and *bon marché*, the apartment was in the 16th, which is held to be a rich, boring, stuffy *arrondissement*. It didn't quite match the down and out in Paris brief, and living in a complete dump in one of the seediest and most dangerous areas of Paris certainly would have sounded better when I came to pen a career retrospective. Then again, F. Scott and Zelda Fitzgerald had lived close by in the even ritzier rue de Tilsitt, just after the launch of *The Great Gatsby*. Four years later, they lived even closer at 10 rue Pergolese. It was there that F. Scott drank heavily as he struggled with *Tender is the Night*, and the increasingly unstable Zelda practised ballet around the clock with an intensity that brought the first of many breakdowns.

Soon I would go weekly to the laundromat in rue Pergolese, exactly opposite the rundown but once luxurious number 10. Each time I would imagine those two aristocratically dressed Americans, beautiful and damned, wandering these streets, visiting these bistros and bars, recklessly spending the fortune that was coming in from his magazine stories and probably already arguing violently about whether his drinking was sending her mad or her madness was making him drink.

Of my two rooms, the less minuscule had an open kitchenette on one side and an aircraft-style plastic moulded bathroom bolted onto one wall. The apartment was described as 'luxuriously furnished'. This was a slight overstatement, but it did have a corkscrew, a bed, a black-and-white television and a small table with two chairs in the kitchen-cum-loungeroom-cum-dining room-with-ensuite that would serve as my office. The writing impulse would be further stimulated by the rent sucking up most of the money that might have otherwise allowed me to go out and enjoy myself. It was 3800 francs a month, or 350 'South Pacific pesos' per week, at the then-poisonous exchange rate.

I unpacked my suitcases into two sticking, twisting, chip-board drawers, and loaded four bags of shopping from the nearby Franprix Supermarché into the tiny fridge and kitchen cupboards. With my hands wrapped around a cup of instant coffee, I looked out the open window onto a small, but unmistakably Parisian, cobblestone courtyard. I felt a cool, gentle wind on my face and smiled. I put my coffee down and leaned out the window. The top ten per cent of the Eiffel Tower was clearly in view. If I leaned out far enough. Less cheerfully, if I stood in the street entrance I could look across at 21 rue le Sueur, the address where half a century earlier the French doctor Marcel Petiot poisoned and incinerated scores of runaways, alleged collaborators and other 'undesirables'.

In traditional Parisian apartment blocks, of which mine was one, the maid's quarters were tiny, without running water and always located on the top floor, which was usually the seventh floor. One of the many un-*belle* things about *Belle Époque* apartment blocks was that they didn't have flushable toilets. The top floor was where they stored whatever the euphemistic French equivalent of 'night soil' is, on the basis that smells rise rather than fall. That's the story I was offered, anyway.

To add to this, the lift – if the building had one – wouldn't go all the way up to the maids' quarters. In some buildings, both the lift and the main stairway stopped at the sixth level. The maids had to walk up an unsheltered outside staircase to access their chambers. In other buildings there was a completely separate exterior staircase all the way from the ground floor for the staff, lest the residents should have to suffer the indignity of meeting a working-class person between the foyer and the front door to their own apartment.

Now, with the age of maids pretty well over, most *chambres des bonnes* had been fitted with plumbing and electricity and converted into self-contained studio apartments. They housed mainly students and foreigners, many no doubt engaged in literary pursuits: the Great Australian Novel here, the Great Uzbekistani Epic Poem there, the Great Moroccan Music Hall Skit somewhere in between.

In later, darker moments I would imagine Paris as one big word factory, its cogs turned by the world's unpublished writers, all quietly, hopefully, pathetically contributing to an immense project that no-one would ever see, no outsider would ever benefit from. From which no return would ever come.

In my building the lift stopped at the sixth level, which was called the fifth level, because the ground floor was known as the *RDC*, or *rez-de-chaussée*. The final three flights of stairs were at least indoors, if a little narrow and slippery. At the landing at the top of these precarious wooden treads there were five or six doors. The one to the left of mine was the entrance to a shared toilet of the traditional French stand-up type, which I avoided at all costs, even though my apartment's aircraft-style contraption made so much noise that everyone on the floor knew your movements, so to speak. The door to the right of mine led to a room that would soon house the loudest, oddest person in the expanded European Community, a neighbour who threatened to make – or if she had her curious and mysterious way, break – my Great Work.

For the moment, though, I was truly on my way, lord of all forty-five square metres I surveyed, my suitcases at last fully unpacked after three months on the road, my first full day spent tapping away furiously at my laptop on the small table, surrounded by the history books I had brought to help make the background of my novel authentic, reading my sentences aloud to ensure the rhythms were right.

I left the small black-and-white television on in the background, its rapid-fire *blehr, blehr, blehr* dialogue providing just the right exotic soundtrack. And I thought the language just might seep in.

I knew it was going to be a hard slog. The literary bench marks I had set myself were only part of the story. I set off on my journey not just holier than thou, but holier than everyone else as well. I was filled with a brutal resolve to steer miles away from the typical Australian first novel, where you sleep with a lot of people and then write about them, or revisit your difficult childhood. Or, in my case, undifficult childhood.

I wasn't going to scrawl in the first person, I wasn't going to set the thing in my own town and give the main character my own past. I wasn't going to take real events and fictionalise them. I wasn't going to get back at enemies by making them characters in my story. I wasn't going to rat on my friends or colleagues by appropriating their foibles, peccadilloes and failed affairs for my own literary ends. I was going to do the full job of an honest novelist: create characters entirely from scratch and put them in wholly invented situations. And I was going to set them against a physical backdrop so real that readers could taste the air and run the earth through their fingers.

Oh, yes. From the time the first letter hit the screen, the warm glow of moral literary rectitude was powering things on.

❖❖❖

At one side of my parents' kitchen, there are three large noticeboards covered with family snaps. Among the weddings and reunions, picnics and graduations, there is one of me at nine or ten, riding a home-made billycart down the huge hill outside our new home by the river. The photo is in black and white; my entire childhood happened in black and white. The eyes are squinting at the brightness, the sun-darkened face is crested with a mop of snow-coloured hair. Looking at this face much later, I could still recall the optimism, the belief that the world was a meritocracy (not that I would have known the word), and that I could do well by being clever, by being somehow special. But I guess if you didn't believe things like that at nine or ten, you were in for a hell of ride. George Orwell wrote that one should never trust a positive autobiography because any life seen from the inside is simply a series of defeats. I couldn't have believed it then. I thought there would be fairness in the high-school yard, justice and equity in the workplace. Mind you, at that age I also thought it was exceptionally cool when I heard that Evel Knievel had broken 108 different bones. It gave me something to aim for.

Being born relatively comfortable – and in safe, peaceful, out of the way Sydney – later became a great regret. It seemed a distinct drawback in the creativity stakes. But I knew I could overcome my many advantages if I only worked hard enough – and eventually moved to Paris.

Partly covered by a faded shot of Oscar and Boris, my parents' much-loved, long-departed and none-too-bright cocker spaniels, that same noticeboard carries a photo of me at the airport, about to depart on the great literary mission. One can never be totally objective about a photo of oneself; we tend to choose the photos in which we look nothing like ourselves, where we look handsome, comfortable, on top of the task. I didn't look any of that; this one is no better or worse than the average, but then I didn't choose it. I am lanky and fairly thin (and about to lose another ten kilograms in my travels). There's a smile, tight-lipped and slightly crooked after the wisdom teeth debacle. The hair is darker and cropped close; short sidelevers, dark brown eyes, pointed chin. I am wearing running shoes and a dark denim shirt with a pen in each breast pocket, no doubt to scribble down every idea, observation and snippet of brilliance that came to mind.

There is a carry-on bag pulling tightly on my right shoulder, loaded down with books and travel documents. I look relieved more than anything, relieved to be finally on my way. After all, tradition and common sense dictates Paris is the only place The Great Australian Novel can be written (other than perhaps an obscure Greek island, or the remote northern coast of Western Australia). You certainly wouldn't want to attempt it in, say, Sydney or Melbourne. Indeed, any decent writer from any country has to leave home to do his or her best work. Not just F. Scott and Ernest, but George Johnston, Christina Stead, Oscar Wilde and, of course, that poster boy for literary obsession and perseverance, James Augustine Aloysius Joyce. Now at last I too had been exiled (writers never leave, they are exiled) and was ready to get on with the task of writing about everything, because my story was set in a place where everything happened: Undermoon Bay.

3

Isabelle and the Bard

Kingsley M. Baker needs to cast some favourable light on a decision that every connective tissue of his being fully comprehends is the worst mistake of his life. It plagues him as he drinks alone at The King & Queen, as he sleeps in the narrow single bed beside the printing press, as he stands or sometimes sits next to a bony gum, listening to the alien birds, rubbing the dry and waxy leaves across his skin, sprinkling the warm sandstone soil into his left and then right palm, placing one hand on each side of the trunk and trying, somehow, to draw some power or message from this strange foreign tree.

The new land haunts him as he watches the three-quarter-inch red ants crawl over his ink-splattered boots, gritting his teeth but failing to resist as these tireless workers occasionally scale and bite the paper-white, hairless skin of his lower legs. It torments him when he lifts his face to the globe of fire slicing relentlessly through the thinly furnished tree, maintaining the pose even when he can feel the flesh sizzle, sometimes even trying to open his eyes to the full sun, like a man in the stocks egging the pillorers to do their worst.

✣ ✣ ✣

I sat at a desk in the reading room of the Bibliothèque Nationale – not the modern piece of Mitterrand monumentalism on the edge of Paris that has four tall buildings shaped like open books, but the seventeenth-century library near the Palais Royal in the centre of the city. It was the very room where James Joyce spent most of his time on his first trip to Paris, in 1902.

I was holding my copy of Joyce's magnum opus. It was the first edition in Paladin, described as *Ulysses. The uncorrected text*. I had read some Joyce before, but *The Dubliners* didn't make much of an impression, not compared with the short stories of Hemingway, or Fitzgerald or Graham Greene. I remembered *A Portrait of the Artist as a Young Man* as being cold and difficult. I'm not sure I even finished it. But I could blame the circumstances. Sometimes we try to read books at the wrong time, when there are too many other things happening, when our mood is not right. They don't get a fair chance.

So many people have said Joyce was a genius, and *Ulysses* his greatest achievement. I had to give him and it a fair chance. I placed the thick, white-covered paperback on the ancient leather inset of the desk. This was the benchmark for literature, and much of it was written at the nineteen different addresses Joyce occupied in this city. There was a gentle crunch as I firmly opened the cover and flicked through to page one, with its chapter head simply declaring 'I'. My seat was in the upright position, my overhead locker secured, and my voyage through Dublin had commenced.

Imbued with the majesty and gravitas of the nine metallic domes of the elegant reading room, I slowly and meticulously started taking Joyce's words in. Everything went really well, too, right up until line six, written in Latin and translated by me as 'this is going to be hard work'. I had to reassure myself by quickly turning to the back of the book and rereading the quote from the *Times Literary Supplement*. 'James Joyce,' it said, 'was and remains almost unique among novelists in that he published nothing but masterpieces.'

With my focus thus renewed I wasn't going to be put off by the early use of words such as 'ouns', 'woful' or 'omphalos'. Nor was I going to be distracted by perspectives suddenly changing. It was simple really: there were two men in some sort of gun tower. The first, Buck Mulligan, was shaving and the other, Stephen Dedalus, fixating about his dead mother. It was art and it was going to last forever. And like the city of Paris itself, it was now all mine to immerse myself in as I chose.

I'd set myself the task of at least an hour of *Ulysses* a day. Ideally I'd write my novel in the exalted atmosphere of the Bibliothèque Nationale too, but it was hard to find a table and there was no obvious place to plug in my laptop, which had a battery life of about three long sentences.

On this day, surrounded by the Bibliothèque's walls of beautifully bound classics, I felt more determined than ever to make my mark as a novelist. With a book you can refine your ideas and your wording over days, weeks, months and years. If anything is not right, you simply go back and change it. There are no budget restraints on costumes or scenery. You can jump from country to country and era to era. And when it is finally published, you end up with something that – if they use a high-quality, low-acid paper

– should last for hundreds of years. When writing a book, you start with nothing and can produce something important, permanent and worthwhile. How many people do that in their jobs? And how many people are lucky enough to say 'this is now my job'?

✣✣✣

A COUPLE OF TIMES a week I walked to the Bibliothèque Trocadéro, near the horseshoe-shaped palace that looks across the Seine at the Eiffel Tower. It was not a fraction as glamorous or significant as the Bibliothèque Nationale. But this nondescript 1950s building was my local library, and so allowed me to borrow books, CDs and language tapes. On one of the noticeboards I pinned up a sheet declaring in French (or an approximation thereof): 'Person with English mother tongue seeks to meet people for English–French conversation exchanges.'

Such exchanges were popular with French students who didn't have much money. And they suited people like me, who had only Australian money. It was still many weeks before the start of the next round of affordable French classes at the local *mairie* (or council); in the meantime I had begun listening to my tapes and reading the accompanying books.

Because English is vital for every ambitious young French person, I figured I wouldn't have too much trouble finding people to meet and converse with. It was important, however, that these people spoke more English than I spoke French, otherwise we could never set up a meeting. There was no such problem with the first person to answer. Her name was Isabelle and she spoke English rather like an

English person. She gave me the address of a café in the Marais, in the heart of the 1st *arrondissement*.

'I have black hair and will be reading Baudelaire,' she explained in a clipped, precise tone. 'I could wear my red jacket, yes, that would make it easier.'

How could I reply? 'I have brown hair and will be reading Joyce'? No, not quite. 'I'll be the one reading nothing,' I replied after a short pause, 'the one looking for someone with black hair and a red jacket and, ah, a book by *Bow-derlairrrre*.'

I felt a disappointment from the first phone conversation. What could I teach this Isabelle? Certainly not how to pronounce the names of nineteenth-century French poets. I walked to the café nonetheless, through the tight cobblestoned streets, past wooden-framed houses thought to be the oldest in Paris, up the kerb, past several rows of tables set up on the footpath, through the steel and glass doors and into clouds of smoke. My eyes adjusted to the comparative darkness. I was surrounded by heavily panelled walls with brass railings and soft, orange-hued hanging lights. There were lines of expensive-looking bottles behind long, dark-grained counters and there was a low, emphatic hum of conversation. A short, dark-haired woman – in her late twenties perhaps – immediately leapt up from her book and said, 'You must be Tony.'

'You found me quickly,' I replied. 'I mustn't look very much like I belong.'

The woman made no comment. She did have a red jacket on. Her hair was a jet black bob and her book looked hefty even from a few paces.

'It is really Anthony, yes?' she said, ushering me to her

table. 'I'd prefer to call you Anthony. I am Isabelle.'

She sounded even more BBC World Service than on the phone. I had no idea why she thought she'd chance on someone to meet her standards on the wall of the local library.

'So you've lived in England?' I suggested. 'You sound like someone who has spent a fair bit of time there.'

'No, but I shall at some point. I study phonetics. I think it is very important when you learn a language. And you?'

'I'm half-English,' I replied in as neutral an accent as possible. It was distorting the truth by no more than fifty per cent, I figured. Anyway, my father was *born* in England.

'But I've been living in Australia for the past few years,' I said, failing to add that I had also been living in Australia in the years before the past few years.

'Oh, I shouldn't like to pick up an Australian accent,' Isabelle modulated.

'Don't worry, I can sound almost as English as you.' Again, no response. Surrounded by clusters of well-dressed students who had read so much Sartre and de Beauvoir it showed in their faces, we ordered espressos.

'I would like you to talk first in French, Anthony,' Isabelle said. Normally I would have been absolutely terrified to utter a syllable. I took the first bitter sip. I was not used to drinking espresso but, with the price a third that of a *café au lait,* I soon would be. I felt the harsh, hot taste hit the back of my mouth and thought: *what the heck? I don't know any of these people.*

In such ancient, solemn, philosophy-charged surroundings I couldn't help but overreach my grammar, pronunciation, vocabulary – and intelligence. It was a credit to Isabelle that she was prepared to sit still while I murdered her mother tongue. I usually first tried the English word for each concept, modified with a suitable grunt and Gallic inflection. Occasionally it was. Very occasionally. But I didn't want to just say 'My name is Tony. I live in Sydney. I am from Sydney. Would you like another coffee?'

No, no, *non*. I felt the need to explain in the language of this city of architectural splendours everything I felt about Paris and writing. I wanted to relay my fascination with the modern steel and glass and tiles and concrete, the pointed towers of St-Germain-des-Près and medieval Paris, the Sun King era's overwrought detailing and strangely sloping roofs, the majesty of the Belle Époque's grand buildings with curvaceous roofs, sweeping arches, wonderful circular windows and huge domes. Even all that ridiculously overbearing Napoleonic egotism moulded into bridges and pillars and squares.

I wanted to explain how some architecture works in Paris but would look silly in almost any other city in the world. And that I believed – or wanted to believe – that a quality of writing was possible in Paris that could be achieved in no other city. But I needed to say it with a vocabulary of only a handful of words, and with only one tense – the present. I had to keep flicking through the dictionary, squinting in the soft light, or ask in English 'what is the word for . . . ?'

'Take a bridge like the Alexander III,' I said, or thought I said. Perhaps I had told Isabelle 'my elbows exist in a vacuum' or something else that might have been mistaken for the deep philosophical delving undoubtedly being aired around us. 'Those golden-winged horses and nymphs of the Niva and candelabras and cupids, I mean anywhere else they'd raise accusations of bad taste.'

Isabelle made no comment on the bridge. Nor on the new *philosophie d'elbowism.* But with each phrase I produced, propelled by facial contortions and wild guesses, she would patiently correct my grammar and syntax, her bob of perfectly even hair swinging heavily from side to side as she spoke, her seriousness positively frightening.

When it was her turn to talk, Isabelle pronounced *la langue de Shakespeare* beautifully, even the 'th' and 'h' sounds that don't exist in French. And she did it with near-perfect grammar. Isabelle was hampered, however, by an apparent inability to comprehend that anything much had happened in the world, or in the English language, since the heyday of the Globe Theatre.

'My current English project is Blake,' she explained, after speaking of Milton and Sheridan and of course the Bard. She seemed to think that pulling quotes from such authors out of the air would be second nature to me, firstly as an English speaker and secondly as a writer. Time sprinted along. We had been talking for two hours, at least a half of it in something we both pretended was French. I was thoroughly exhausted but felt I had accomplished something. It was time to go.

'L'addition,' called Isabelle, before turning to me and saying with her small, precise voice, 'I'm afraid you will have to invite me.'

I didn't know what this meant.

'That is how we say it in French,' she clarified. 'I have no money today so, Anthony, *vous devez m'inviter,* you have to invite me.'

✣✣✣

I CAN'T REMEMBER WHERE the title *Undermoon Bay* came from, it just seemed right. So did the idea of two families, the pragmatic Wheelers and idealistic Joneses fighting it out and dividing the population into two camps, to the ruin of all concerned. I also planned a lovable rogue, Henry J. Smith, who would charm both sides to their considerable cost, and a writer, Lancelot Branch, to keep the minutes.

The approach would be unlike any other novel. It was going to be a documentary, a feature film and racy literary narrative all in one, with contemporary reports, modern perspectives and breakout boxes containing poems, songs, speeches and technical treatises. I was going to inject the language of screen – small and large – to create something truly innovative, to attack the senses from every angle, to make you feel you were truly there. Ambitious? Not at all.

I believed I needed at least 100,000 words to tell the story and not just any 100,000 words. They had to be perfect. But there was a further catch; before your humble author could incisively expose human frailty and, in doing so, change the world, he discovered he needed to spend huge slabs of time on the most turgid aspect of novel-writing: compiling lists of character attributes and place-names, and creating chronologies and character timelines. No desk is ever quite big enough for this task. You need the floor as well. As I sat and looked at this archipelago of charts, lists and inventories stretching across the small sea of cheap nylon carpet, I couldn't help but reflect how much easier it is to recycle your own past. It's already in your head. If something doesn't quite fit the narrative, you just change it; the only people able to complain are family and friends and they will be too shocked by the character assassinations in the early chapters to be bothered about a couple of wrong dates.

I was above cheating like that, I thought as I scratched my head and tried to work out what year A.O. Wheeler would have had to marry for his legitimate son Roy to have first met and been taken in by Henry J. Smith before the fateful events of 1890. Or would it be better if I made the fateful events of 1890 occur in 1899? Would that make them more fateful? But, then again, would Roy's wife Simone be too ill by 1899 to have the affair that she needed to have to convince Roy that . . . you get the picture.

Perhaps inevitably, the first character I properly fleshed out was the writer. Undermoon Bay's best known literary figure, Lancelot Branch, was popularly likened to a bottle of the finest red wine. This was not because he became better with each passing year, but because on any given evening, he was usually drunk first.

Being an Australian (albeit an un-Federated Australian), Branch needed flaws, big flaws, if he were to be respected. And these flaws had to include being a slob and a booze artist and someone who always managed to undermine his own best interests. If he became too successful, he'd need to be knocked down.

Branch knew he had an inescapable role in life: to serve the gods who required so many pages. Most of his literary motives were nothing unusual – slaying dragons, getting back at people, showing off – but more than anything, Lance Branch wrote because he desperately wanted to believe in something. He hoped that if he kept emitting words a pattern would emerge. The gift, or burden, of life would start to make sense.

Branch's existence, like that of all others, was short and bereft of control over almost anything that really mattered. But he told himself it could all be proved worthwhile if he produced just one perfect piece of work, if he could hammer his shingle to a single unquestioned triumph, an impeccable concoction of words in which not a sole one was wasted, nor a sole one anything other than the right one. An entity as delicate and perfectly formed as Pradier's *Three Graces*, as simple and strong as Goya's *Colossus*, or as technically stupendous as a Bach prelude.

Yet Branch knew that every article and poem and story and book he ever produced was compromised by deadlines, diminished by his own wretched need to slay dragons, to get back at people, to show off and, of course, to sell each word for the highest price. Worse still, there was the gnawing notion that perhaps he was not really a Pradier or Goya or Bach, just a small-time, small-town wordsmith.

As I said, there was no way I was going to write anything autobiographical.

✣✣✣

The 16th *arrondissement* is also known as the Étoile or Star district, on account of the twelve roads that radiate from the Arc de Triomphe. It is an old and conservative pocket; even the prostitutes who double-park with hazard lights flashing on the side-streets of the Avenue Foch are well-dressed and favour German cars.

As a resident I discovered that although it may have been haughty, it wasn't quiet. Most of the city's motorcycle showrooms were housed on the nearby Avenue de la

Grande Armée (a name that obviously dated back a very long time indeed). It was a point of honour that customers arrived and left these showrooms on their own motorbikes in the manner one would approach the final corner of the race that would decide the World Championship.

Aside from the incongruous racket of motorcycles screaming at wide open throttle, and the posh nature of the district, which by convention impinged on any artistic credibility, it was the perfect place to live. I had the world's most famous arch and the top of the Avenue des Champs Elysées almost on my doorstep. Any short walk would take me past a dozen major landmarks older than any building in Australia, or Undermoon Bay. On the most unassuming corners I could find plaques honouring the achievements of some famous philosopher or artist, commemorating some historical event – usually a massacre – that occurred on that site, or honouring a hero of the Resistance that was *fusillé par les Nazis* right here.

Not only did someone who was someone always live here and someone else who was someone else always die there, almost every street had been lined up to give a perfect view of a jaw-dropping monument. Standing in the centre of my *rue*, I could stare straight at the top of the Eiffel Tower, evenly framed by buildings of a uniform height. Okay, Napoleon III had to bring in the nineteenth-century equivalent of bulldozers and make a few tens of thousands of people homeless to achieve such magnificent city-wide symmetry. But that was no skin off my nose.

And when it came to mixing the old and the new, I could delight in Paris's outrageous boldness. It didn't always work, but so very often did. There was no reason the mirror-finished collection of curves and steps that was the Opera Bastille should sit so comfortably at the edge of the history-steeped Place de la Bastille. But it did, like the modern pyramid that rose in glass and steel from the ancient square in front of the Louvre, and made everything – I thought – look better for being there.

'Why would any sane person want to live anywhere else, or in any other fashion?' is the general French line of argument. It is easy to see the strength of that logic when you are walking through a city of wonderful bridges and ancient islands with tiny cobbled courtyards, of street markets with overflowing tables of fruit and vegetables and sausages and seafood, of old men playing *petanque,* hurling their bowls with a slow, deliberate air onto a white, sandy surface with the consistency of dry rice.

But, as I was learning, there are other times too. Times when you are a foreigner dealing with the Préfecture de Police, the organisation that handles most immigration and visa matters. The bureaucracy of Paris was everything a fervent Francophobe would expect. It meant dealing with electricity and phone companies determined to bury the *ennemie* (that's French for customer) in mounds of paperwork. It encompassed endless trips to the Préfecture de Police to obtain the *carte de séjour* that, in strict terms, I was supposed to have if I planned to stay more than three months.

The Préfecture's forms were written in such complicated French that even university-educated Sandrine struggled to decipher them. Bad luck if you were African and alone. And no number of supporting documents ever seemed enough to get to the next stage. At one point I paid 100 francs, which seemed to merely give me the right to later pay another 200 francs. But even this 200-franc fee mysteriously increased to 400 francs between when I was given the form and when I returned it.

Sandrine and Gilbert cheerfully helped me with each new stack of questionnaires and seemed unsurprised by their volume or degree of difficulty. It made me realise the French are ruled by forms and permits and ID cards in every sphere of life. Sandrine shook her head in disbelief when she realised that I was happy to walk around Paris without my passport or any other form of identification. And she had always been bewildered by the lack of an Australian *carte d'identité*.

'But what if you are stopped in the street?' she asked, 'How do you prove who you are?'

'Who is going to stop me in the street?'

That didn't seem to be the point. You had to have a *carte d'identité* because, well, you did. So in France I made it a matter of principle – a small principle admittedly – to never carry any papers with me. What were they going to do: throw me in a French jail?

'Warder, this wine is corked.'

4

A Gamble Against Reality

The problem had started in Birmingham three and a half years earlier. Baker's wife, Louisa, and his business partner were becoming too well acquainted. It was a poisonous time; denials were made but not accepted, and Botany Bay was the harsh and rigid ultimatum. But the bluff was called and Baker's pride forced him to climb onto a barque and head beyond the seas, threatening – or promising – never to return.

Having sentenced himself to 1000 lashes over something based more on instinct than evidence, the need arose to tell himself – and the cool, milky, nippled surface of the gum – that this was a land of opportunity. Just the place where a man could start afresh with his trade and operate on his own terms. As he stroked the native hardwood or hand-fed his heat-warped press, Baker also felt compelled to conjure images of Louisa committing obscene acts with Robert McLaughlin, Master Printer.

When J.H. Wheeler came to call, Kingsley M. Baker was swinging the pressman's bar through a large arc to place pressure evenly across the entire forme. At the same time, he was visualising Louisa dropping her whalebone corset to expose her bounteous, mellifluous breasts to

McLaughlin's flapping, beetroot lips. The scene was suddenly put on hold, as was the daydreamer's rage.

✣ ✣ ✣

AFTER THAT FIRST ENCOUNTER in the café in the Marais, I met Isabelle regularly. When it was warm we went to parks. Her patience remained solid, her financial situation precarious. When she had money she 'invited' me. I realised I needed to talk about simple things. Even then, I remained stupid in French and had to hope to claw back some dignity in the English conversation. Soon there were moments, tiny moments, when I was sure I was talking in French without translating anything in my head. Sure, it was only a word or two, or a prefab phrase here or there, but it was progress.

Like so many people in a country with a written law code and an *Académie* to ensure linguistic rules are not bent, let alone broken, Isabelle instinctively believed that English must be underwritten by some sort of sacred system. She brought with her lists she had assembled of English verbs and plurals, trying earnestly to identify and apply conventions that simply didn't exist. Likewise, she believed I should be able to recognise grammatical patterns in French if they were only pointed out. For every subclause I generated, Isabelle had a long explanation I wouldn't have understood in any language, including my own.

'It's simple, Anthony,' she insisted as she pointed out that one of my French pronouns wasn't reflexing properly. 'It's the same as you learned in English.'

'What, to copy what other people say and change it only if someone corrected me?'

We were sitting under a lattice awning in the Tuileries, on spindly green chairs plonked seemingly at random on the white pebble surface. Isabelle opened her book of poems by William Blake. 'I love this part where the stars throw down their *spares*.'

I blinked and looked over her shoulder.

'No, *spears*. The stars are throwing down their spears.'

'Yes, *les lances*. I know what they are, but the phonetic transcription I've made indicates . . .'

'No.' I had found a mistake to correct. It was a brief victory. Isabelle pointed out another phrase. 'What's the rule here?'

'Well there isn't one,' I had to reply. 'We say it that way because, well, it would sound wrong to say it any other way.'

'Though in other cases,' I added after giving it some thought, 'we do the opposite. And to not do that would sound just as wrong. It's just the way English is. Tomatoes with an e, pianos without one, and two childs is one children.'

I could find no real way of explaining to Isabelle the peculiarities of English syntax: 'What you've just said is perfectly correct in every grammatical sense, but no-one would have a clue what you were talking about.'

'Why?'

'Er . . .'

'But you are a writer, surely you should know.'

I was stunned and a little ashamed that Isabelle talked so comfortably about subordinate clauses, dangling participles, and other things I had heard of only in whispers behind the bike sheds. 'Today,' Isabelle once announced, 'I should like to discuss the subjunctive mood.'

Why, does it seem like I'm in a subjunctive mood? A little tense perhaps.

✣✣✣

FOR THE YOUNG PHILOSOPHER, secondary school beckoned. He had by this stage begun to acknowledge the self-indulgent meaninglessness of aphorisms, dictums and maxims and, as a veteran of two novels, he clearly needed a break from that literary form as well. Instead he produced poetry, comedy skits, a radio monologue or two, and wrote and edited a school newspaper which possibly helped him gain a journalistic cadetship at seventeen with Rupert Murdoch's curiously named organisation News Limited. At twenty, it was a musical he turned his hand to: a full-blown singing, dancing extravaganza that was as successful as it was musical. It was set in the 1920s and filled with insanely complicated songs laid over an inanely simplistic story about a wheelchair-bound man who discovered he had a musical gift and became a songwriter. Why he was a paraplegic I don't quite remember, but he found stunning success in the midst of the excitement of the roaring twenties. Wealth and fame didn't prove enough to capture the girl of his dreams, though. She was, after all, the girl of his best friend's far more able-bodied dreams too.

A Broadway production did not eventuate. Maybe it related to the difficulty in finding someone in a wheelchair who could tap-dance. Or the fact it never really left my bottom drawer. There was a second musical, now that I'm spilling my artistic guts. And did I mention a couple of children's books? Well, three actually. More importantly, the occasion to write my third novel arrived, and this time it was serious. It had to be, as I'd thrown in the first and only full-time job I'd ever had with the depressing realisation I'd never be able to smoke enough, drink enough or say 'fuck' often enough to impress the people at the newspaper. I had wanted to be a professional writer almost all my life and had secured what seemed the perfect break straight from school, yet had decided in just four years that newspapers weren't for me. It was a huge blow and I dealt with it by putting my energy into *New Worlds*, a story about an attempt to win a prize for being the first person to drive a complete lap of Australia. It was told through the perspective of the mechanic/chauffeur who had been employed to 'ghost drive' the lap by a rich retailer, who wanted the honour and to promote his opulent department stores.

In *New Worlds* I was back in the 1920s. It was an era that seemed to make a lot more sense and had a great deal more style. I undertook vast amounts of research to authentically set the story. I became fully conversant with the foliage and soil types west of Adelaide, the tidal movements of Broome and the boundaries of Queensland cattle stations during the mid-1920s. Yet I never succeeded in making the subject of the narrator's scrutiny – the rich retailer – nearly as convincing as my well-researched backdrop. He came across as *The Mediocre Gatsby*.

The prize – some tens of thousands of pounds – was offered by a newspaper. This may or may not have given me the chance to rail against the industry that I had just left. I'm not sure, but have no intention of ever going back to look, even though *New Worlds* is probably still sitting in a crumpled cardboard file somewhere, one of those hundreds of things we truck from home to home in boxes that we never open but are not quite game to throw out.

The next novel, *Just Managing,* was completely contemporaneous. It dealt with a spiky-haired cabaret artist named Hate Winchester and his manager, a businessman as incompetent as his charge was unruly. Many years later I found a copy and re-read it. I was pleasantly surprised how good it was. In parts. But I was even gladder no-one else had thought it was as good as I thought it was when I was twenty-two or twenty-three. That's the thing about a bad novel, you can never get rid of it. If someone had published *Just Managing* it would be out there haunting me for the rest of my life, ready to jump up from a remainder bin and bite. At any time, the spine could peer out from the shelf of someone whose respect I thought I had earned, only to suddenly realise that they couldn't possibly have anything but contempt because they knew the dark secret behind my life.

This time there would be no excuses, and no banalities. This would be my first *real* novel. And there would be no easing up, even though at roughly the time I arrived in Paris I read an article in which an English academic said that writing a first novel was a 'gamble against reality'.

I made the decision that I would write each and every morning except Sunday from six until noon without a single break or distraction, except to get a baguette from the corner *boulangerie* and have some of it for breakfast with jam and black coffee. At noon, I would turn off the laptop to eat the rest of the baguette (this time with cheese, paté, cold sausage and various other things that French law dictates must be eaten for lunch). And then after those six hopefully productive hours pursuing my vainglorious gamble against reality I would go out for two or three hours to be a tourist, even if only to aimlessly wander among the back streets or take a walk in some of the parks and squares around the apartment.

There are worse things in the world than sitting to read, take notes or think about the big issues of life, or the small ones, in a place like the Bois de Boulogne, the massive park that borders the western end of the city. Or walking around Parc Monceau with its huge shady trees and follies and statues and swept gravel avenues and its monument to the brave man who strapped on the world's first silk parachute and jumped out of a hot air balloon and landed there in 1797.

From about 3 p.m. I'd return home to work on my French until the evening news, which I couldn't understand, and an evening drink which, after all that cramming, would speak to me very clearly indeed. With the Aussie dollar fetching so little, there remained one huge bargain in Paris: low-cost, high-quality wine of innumerable varieties. I could then read, or go for another walk, as it was light until after 10 p.m. Or write some more, which I frequently did.

'I will produce a *tour de force*, a *pièce de résistance*, a Great Work. I will. I will.' A mantra had worked for Cassius Clay and I hoped it would work for me. I figured I needed one. At school, I had relied on ability rather than effort. It worked really well for, let's see, at least the first year. Alas, even by Second Class I didn't have the jump on the class that I did in First. And by the time I looked up six or seven years later I'd been well and truly overtaken. Even by the stupid ones. Who now had me to call stupid.

It seemed ridiculous that I should have been sitting in a tiny apartment repeating a mantra not too many notches up the scale from those daft affirmations penned by life coaches, or ten-year-old philosophers with a keen eye on the flip-over desktop calendar market. But I knew I had a chance of succeeding only if I backed up my plan by sticking strictly to the hours I had set myself, and told myself repeatedly I was going to produce a Great Work. But, then, what was I going to tell myself: *I'm going to write an average novel that will be reasonably well received*? No, if I was going to beat a far more competitive bunch than my classmates – namely, the international army of hungry and highly-drilled unpublished novelists – I had to live for my art. This did not necessarily mean dressing in black like Nick Cave circa 1988 and existing on heroin and dry biscuits. But it did mean making the job of writing fiction the single most important thing, and indeed the only thing, in my professional life. I knew there were others doing just that, so I had to be either obscenely talented to beat them all in my spare time, or I had to work at least as many hours as them. I figured I had to work at least as many hours as them, and probably more.

'I will produce a *tour de force*, a *pièce de résistance*, a Great Work. I will. I will.' I had to aim for the heavens, if only to increase my chances of actually leaving the ground. And, who knows, I might just make it over that difficult eighteenth car.

⁂

LEARNING ANOTHER LANGUAGE WAS a far bigger task than I had imagined. The questions thrown up at me during the conversation exchanges made me wonder how I'd ever learned English. My French-born grandmother should have been an advantage, but she left France as a child to live in the US then the UK. I met her only four times, lastly and terribly sadly in a south London retirement home on a cold and bleak English afternoon.

'This is my oldest son,' she'd said to the nurse, before complaining that she hadn't been given the lunch she had just eaten.

But to say I arrived in Paris with no French would not be entirely true. Way back in First Form, when I was twelve years old, I completed a compulsory term of French and another of Latin to see whether I had any interest in, or aptitude for, languages. I didn't, though my marks in French included ninety-seven per cent in one test. The teacher was Brother Kevin, who talked at a million miles an hour and was the designer, inventor and presumably the patent-holder of a punishment system called 'The Brother Kevin Special'. This involved a lightning snap of his closed knuckles over the top of the forehead if you were mucking up in class. Sporadic outbursts of violence aside, Brother Kevin was a liberal soul. His exams worked on what was, when dealing with twelve- and thirteen-year-old boys, a particularly optimistic principle: the honour system. Students marked their own exams and it was during the course of assessing one of my own deeply-flawed test papers that I granted myself what I thought was an entirely reasonable ninety-seven per cent. Trouble was, even that made me third last.

Under the same system, classmate Colin Laycock once scored zero. 'If I don't mark myself harshly,' he explained, 'I'll never improve.'

If the more I studied French, the more I realised there was still to do, exactly the same was true with my novel. Still, there were no deadlines and no more pressure than I put on myself. Which was probably pressure enough, as I was a man on a mission. Fortunately, I could restructure the day any way I liked, as long as I met my target of 6000 new words every week. It was rather like undertaking a university course and setting your own subjects and hours. It was a wonderful feeling to know that if I wanted to spend an hour chasing up the meaning of just one word or a whole day getting one paragraph just the way I wanted it, I could. And often did.

Somewhere along the way – in that cheerful, optimistic false dawn that was my early period in Paris – I was also going to read as many great novels as I could, as long as I also spent an hour each day slowly taking in Joyce. The first, appropriately, was *The Great Gatsby*. I hadn't read it since it was on my high school syllabus. I had been the sort of schoolboy who took it as a given that anything on the academic syllabus was the literary equivalent of green vegetables and that any writer without a proper first name must be a pretentious turkey. Yet F. had proved a revelation. Within a few years I had read every other book he wrote, even those propelled by low-cost, high-quality wine of innumerable varieties.

In the golden era, the young, handsome F. Scott had dazzled everyone with his otherworldly talent, otherworldly charm and otherworldly drinking. And in my little Paris apartment I set about rediscovering his jewel from the 1920s, those 170 or 180 pages of perfect Art Deco writing which, it had not escaped my attention, were also written in

France. I was reminded how Daisy's voice was described as being 'like a tuning fork struck against a star'. Nobody writes like that any more. Audiences are too cynical. Today's reader wouldn't sigh with the delight of such rare poetry. They would think: *but a tuning fork is small and a star is big and hot and you couldn't get anywhere near close enough to bring them together, let alone deal with the differences in size. And the sound of a melting tuning fork is hardly going to be resounding, or even on song, so why would you want to risk everything for a women whose voice sounded like that?*

Re-reading *The Great Gatsby*, Hemingway's *The Sun Also Rises* and *The Old Man and the Sea*, Graham Greene's *The Basement Room*, and almost getting through an annotated Penguin collection of Shakespeare tragedies were merely diversions, however. The main game remained *Ulysses*, although some days I could finish only a few pages in my hour. On those days all Mr Joyce proved to me was that he'd be a bastard to play at Scrabble. *Gee, James, a multilingual pun on a triple word score. Very clever, very hard to do. But are we really having fun here?*

The conceit of *Ulysses*, as I understood it, was to look at every single thing a man did in one day, likening his twenty-four-hour journey to that of the Ulysses character in Homer's *Odyssey*. But the man in question – Leopold Bloom – didn't even rate a mention in the first sixty-four densely packed pages, some of which read like *Roget's Thesaurus* played on 'shuffle'. When I found it hard going, I did the only noble literary thing. I blamed myself as a reader.

When it came to keeping up with the wider world, the television news was not much help. Very little from overseas was shown unless it affected the French and even then I had to guess what was happening by following the pictures. Or by ringing Sandrine. When they showed someone speaking English, I had to try to listen under the translator's voice-over.

A couple of weeks after the election, François Mitterrand invited Jacques Chirac into the Elysée Palace for the handover. This handover is a quiet affair, where the outgoing president divulges various state secrets to the only other person in the world he is allowed to tell, then hands across the atomic codes, the house keys and, one supposes, the fridge magnet marked with the garbage bin collection nights. The outgoing president then walks out of the official residence and resumes life as a private citizen.

Chirac was now the boss and soon announced his new prime minister. The president was able to choose – and, if he liked, replace at any time – the prime minister. This was because of the way Charles de Gaulle had set up the mechanics of the Fifth Republic in 1958. As De Gaulle saw it, the president should do all the interesting work (such as international affairs and overall strategy) and the prime minister should do the grubby day-to-day stuff and receive the blame for all domestic problems. Chirac's new P.M., Alain Juppé, enjoyed exactly seven days of industrial peace before the French public service called a big *manif* to protest, well, everything. The train workers followed a couple of days later.

✣ ✣ ✣

WHEN MY WRITING WAS going well, I took all the credit. When it was going badly, I blamed Melanie, whom I had never met and was slightly scared of. The story of Melanie started a few days after I moved to rue le Sueur. I had walked out of the lift, up the stairs and onto the landing to find a well-dressed forty-something woman standing there. She looked stern and unmistakably Parisian and appeared to have been waiting for me. It was a surprise to see anyone on the landing. Other than the concierge, I had scarcely seen another living soul in the entire block and certainly none of my direct neighbours. Even my landlord, Alberto, managed to make his way in and out of the building invisibly.

'*Bonjour*,' the woman said. 'I mean good morning, 'ow are you?' It was a perfunctory question. She continued without offering even the hint of a gap for a response. 'You are from Australia, I believe. From what city?'

'Sydney.'

'Ah, Sydney,' she said with a lowering inflection. Exactly what this lowering inflection inferred, I couldn't gauge, and she didn't elaborate. 'And now you are in Paris.'

It was hard to argue. 'Yes.'

'Melanie, our daughter, is about to move into the *appartement* here, next door to yours. We are just setting it up for her.' The woman reminded me of a school teacher. I felt ten years old.

'Does your daughter speak English?' I asked quietly, pathetically. 'If so, she should knock on my door and say hello. If she is learning English, we could possibly help each other.'

'She already speaks English,' the woman responded crisply. 'And Spanish. She has worked for an airline and studied in America. I'll tell Melanie that you are there. But can I ask you, finally, do you live alone?'

I was amazed this woman knew what language I spoke and what country I came from (is our national dress sense that distinctive?). And even more so that she needed to know my domestic arrangements. After that day I waited for a knock on the door from Melanie, though with a sense of unease. Something wasn't quite right. In fact, something was very wrong.

5

Madagascar

Quatrefoil, the suburb that provided the site of Undermoon Bay's first cathedral, took its name from an architectural term for a four-leaf clover carved from stone. The former cathedral, now the main Undermann branch of the National Australia Bank, features two beautiful examples of this Gothic device on its west wall. The lower of the two quatrefoils, which encloses an additional security camera for the automatic teller machine, is the larger and features an elaborate inset stained-glass window depicting early European settlers coming to the area under angelic guidance.

✣✣✣

Today I was writing from a late twentieth-century perspective, lookeng back at the major architectural works of the early nineteenth century. Not that I was writing the novel in order, and not that any two sections were in the same style. I was spitting out straight narrative history, interviews with early residents, break-out boxes on events and oddities, and self-contained incidents from the town's recent (and far less colourful) history. This later category included the visit to town during the 1980s of a second-rate tribute band based on the notion that Elvis Presley's twin brother survived and became half of a musical duo known as Elvii the Pelvii.

I was trying to cover the entire history of the area from the First Fleet to last week. Much of it was seen through the pompous pen of a small-town historian, though there were narrative passages such as the tale of Kingsley M. Baker, intended to give warmth and an extra slice of realism. Baker was slowly going mad, as it turns out, to allow an opening for the impecunious J.H. Wheeler to acquire a printing works as a prelude to creating a dynasty, the characters of which would drive the novel. I hoped. Novels, when broken down like this, are very silly things. In more frustrated moments I wondered why we didn't just say what we mean and do away with the elaborate fictional dressing. Joyce didn't have to write 933 pages. He could have just written 'The string of challenges and complexity of emotions that face every man every single day approximates in a very approximate way the stuff that Greek guy faced in Homer's epic. So there.' Think of the pages saved, the years not spent on PhDs about Joyce and critical essays on *Ulysses*.

On that front, Leopold Bloom was now eating a kidney in between doing chores for his wife, Molly. She, by way of thank-you, was planning to have it off with one of her theatre colleagues while her husband – importantly, a Jew – was out selling ads. It was slow going, partly because I was trying to do every sentence justice, and partly because it was slow going.

If Joyce had run into my father he would have been told 'no-one should ever have to read a sentence twice to know what it means.' And he would have been told it many, many times. I would read other books in one hit, return for a few more pages of Joyce, then start itching again for something more fluid, more involving – in a word, easier. Leopold was thinking a lot about offal and sex until page eighty-three when I was treated to the famous defecation scene. This seemed to expose a flaw in the outwardly clever conceit of running with every single thing a man thinks and does in a day. Most things a man thinks and does in a day are boring and/or not something you'd want to read about in detail. Like dumping. I was still in trouble. A great writer had to be able to recognise another one. And I was struggling. I resolved to read even more slowly, even more thoroughly.

❖❖❖

MY FIRST LIFE AS a novelist petered out in the 1980s. A real job beckoned. It had to. But I didn't give up, even when I co-founded a small technical book publishing business and did normal 'man in his late twenties in the late eighties' things such as getting married and buying a house. I even returned to newspaper journalism (albeit as a freelance to pay for the house, and as a sideline to the business). Yet all the time I was tinkering, dreaming of the day when I could leave an office job behind. There were short stories, collections of Milliganesque poetry, dozens of songs, a play or two. Yet there was always a reason I had to stay in Sydney, toiling away ever harder during the day just to stay on the level as the economy dropped away and the publishing industry did likewise.

It might have been Otto von Bismarck who first said 'If you enjoy sausages or laws, never watch them being made.' It might have been his press secretary or ghost biographer. Whichever, the same can be said for books. I had been drawn into the publishing industry for the right reason: a love of the finished product. I dreamt of being a gentleman publisher. There would be nothing as brash as 'launching titles'. It would instead be a case of gently releasing tomes, rather in the manner of returning rare and delicate species to their natural environment. I would use technical books, where I had some experience and contacts, as a springboard into a wider, more appealing world. Eventually there would be essays, short stories, novels and poetry. Okay, not poetry; this wasn't going to be complete financial suicide. But as it turned out, no essays, short stories or novels made it through the process either. The realities of a tough business market instead funnelled the output into an ever narrower niche, where numbers ruled. It would only be until the business was on a firmer footing, I kept telling myself. But after a while I came to believe there were two types of books – good books were ones that sold, bad books were ones that did not.

This was a complete betrayal of my noble aims. I was helping to pump out a constant stream of publications designed to plug gaps in the market, gaps that I felt often existed for a very good reason, but which we filled anyway against a 'firm sale' order from a distributor. And while working in publishing I discovered that everyone had not so much a book in them, as a long-winded conversation about a book in them. People would ring regularly and say 'I've got this great idea for a book about . . .' After a while I'd know to interrupt with, 'Grab a pen, write down this address and send me a synopsis.' The synopsis would rarely arrive because all the person on the line really wanted was to have a half-hour chinwag to propel their romantic notion of writing a book they would never even start, let alone finish. And half the time they weren't even proposing a book about a subject our small concern was likely to touch. They had just seen the listing in the *Yellow Pages* that said 'Publishing'.

There was also a steady supply of envelopes containing long-winded rants on flyweight paper with key phrases in capitals or underlined, or both. They usually mentioned at least somewhere in their closely typed text that government technology ALREADY IN USE could read minds and invisibly barcode the genitals OF EVERY AUSTRALIAN to monitor reproductive activity in the lead-up to the repopulation of the continent by aliens, the leaders of whom were even now disguised as humans and IN POSITIONS OF POWER. It was these very people – arguably the least likely to have their work stolen – who would litter their text with handwritten Trademark, Copyright and Patent signs. The attached disclaimers and caveats with these so-called book synopses would also demand some outrageously fanciful payment and that the author be enrolled in the publishing equivalent of the Witness Protection Scheme.

The term 'small business' means different things to different people. We peaked at five full-timers, and in the early days I would write many of the books, lay them out (it was the dying days of cut-and-paste design, in which typeset text and screened photo 'bromides' were cut up and waxed onto grids), broker a print deal, organise the distribution and help unload the truck when the final product arrived. At the bleakest nevergoingtogetoutofhere moments I used my real name on the front of books because, well, I was never going to have the opportunity to do anything else with it. At more optimistic times I wrote under assumed names so that when people read the 'Also by this author' note on the ornate frontispiece of my eventual Great Work, they wouldn't see mention of *The Holden Torana Performance Handbook*.

Remember *The Holden Torana Performance Handbook*? I guess not. The bright yellow cover attributed the work to one Eric Blair. I figured if George Orwell hadn't used his real name, then it was available to others. There was nothing intrinsically wrong with the work in question. If you wanted a Torana performance handbook, it undoubtedly was one. And there are still some who would put it firmly in their Top Ten list of technical books about mid-sized, Australian-built, rear-drive automobiles. But performance handbooks, compilations of industry data, consumer guides and biographies of engineers and aviators were not what I most wanted to write or edit or publish. I didn't want to be in the unglamorous but potentially profitable technical-literature end of the business. I wanted to be in the unglamorous *and* unprofitable literary-literature end of the business. And here I finally was.

✣✣✣

'I AM LOULOU,' THE woman said, tilting her head to one side and smiling. She was short and looked somewhere between Asian and Indian and Northern African in appearance. Her mouth was impossibly wide, her rows of broad white teeth seemingly too big for her gums and lips. 'But not real name. French name. I from Madagascar.'

Loulou had also answered my 'conversation exchange' notice. We met in a small park near the library, she having explained she couldn't afford a café. Her actual handle – which she immediately, excitedly showed me typed out on her student card – had eighteen syllables, most of them repeated two or three times during the course of her three extravagantly long names. This show-and-tell came with an even longer explanation delivered in rapid-fire French. I wasn't sure if it was the accent or the speed that prevented me understanding a solitary word.

Loulou could have been twenty, thirty or forty. She had said on the phone she would be wearing red *pantalons* – and she was – but she didn't mention the tall boots with a leopard-skin pattern or the heavily framed, white rectangular glasses with chrome highlights.

'I do *tourisme*,' Loulou said. Her English was at least as bad as my French. It took two hours and two languages to discover, or think that I had discovered, that Loulou was studying tourism in Paris, having previously studied business and anything else she could. Simple reason: as a Madagascan she was not allowed to work in France, and couldn't stay unless she was studying. There were negatives about going home – the state of the nation, for a start – but she would soon reveal the more curious motive that was keeping her in France. In the meantime Loulou gave me almost as much grief about English as Isabelle.

'The *passé compose* of take is took, yes?' said Loulou, 'so why is not make *mook*?'

'Because that would sound silly,' I offered, in what would have to stand in for a grammatical argument.

For all the frustrations, I was glad I was putting the effort into my tapes and conversation exchanges. When someone in Australia speaks a second language, it tends to be

English. As a typical 'Anglo', I spoke in just one tongue and as I became older it was increasingly a cause of shame. I was in my thirties by now, for goodness sake, and needed to learn some other way of expressing myself, if only to confirm that my brain hadn't hardened, that it wasn't only under-tens who could learn new languages.

It was like sending my mind to the gym. I felt my brain becoming stronger and more supple, though sometimes at the end of a long session it also felt dehydrated and it occasionally pulled a muscle. But my achievements were all put in depressing perspective when I saw an information booth in Les Halles with a sign saying 'We speak English, Dutch, German, Spanish, Russian and Italian'. I looked into the small glass box. Inside was one teenage girl sitting on a wooden stool.

✣ ✣ ✣

I WORKED HARDER AND harder. I wrote thousands of words and the whole first month disappeared in a blur. By noon each day my temples throbbed with the effort I'd put into the story and I could scarcely have continued if I wanted to. For most of it, I was wondrously happy. But not one overcast Thursday. I was in a filthy mood and a *métro* ride home late in the afternoon exacerbated it.

I'm sure it wasn't just the stuffing around with the Préfecture de Police when I could have been writing or playing the tourist that irritated me. Perhaps it was the fact that Australia wasn't shining in the Rugby World Cup, or that the French language was proving more difficult than I thought, or that my bank account was already heavily dented. Perhaps it was that the initial excitement of being in Paris was now tempered by the mundanities of everyday life. Or that the war in Bosnia and other parts of the former Yugoslavia – that depressing background roar of the past few years – seemed set to flare again after a few months of relative peace. Whatever the cause, the buskers and beggars were literally queued on the platforms, swapping carriages at each station. For the first time the musicians were dreadful, the beggars ugly and aggressive. A man with no legs rolled right up to me with one hand out, while using the other to pull back his trouser legs to expose two mangled stumps. What do you do in a circumstance like that? You ignore them and look the other way, of course. It's too confronting. The locals were well on top of it. They would walk past with rigid hearts and not offer even a glance. The same was true of most seasoned tourists.

Charity overload comes quickly when you are feeling low anyway and the *métro* is filled with forceful misfits trying to sell magazines which they claim will fund their next feed because they have fallen on hard times, or ribbons for *SIDA* (AIDS), or collect funds for homeless people in the former Yugoslavia or limbless children in Central Africa or displaced people in Eastern Europe or the old, the starving and the diseased right on the doorstep.

There were gypsy women in dirty multicoloured rags, who would sit in the one place all day holding a two- or three-year-old child who didn't move at all. One of these women reached across the body of her drugged kid and clutched at my legs as I walked past. Everyone in Paris was out to get me and I was starting to think that if one more person asked for something, I was going to knock them off their crutches.

It seemed as though the whole city had its hand out, and it was a great deal easier to hate the beggars wrecking my journey than the circumstances wrecking theirs. I cursed the French, I cursed their stupid capital, and I cursed myself for moving to it. But when the bad day was over I could see that beggars were just part of the unique chemistry of the City of Light, as was the sight of smartly-dressed, well-off Parisians quite openly throwing their rubbish on the ground, or nonchalantly bashing their car into somebody else's as they parked half on the footpath and half on a pedestrian crossing. Or calmly smoking a cigarette while a Gucci-brand miniature dog, which they were dragging at the end of a Gucci-brand leash, shat at leisure on somebody's doormat.

The next day Paris was everything even the hardest-marking arts reviewer could demand: a ballet of Citroëns and Renaults and bicycles and taxis weaving around striding businessmen in suits and trophy wives in couture fashions who carefully placed one expensively shod foot in front of the other while being overtaken by tall African women who loped along to a completely different rhythm. These magnificently erect females with their brilliantly coloured headgear and clothing, and often a baby or two wrapped somewhere within the folds of their garments, crisscrossed paths with middle-aged office workers shuffling with their own unmistakably Parisian gait and old men with Gitanes hanging from the sides of their mouths, looking almost exactly like they were from Robert Doisneau's photographs of *boulangers* and factory workers of the 1940s.

There were the stylish blue street signs too, and huge posters of naked women advertising anything from perfumes to cars and giving the finger to the politically correct. They ensured even a walk down a modest street could offer a tiny hint of what the Lido, the Folies-Bergères and the Moulin Rouge should be, and once were. Arses, tits, feathers, Champagne, Josephine Baker, and rows of bare legs swinging to accordions.

Even the graveyards were enticing. Père Lachaise is the big daddy of them all, *the* place to be seen dead in Paris. One afternoon I caught a *métro* across the city to the massive site to the west of the city. I slowly strolled up the wide, shady, gravelled avenues and stopped at the graves of Balzac, Abélard and Héloïse, Yves Montand and Simone Signoret, Molière, Gertrude Stein, Frederick Chopin, Edith Piaf and Sarah Bernhardt. I lingered at the gaunt, twisted, tortured statues commemorating the deported French Jews and World War II Resistance fighters and stared at the wall against which the last members of the Paris Commune were shot. I ignored the graffiti on tombstones saying 'Jim Morrison this way →'. I wanted to reach the Art Deco monument marking the last resting place of Oscar Wilde.

I was pleased that Wilde resided in a different and quieter part of the cemetery. I was completely on my own as I walked around his monument, the tall white rectangle not built until years after his death because few had much interest in, or sympathy for, a bankrupt old pansy in 1900. I read the inscription etched into the marble, which dealt only with Wilde's academic achievements. But I also read at least a dozen of pieces of paper that had been left, held down by small stones. 'To Oscar, poet, genius and victim of bigotry' read one, and it was typical. I stayed next to the crypt for a long time, sitting on the gravel with the soft spring sun filtering through the Père Lachaise trees. I was trying to throw myself back ninety-something years to the time when Wilde lived in this city under the pseudonym Sebastian Melmouth, wandering the surrounding streets with the lonely steps of an exile, yet with still enough of his old self intact (I'd like to believe) to have breathed his last in a hotel in the fittingly named rue des Beaux Arts with a line that never allowed you to look at wallpaper in the same way again.

Hemingway said this was the best city in world to write. No argument there. But Oscar was a broken man by the time he arrived and never really had a fair chance.

I did have a fair chance, and had to make sure I didn't squander it.

✣✣✣

TODAY WAS A GOOD day to be writing in Paris. The breeze through the open windows was just cool enough to be pleasant, and I was typing away with confidence about a plan to construct the tallest building in the Southern Hemisphere. It was to be a monument to 1920s progress, according to Roger Forbes, the entrepreneur behind it. It would require only a few planning laws to be overlooked, he explained, and a small number of government grants and tax concessions. 'But what an asset for the people of Undermoon Bay!'

As I wrote about the building's four varied façades, each in a different style to represent the four claimed virtues of Forbes' Number One Corporation (Enterprise, Innovation, Goodwill and Integrity), I became aware of an irregular thumping noise. It was coming from the apartment next door. I knew a girl called Melanie lived there – her scary mother had told me – but I still hadn't met her, nor passed her on the stairs or landing. The noise was very close and peculiarly irritating. I clasped my hands over the keyboard and waited for it to stop. I'd heard a few odd and slightly creepy noises from next door in the previous couple of weeks: a short squeal here, an unexplained clanging there. But they were never quite this loud. And they usually stopped after a few minutes. This time they did not.

I started writing again but my progress was slow and the pounding was overlaid by a whimpering noise. 'Shut up,' I seethed, though only for my own benefit. 'Don't you realise the mornings are my time to write . . . and things are going well?'

The Enterprise façade, I typed, was penned as a piece of pure classicism, influenced by many of the new skyscrapers going up in New York at that time. Integrity featured hints of Greek revival style, which Forbes, who had suddenly styled himself as an expert on architecture, explained away as . . . *thump, crash, wallop*. The noise from next door dramatically escalated. It sounded exactly like a forehead being firmly butted against our shared wall. My pauses became longer as I tried to take in what was happening. After maybe ninety minutes the thumping was replaced by the sound of gentle sobbing.

Until then I had been mildly annoyed; now I wondered whether I should knock on the door and ask if help was needed. I eventually reasoned no. This was Paris, where it is considered polite to ignore other people's misery.

✣ ✣ ✣

AFTER TRYING TO REINVENT adult literature in the mornings, in the afternoons I was struggling through books aimed at five-year-olds. *Mon petit Père Noël* was about a little girl who found a pint-sized Father Christmas who had fallen out of the sky and didn't have any presents to give to children. She presented him with her most prized doll. It brought a lump to the middle of my forehead. There was also *Il y a un alligator sous mon lit*, the exciting tale of a deluded boy who thought there was a giant reptile under his *lit*, and . . . well, you get the idea.

It was particularly discouraging to learn that in French there were (and perhaps still are) seven simple and seven compound tenses, and six conjugations of each verb in each tense – and not all the verbs are regular. They also have outrageously unnecessary things such as adverbs and past participles, which they use at will with little consideration for foreigners. Still, I continued practising my conjugations, listening to my tapes and attending conversation exchanges.

Loulou told me about her homeland, and I wasn't tempted to make a holiday booking.

'There are eighteen ethnic minorities, and they each hate the other seventeen,' she explained, as we sat on the grass near Trocadéro (the grass is normally a no-no in Paris) and madly flicked through dictionaries to say or understand the next word. 'And even the rich people are always sick because of all the dust in the air.'

In the tough times, and now was one, most people ate roots because they couldn't afford plain rice. Loulou went on to describe a country that was dirty, poor, violent, overpopulated, corrupt and riddled with superstitions. 'It is very, very, very hot,' she sighed.

'But you have beaches, like in Australia.' I was sure I'd seen long surf beaches in a *National Geographic* article on Madagascar. Long surf beaches and lemurs.

'People living near beaches don't swim at them,' Loulou explained. Or I think that is how she explained it – filtered as it was through Loulou's limited English or mangled through my poor comprehension of French. 'They think the spirit of the water will pull them down to the bottom.'

Conversations with Loulou were much like watching French television shows or reading French newspapers. They made me a master at half-knowing things, and whetted my appetite for the other half. Most of the time I could attempt to satisfy this hunger for knowledge in clear English only among the limited materials at my local library. The Bibliothèque Trocadéro had *Newsweek*, some copies of the *International Herald-Tribune*, a few slightly yellowing London newspapers and one encyclopaedia in English: *The New Encyclopaedia Britannica* in thirty volumes, fifteenth edition, from the early 1970s.

On many afternoons I sat there and read. I read till my eyes hurt. I threw my neurons into treatises on the second Globe Theatre, James Watt's rotative steam engine, Iran under the Shah, the laws of copyright, General de Gaulle, Marshal Pétain, architectural styles (and scores of other things needed for *Undermoon Bay*) and, after meeting Loulou, Madagascar.

Thanks to the *Britannica* I was able to glean that Madagascar had more than ten million people in 1972 or 1973, which was rather a lot for a small country moored off the side of Africa. Madagascar used to be what the French called a 'possession', which means there is a street named after Victor Hugo, a couple of grandiose town halls and the place is completely buggered. You don't have to read a lot of history to know about the French attitude to decolonisation: 'When we finish loading these valuables, we're leaving'.

And did Madagascans really avoid the beach even in the fiercest summer, further adding to misery that was already miserable enough? I never managed to find out.

Meanwhile, it was the weather in Paris that was becoming remarkably hot. Or, as Joyce might say, the darkrimmed sevenfigure of *rutilantium* was tambourining the ungentlemanly hayjuice of Xanthippe.

6

Murder and Mayhem

'Go, Jesse Garon, go', yelled Elvis as he twitched his top lip and waved his sequinned cape towards his guitar-wielding twin, who was a head and shoulders taller and, hairstyle aside, didn't look at all fraternal. Jesse Garon hulahooped his knees to the ample beat then traced a large arc in the sky with his right hand, all the time surreptitiously scouring the floor in front of him. There followed a carefully practised flick forward of the slicked black hair, another quick look down at the dark floor and a dramatic slide of the left hand down the guitar neck to complete the last chords before the solo in 'Jailhouse Rock'.

The burst of staccato guitar notes was best when enlarged with reverb, but Jesse Garon was having no success finding the pedal among the leads and legs of microphone stands. He wished he could wear his glasses but Elvis said they didn't look the part.

They had been on stage now for forty minutes, in a room containing maybe eighty people, every one a smoker. There was almost no air movement and the door at the other end of the hazy hall, the full length of a cricket pitch away, was the only opening. It led into the bar. A continuous stream of men carrying full jugs of beer walked through it, crowding around the ten or so lean-against-high tables randomly scattered across the nondescript pub carpet.

A dozen or fewer people stood on the dance floor adjacent to the stage, but only one or two attempted to dance. It came in fitful drunken bursts, sometimes between songs. At the left of the stage Jesse Garon had noticed a singletted man push a short, dumpy woman away from a cigarette machine and start to shake it. The long view wasn't a problem. It was the area around his own feet he couldn't see.

✣ ✣ ✣

I WAS LOST IN a typical Australian country pub when the slamming of Melanie's door hurled me straight back to rue le Sueur, Paris. I quickly, quietly stole across the floor to look through the peephole but missed her. The next time I tried she walked so close I could see only blackness. How did Melanie and all the other people in the apartment block come and go without me ever seeing them? The only person who seemed to exist in three dimensions was the small and almost silent Portuguese concierge.

It wasn't Melanie alone upholding the strange quotient in rue le Sueur. The day after I moved in, I walked out of the lift, through the front door and onto the street. As I turned right I noticed a pair of knees jutting out of a small alcove three or four metres away. The knees appeared to be wrapped in brown paper. I walked further and subtly looked to my right. It wasn't just knees that were wrapped in brown paper. There was a whole man wrapped in brown paper. He could have been seventy, with thick stubble and a scrappy stub of a homemade cigarette in his mouth. I came to a complete standstill. He sat there calmly, silently, reading what may have been that day's copy of *Le Monde*. Or one from last year.

The man had a brown-paper shirt and brown-paper trousers which exposed pasty, impossibly thin ankles. Below these were cardboard shoes fabricated from boxes and paper and string. I felt like covering my nose, even though there was no obvious smell.

'Don't you realise this is a ritzy part of town?' I said in my mind. 'Shouldn't you be in a corridor in a train station somewhere?'

Not your standard issue warb, I decided. Probably a former mental patient who had been judged fit to go home, without anyone bothering to ask him if he had one. Or perhaps the brown-paper man had been around here in March 1944, and had never quite recovered. It was then that residents started openly complaining about the smoke coming from the chimney of number 21, across the road. The smoke had a particularly foul stench and didn't let up for days. Police were called and when they couldn't raise anyone, they brought in the fire department.

One of the firemen entered the building through a second-storey window then clambered out and threw up. What he had seen included a roaring furnace with a human arm hanging out of it, a pit of quicklime mixed with male and female remains and a sack filled with body parts. Even the pile of coal next to the furnace had bone and flesh in it. When the owner of the house, Dr Marcel Petiot, turned up, the police grabbed him. In a short time he was able to convince them that, although there did appear to be numerous body parts in various rooms, and in the basement there was what could be fairly described as a soundproof chamber, plus purpose-built sinks for draining blood, everything was in fact just hunky-dory. The police let Petiot go, subject to further investigation, at which point he went into hiding.

It's a curious thing about city life that you can live so close to another person – Dr Petiot or Melanie or the brown-paper man – and know so little about them. In the case of Melanie, serious disturbances were coming at least once or twice a week. I could hear every scream, thump and sob and still had no idea what she looked like or what the hell was happening.

Marcel André Henri Fèlix Petiot had been classified mentally ill in 1914, but that was considered no impediment to being slaughtered in the World War I trenches, so he was duly enlisted to do his duty for France. His time in the army was eventful: wounded and gassed, arrested for stealing army blankets, committed to a psychiatric hospital then pushed back into the front right at the end of the war, at which point he shot himself rather than any Germans.

Petiot survived the bullet and in return for his army service was entitled to join a special accelerated education program. In just eight months the former mental patient became a psychiatric doctor. In his new role, according to the material I could find in English, he prescribed huge quantities of addictive narcotics, often with fatal results. Petiot was investigated over a murder in 1926, when a woman he was having an affair with disappeared. In the same year he used his charm and a series of arson attacks on opponents to be voted mayor of Villeneuve-sur-Yonne, near Auxerre. Despite widespread and often quite open embezzlement of town funds, many voters and fellow councillors remained loyal supporters. When Petiot lost his mayorship in the 1930s he moved to Paris, where he embellished his medical qualifications enormously on a sign outside premises in rue de Caumartin. There, it is believed, he provided abortions and continued with a few other favourite pastimes, including theft, tax evasion and murder. When he was charged with over-prescribing addictive medicines the case fell down because two drug addicts who were scheduled to testify against him disappeared.

Petiot spent the early years of the Nazi occupation of Paris inventing what he later claimed were secret weapons that could make Germans instantly drop dead. He also provided false medical certificates to Frenchmen who had been conscripted to work in Germany. But his main business concerned a supposed escape route out of France. For only 25,000 francs he could deliver anyone to a new life in Argentina, via Portugal.

The Jews, fugitives and common criminals who turned up at Petiot's house with 25,000 francs and every valuable they could carry crammed into their suitcases were told that to enter Argentina an inoculation was required. But that wasn't a problem, because as well as being a Resistance figure, death-ray inventor and international travel agent, Petiot was a qualified doctor. The would-be voyagers were injected not with a vaccine but with poison. When the numbers became too great to handle at rue de Caumartin (the bodies being fished out of the nearby Seine were arousing suspicion), Petiot bought the rue le Sueur premises and had builders adapt them to his specialised requirements.

After an inoculation at rue le Sueur, the victim was led into a waiting room and a heavy door slammed behind him or her, and in some cases him *and* her (fleeing Jewish couples were among the victims, perhaps because those already in hiding were the least likely to be missed). The waiting room turned out to be an octagonal chamber. It was soundproofed but a small window allowed Doctor Petiot to watch the screaming and thrashing that accompanied death. After this, he could help himself to the contents of the suitcases – on top of the 25,000 francs each had already paid.

In 1943, when the Gestapo got wind of an apparently successful escape network (well, no Jews had been seen again after they had signed up), Petiot was arrested and jailed. Even under torture he didn't give up the names of Resistance workers, almost certainly because he didn't know any, and after eight months he was released.

When policemen turned up to the smoking building in 1944, the doctor quickly ascertained they were all French and that there was no Gestapo representative among their number. He then explained that the bodies belonged to Germans, collaborators and other undesirables. He was actually a hero of the Resistance – he'd been jailed for it no less – and was doing the work of France.

Petiot was finally arrested after the liberation of Paris and charged with twenty-seven counts of murdering for profit. His own claim was that he had killed sixty-three 'enemies of France'. A jury didn't believe the 'I was helping France' defence. They thought Petiot was helping Petiot. He was sentenced to the guillotine and executed in May 1946, insisting he had nothing to apologise for, and supposedly smiling as the blade fell.

❖❖❖

DR PETIOT'S ELABORATE THREE-storey house from the nineteenth century was replaced in the 1950s by a nondescript apartment block, still bearing the number 21. Unlike other significant sites in the vicinity, it had no plaque.

A couple of times I walked up close to have a look, all the time worried someone inside would think I was a prowler. Rather than, say, a ghoul. I was intensely aware that the story of Undermoon Bay lacked the bizarreness of Dr Petiot's. And the body count. Against real stories such as Petiot's or countless others, fiction often seemed so slight and inconsequential. Sometimes I felt like Lancelot Branch, the writer in *Undermoon Bay*. Or to be more accurate, perhaps sometimes he felt like me. He would despise the blank page, would harbour the wish that the sky would fall in, a tidal wave would wash overhead, or something else would happen that meant he didn't have to keep working on the unwriteable chapter or poem.

Journalism, for all its difficulties, comes with a map: bash out 500 words on this, knock up a profile on that. I knew where I was going. Large-scale fiction was new, and something else entirely. However, at least I had a computer. With paper and pen, the first sentence can take ages to arrive. With a computer, if the first sentence stubbornly refuses to arrive, you can start on the second, or the third or even the fourth and re-order it later.

It wasn't always so. First there was handwriting, a dreadfully inefficient method that in my case produced a vile scrawl no-one could read. In Second Class I learned to write in Italics, taught by a nun – another mad nun, in fact – who hit you with a cane if you committed the greatest sin of Italics: you blotted your copybook. But there was a world beyond handwriting even then. My father worked in an office and we sometimes went there on weekends. Everywhere, there were complex mechanical adding machines that printed out their answers on little rolls of paper. There were little carousels of paperclips and staples, boxes of carbon paper, evil-looking paper spikes and an IBM computer the size of a London bus, which had its own sealed, dust-free, climate-controlled room. It chewed up and spat out punch-cards and probably wasn't as smart as the mouse connected to a cheap modern PC. And there were desks – rows of desks – bearing typewriters that were tapped during the week exclusively by women, all of them seemingly plump and with beehive hair.

On weekends, while my father was working in his smoked-glass office at the end of the corridor, I would sit in the middle of the ghost typing pool with a cushion or two under me to reach the keyboard and tap away with one finger, then two fingers, then four. And it was with those original four typing fingers I would later produce the class newspaper. I was editor, which may have sounded grand, though the real role was grander still. The title should have been Writer, Editor, Designer and Distributor, because the contribution of classmates rarely extended beyond submitting dirty jokes – verbally – and telling me what the final product was a heap of.

Back in those low-tech days I used a manual typewriter

directly onto a master stencil, which was uncorrectable. This stencil would be clipped onto the roller of the school's hand-cranked printing machine, which looked primitive even in a manual typewriter world, and usually coated everything except the paper with ink. The stencils were expensive. So Mrs P, the fire-breathing admin assistant who slurred her words and was said to belt the bottle, allocated me just four stencils to produce the two-sheet, double-sided extravaganza. That gave me, let's see, none spare.

If I typed the wrong word, I had to reword the rest of the sentence to make it seem like it made sense. Elsewhere, straight-out unsaveable mistypings (say, words that started with 'sxqp') required all sorts of low-tech subterfuge, such as using a thick black line as a design element. It would fortuitously wind its way through the offending word or sentence but leave room for something like 'story continued overleaf'. Then there was the audience to deal with. They were critics so hardened they didn't need to even read the paper to know it wasn't any good. They just had to skim the bragbox: Editor, T. Davis. If Davis knew anything about what made a publication worth reading, he would have included Michael Roman's joke about the Irishman with three testicles.

The people who did read the class newspaper from cover to cover – or would have done if there had been covers – were the teachers. And they sometimes, with complete disregard for normal freedom of expression for the fourth estate, suppressed publication or, in the most extreme cases, detained the editor. These incidents were never investigated by Amnesty International nor the Press Council.

Through this hard-earned editorial experience, I realised the power of the written word. Although small and seemingly innocuous, the written word could take up all your time, have you pilloried, ridiculed and punished, while bringing you no glory or material gain. That's powerful by any standards. And yet I continued writing and putting out the silly little publication.

Years later, at the real newspaper, we used manual typewriters to type onto little oblong stacks of five sheets of paper, separated by four sheets of carbon. The rule was: one paragraph per 'five'. This was a great leap forward because it meant you could shuffle paragraphs after the event. If you made a mistake, you could throw that single paragraph away, without incurring the morning-gin wrath of Mrs P in the school office.

The advantages were fewer when deadlines were close. At times like those you had to type your first paragraph and immediately yell 'copy'. At this point, a copyboy would appear (a copyboy – later copyperson – was a sort of low-life, shit-kicking, lunch-fetching ferret, which all future journalistic cadets had to start as). The copyboy would run to your desk, pick up the little green wad, rip the staple from the top left-hand corner, slide out the carbons and bin them, then distribute what was left.

One sheet was left with the journalist, another given to the chief of staff, a third slammed onto the famous hand-piercing spike as a record of the journalist's original words (in case of lawsuit), but the most important was hurried to the sub-editor's desk. There it would be covered with Sanskrit-like markings, put in a little steel canister and slotted into the 'chute' to be spirited by air along whistling tubes to the people downstairs whom the older journalists called 'grubbies'. Those were the final days of hot metal and some of the grubbies, the ones more politely called Linotype operators, sat in their blue overalls at huge and complex machines that looked like a cross between an old-fashioned typewriter and a combine harvester. These men – always men – retyped our stories on a strangely configured keyboard, somehow producing the exact typography and sizing demanded by the sub-editor's Sanskrit. I'm sure no-one except them ever really knew how it was done. And now it's a lost art.

The difficulties for journalists were obvious: once your first paragraph was gone, you couldn't change it. Any deficiencies had to be addressed in your second par. It was rather like working on the uncorrectable stencils of days gone by except the circulation exceeded the print runs I used to produce at school (where I think the strongest audit showed a readership of forty-eight). And by the time you were working on your second par, you had no idea what changes had been made to your first.

Within months of me starting, we journalists went on strike for six weeks to fight 'the bosses', who wanted to replace this system with nasty, nasty computers. The bosses won.

✣✣✣

I COULDN'T NOW IMAGINE tackling something like *Undermoon Bay* without word-processing technology. Writing by hand requires a whole different way of thinking, of constructing things in your head. Despite this, there were now long moments I was staring at the screen, not producing anything. After five weeks I already sensed trouble. The first symptom was an increase in the number of times I went for the mail.

For reasons of security or job creation, Parisian apartments are not usually individually numbered. Once the mail has reached the right street address, a concierge – usually Portuguese, female and doing the job in return for cramped ground-floor accommodation plus a token wage – directs the mail to the right occupants. The concierge at rue le Sueur silently went about her business, never saying more than *bonjour* as I passed her in the dark foyer or opened my door just as she was distributing the mail. And I started opening my door far more often than I should have, because I needed excuses to leave the laptop and do something that could be vaguely classified as work, yet didn't involve trying to push the story forward.

I didn't have email, otherwise I could have checked that every thirty seconds and felt like I was achieving something. Another method of cheating was to momentarily switch to other writing projects during the mornings, such as a collection of children's poems I had been sporadically working on. That was something I had earlier assured myself I would only ever do only after noon. 'Novel time' was meant to be sacred.

The original concept had all looked so simple: a faux history of a faux town in an unspecified location somewhere on the east coast of Australia. The town would have all the problems of today delivered in microcosm. Initially I had this vague notion that the characters didn't need to develop, that the town itself could be the thing that developed. This sounded wonderfully clever right up until the moment I tried it. So did many of my other ideas.

I should have been sitting in a café discussing the challenges with someone who had more experience in structuring novels, who could have given me some worthwhile notions about which of my more radical ideas were going to work. Or even someone who would just listen while I tried to articulate what I was attempting. I was in Paris, for goodness sake. I should have been wrestling with such issues in a smoky bar, surrounded by people in berets, sipping a local rosé to the beat of a distant jazz band. But it wasn't happening like that at all.

It was just me in a tiny flat trying to make my way through the maze entirely alone and determined not to mention a single detail about what I was doing to anyone lest the magic, such that it was, should be destroyed.

For the first time I started to think, however briefly, that perhaps I just might not pull it off.

'No,' I repeated to myself again and again with added force. 'I will not fail. I will produce a Great Work.' I had to prove to myself I could do it. And, to be frank, I had to prove it to anyone who might have been sniggering as the jet took off. Sure, people bought me drinks at the airport and wished me luck. But maybe they thought that luck provided my only chance.

7

Saving Darwin

'Jailhouse Rock' had thus *far been a sloppy affair. Elvis had been singing flat and had mixed up the verses. Jesse Garon squatted to get a closer look at the floor but felt the back of his white jumpsuit start to burst its stitches along his spine. The drummer – a late substitute – took Jesse Garon's crouch as a signal to wrap up the song. He gave the cymbals four crashing blasts with the thick ends of his sticks, snapped his towel from his shoulder and bounded up to grab his beer from the top of the speaker stack.*

The moment the drummer made his decision, Jesse Garon finally located his reverb pedal and twanged the first two notes of the solo. In desperation he added a few more notes which made the sudden finish sound vaguely planned – or might have if the bass player hadn't kept plodding on for what seemed like eternity. Elvis pushed back his hair with his hand, pulled in his distended stomach, yelled 'Shit-a-brick' into his microphone and stormed off the stage. This meant stepping down on to the pub floor, as there were no wings.

The audience members, who had until now failed to do more than vaguely put their hands together, let out the most enthused whoop of delight that the night's act was likely to muster. It had been the same for the folk singer earlier. The only time they cheered was when she bent over to retrieve a dropped guitar pick.

✣✣✣

AND SO THE STORY of the King-and-his-late-brother impersonators went on for another few hundred words. 'Jesse Garon' had ability but no direction, 'Elvis' was graced with ambition and determination but a wholesale lack of talent. And both of them were on a losing wicket. It was one of many scenarios I wrote as I frantically tried to find form and rhythm in *Undermoon Bay*. Admittedly Elvii the Pelvii was one of the more unlikely segments, but the choice was sit and stare at the screen, or write something.

May turned to June. I was receiving fines from France Telecom for not paying bills that arrived after the fines and I still didn't have my *carte de séjour*. Apparently I hadn't jumped through a sufficient number of hoops. It looked like the only solution was to go to the French Embassy in London and apply for a *carte de séjour* there. 'That would be easier,' explained an official in the Parisian *Police Préfecture*, neatly avoiding mentioning for whom it would be easier.

I continued the quest to produce great art amid such frustrations, further industrial stoppages, the screaming and screeching of motorcycles, honking horns and the thumping and whimpering from next door. Helping me along with *Undermoon Bay* was the reinvigorated belief that things such as structural problems were the small issues and I was completely on top of the big ones. That, and self-delusion. Sometimes I was tempted to cheat and start writing what was happening around me. Alternatively, I could retell or, to use the motion picture term for plagiarise, *reimagine* the story of Dr Petiot. That would give me a tale of murder as amazing, bizarre, strange and disturbing as any from England, the traditional home of the quietly spoken, perverted doctor who despatches his patients with unspeakable cruelty. And no-one back home would realise I hadn't made the whole thing up.

Getting to the top of my chosen field was going to be particularly hard because my field was badly chosen. Even if I made it all the way to the finish line and completed my novel, I knew most unsolicited manuscripts were never read, that most publishers used agents as poison tasters and that most agents had little interest in new authors unless there was some marketing hook. They wanted not just a book, they wanted 'the whole package'.

Where could I find such a hook? I was neither excitingly young nor old. Nor was I spectacularly rich nor breathtakingly poor. I was white, male, mostly Anglo in origin, of a stable temperament and moderate habits. I hadn't become famous doing something else. Nor was I related to anyone who had. I was heterosexual, despite a slightly disturbing fascination with Broadway show tunes. And I was a journalist. That might seem a profession likely to attract a fair share of people who know how to write, yet journalism is somehow held up as being separated from real writing by an unbridgeable divide. I was sure that was why many author biogs in novels contained a long list of menial jobs undertaken before the author was published. Sure, it was also there to imply experience born of hardship, but was mainly to disguise that the person in question had spent most of his or her professional life working as a journalist.

I had spent most of my professional life working as a journalist. I lacked a PR hook. In some ways it looked bleak already – and I'd scarcely started.

❖❖❖

GENEROUSLY, THE FRENCH BUREAUCRACY did everything it could to take my mind off problems with The Great Work.

Another day, another queue: I was waiting to hand over the final pile of dastardly difficult-to-compile documents, certificates and references. I thought I had at last completed the impossible task, but was still wary enough to feel the top of my ears burn and a throbbing in my neck as the woman at the desk turned over the differently sized and shaped pieces of paper in freeze-frame slow motion.

One, two three, four, five . . . She languidly flipped each over until she arrived at the last vestige of my official life in print. Then she started again. And when she finally looked up, the silence lasted a full minute. 'But where,' the woman suddenly asked with the delicacy of a camp commandante, 'are your inoculation certificates?'

I could scarcely reply. 'Inoculation . . . no-one has ever mentioned these.' She handed back my miserable pile of papers with a look that said *get out of my sight, you English-speaking nobody*.

'We must have them,' she said, 'it is the *r*egulation.' She commenced the last word with a demonic, guttural 'r' that came from deep within the hellfires of her administrator's soul. Inoculation certificates! Didn't my shiny coat, wet nose and wagging tail make it obvious I'd had my worming shots?

I was supposed to be a writer, but I couldn't find the

words to explain how angry things like this made me, and when I was angry I couldn't write, and when I couldn't write, I became angrier.

The anger was real but even fury has degrees. When I stood in a long and unmoving line at the *Police Préfecture* behind a small woman who was clutching a Bosnian passport and visibly quivering, I could appreciate how little real importance was attached to my application to live in one rich, safe country rather than another.

❖ ❖ ❖

WALKING WAS THE BEST cure for many things, and it was good to walk with Sandrine, who could easily keep my mind away from my book (and her country's bureaucracy) with an almost limitless knowledge of Paris. Some days I would be not only exhausted when I finished writing but despondent. Though I'd never admit it to her.

'You look horribly tired again today,' Sandrine would say, as we walked over any of the wonderful bridges that cross the Seine, past the fold-up bookstalls that line its banks, or into the tiny galleries and shops on the rue Vieille du Temple. 'I don't know why you are trying to do so much.'

Sandrine's main hobby was taking photos, thousands of them. She would photograph the same buildings and monuments time after time, recording the way the light interacted with them at different times of day, the unique banners or flags that were attached at certain times of year, or tiny changes that she had read about in newspapers or architectural magazines that most people wouldn't notice. And she would file the photos in neat folders and stack them on her bookcases, for her eyes alone.

'These are the Wallace fountains,' she explained, pointing to one of the ornate green cast-iron sculptures I had noticed all over the city. 'A wealthy Englishman named Wallace donated them to Paris in the 1870s so that everyone could have clean drinking water. It was after the siege and the Commune when, *oh-la-la,* everything was destroyed. You can still drink from them.

'I love the goddess on each corner. There was once a glass on a chain in the middle to drink from but the health department changed that.'

Sandrine photographed each goddess separately then shot the entire fountain and square from various angles.

'You know that this, the Place Saint-Germain-des-Prés, was where Jean-Paul Sartre and Simone Beauvoir lived and worked,' said Sandrine.

'Yes,' I replied. 'I've been reading about them. And the more I read, the odder their private lives seem.'

'But they were artists and intellectuals,' Sandrine said. 'We make different rules for them.'

It was Sandrine who led me to Point Zero, the little marker in the stones outside Notre-Dame cathedral from which all Paris distances are measured. She also took me to the few surviving examples of the original Hector Guimard-designed *métro* stations, with their wonderful Art Nouveau touches, and told me about little Paris secrets such as the roof of the Samaritaine department store, next to Pont Neuf. On a good day you could buy a ten-franc coffee and sit and enjoy a sweeping view over all of Paris for as long as you liked.

We would walk to the Eiffel Tower regularly. Sandrine would photograph it while I merely admired it, not just for itself but because the Parisians have so sensibly put enough space around it to make it look important and significant. The same was true of the wonderfully refurbished Louvre and that train station-cum-gallery called Musée d'Orsay, which gave the feeling I was standing in a tube of light. And there was Notre-Dame cathedral too. Its towers were surrounded by scaffolding and closed for renovation, yet I could sense every one of the 900 years of its existence in every other corner.

I could never be bored walking in Paris: looking at the bicycles, the motor scooters and oddball cars that couldn't be more different from the mainstream if designed with nothing more than that in mind. I delighted in the dual pace of the place, in which people racing through the streets at wide open throttle could exist side-by-side with others sitting in cafés and restaurants and in no hurry to go anywhere. The way the women dressed may not have quite matched the myth, but it was impressive. As was their thinness and beauty. The couldn't-give-a-rat's disposition of the men was also oh-so-Parisian, as was the intricate lighting of monuments at night, the constant parades and feasts and celebrations, and the almost universal acknowledgement that people shouldn't spend their lives inside, being eaten away by the cancer of four walls.

After one long walk I returned near dark and noticed that the brown-paper man was still awake and sitting in his doorway. I stopped in front of him and held out a small bag of chocolates I was carrying. He lifted his grey, unshaven face slightly and looked at me like a wounded puppy. Then he firmly shook his head and turned away. I had never looked at him that closely nor noticed how his knees knocked rhythmically. All the paper was held to him with string, neatly tied up in little, perfectly-formed bows. His face remained hidden. I quickly walked the last few steps to the doorway, punched the numbers into the Digicode that kept people like him out, and hopped into the lift.

❖❖❖

ON JUNE 13, IT was announced that the French military had decided, on mature reflection and having considered all possible options, that it should blow things up. Yes, Blacques Jacques Chirac really was going to allow the resumption of nuclear testing – and not in Marseilles, the Loire Valley or Brittany. He was going set off eight nuclear bombs in the Pacific Ocean, Australia's tropical fish tank. I couldn't believe it. Neither could most of the rest of the world, particularly those living anywhere near the Pacific rim. Protesting Australians became a nightly sight on the news, which also showed, among other things, tonnes of manure being dumped on the lawns on the French consulate in Canberra. Even my level of French didn't allow me to miss President Chirac using the words *Australien* and *irrationnel* in the same sentence. Sure, I struggled with the words in between, but those two were as clear as *le jour*.

Australian foreign minister Gareth Evans was on the teev, but the commentator talked over the top of him. Australia's Minister for Pacific Affairs or some such thing (I had to de-translate his title from the French at the bottom of the screen) was actually speaking in French, though I couldn't understand him, and he looked like everyone's worst nightmare of an Australian slob. The news reports showed an Australian newspaper headline crying out 'The

Arrogance of France', and you could detect the surprise and mystification in the voice of the newsreader. Even those French people opposed to nuclear testing seemed to lack passionate opposition. The attitude seemed to be 'It's so far away and we've got all these more important problems here, like the strikes.' Alberto the Italian landlord, however, made a surprise visit to my *chambre de bonne*.

'It is madness,' he said in faltering English. 'I am very sorry. And could you please not hang your washing in view of the window as it is against the rules of the *maison*.'

Isabelle offered no opinion on nuclear issues – 'I don't like anything to do with politics, Anthony' – but there was no such reticence from my latest French conversation partner, Benoit.

'We French have every right to do whatever we want on French soil,' he said in a voice so forceful that my saucer rattled under its cup.

Benoit, a stocky law student with a round, wide-eyed face and windmill hands, had answered the conversation exchange notice and was now sitting opposite me in a small café off the Avenue de la Grande Armée, drowning out even the motorcycles.

'Arguing is good practice for me,' Benoit explained, as he ran his hand through his thick black hair, cut in a curious 1970s helmet. 'I speak more fluently when I am passionate. You should try this too, you will find you won't need to stop and translate in your head first. You can say anything to me. I don't want you to be afraid that you will shock me.'

While I stumbled in infantile French, Benoit used his far superior English to explain, in ear-thumping terms, the need for the French nuclear arsenal to be upgraded, and why it was so important to conduct real explosions. He also used his French to order food, and lots of it. Real live nuclear explosions in the Pacific were, he continued, the only way to calibrate equipment that would allow the French, in future, to conduct its testing solely via computer simulations.

No-one ever turned around and looked when people such as Benoit talked loudly in cafés. It took me a while to learn this, just as it took me a while to realise that in France you can sit there for an hour or more with your single cup of *café* and watch the world go by. It's the ambience of a Parisian café rather than the coffee itself that makes Paris such a civilised place. Yet the first thing that stands out at a traditional tables-on-the-footpath café is the rudeness of the servers. *I'm not 'ere to do what you want,* our waiter seemed to be saying as Benoit kept calling him back. But I now knew the rudeness was merely a cultural thing. Like, say, ritual disembowelment or female circumcision. The server always eventually, ungraciously delivered my coffee and Benoit's food and then did not annoy us again, unless Benoit demanded his attention. Which he then gave very slowly and begrudgingly.

'You could use the American programs for simulation, like the British do,' I suggested. Being passionate wasn't helping my language. I had switched to three-quarters English and the occasional French-sounding grunt. 'And anyway, if you exploded bombs just a few years ago without getting the necessary information for simulation, what makes you think you'll get it this time?'

'Stopping the original tests was Mitterrand's fault,' Benoit replied, thumping his chest rhythmically with his open right hand as he spoke. 'Mr Mitterrand stopped the tests for political reasons before we had all the information we needed. And we can't use American facilities. We must be independent.'

'Why? I mean the American software is going to be at least as good as anything you will develop from eight tests,' I replied, now entirely in English. This was about learning French, I had to remind myself. Benoit was entitled to his opinion, no matter how wrong it was.

'Yes, but it is not so simple', Benoit said pensively, though not quietly. 'You see the military aircraft who we sell to the other countries . . . no, *that* we sell – or is it *which* we sell?'

I didn't take up the opportunity to correct Benoit's grammar and not only because I often struggle with *that* and *which*. 'The military aircraft,' I said instead, with all the authority of someone who had just read an article on the subject in a library copy of *Newsweek*, 'which, along with various guns, rockets and tanks have made France the biggest supplier of arms to the Third World . . . the biggest, even bigger than the US.'

'Perhaps that is true,' Benoit said with scarcely a pause. He appeared neither shocked nor embarrassed. Clearly somebody had to sell weapons to Third-World despots, and Benoit looked pleased they were receiving high-quality and stylish French ones. 'But I was trying to explain,' he continued, 'that the planes that – which – we sell to other countries are not, let me say, as *interesting* as the ones which we keep for ourselves. So we can't rely on the United States to sell us things or to conduct our computer simulations. We must be independent.'

Speaking like the lawyer he was determined to be, Benoit explained that debating is considered an art form in France, that it is considered very important to construct a proposition formally with an introduction and a conclusion and a logical structure in between. 'People who do that are much admired.'

'It's a bit different where I come from,' I explained with perhaps just a little overstatement. 'The most important thing in Australia is not to have an introduction, a conclusion, and a logical structure in between, but to be glib and funny and tell a good story. The people who are most admired, even at the top of the corporate tree, are those who can rattle off a laugh-out-loud anecdote or reduce a complex argument to a dark comment.'

Benoit looked at me intensely then blew air out between his lips and made a common French hand gesture that looks like the person is throwing something over their shoulder with their right hand. Probably their rubbish.

He ordered another *croque-monsieur*. 'Hate your food, don't you?' I blurted out as his fancy and very expensive toasted-cheese sandwich arrived. Well, I hadn't shocked him so far.

Benoit looked at me with genuine surprise. 'No, no, no, I love my food.'

'Sorry. A bit of Australian irony.' My explanation didn't seem to gain any traction. Benoit looked at me like a man who couldn't work out why anyone would think someone who ate so much didn't like food.

'Why do you need to test bombs, anyway?' I continued, without bothering to use a single French word. 'We already know that nuclear bombs are the business, entirely capable of blowing up an entire city. So what is Chirac aiming for? A city and a half? I could understand testing triggering systems or delivery systems but I would have thought that the one thing not in doubt was the power of the explosion.'

'You may think that, but if Australia is ever attacked, you'll be pleased that France is an independent nuclear power.'

'Yeah, sure,' I said, 'I can just imagine you lot risking Paris to save Darwin.'

Benoit leaned forward. 'I went to Darwin when I visited Australia on my package tour two years ago,' he replied, his circular face breaking into a small smile. 'I don't think you *antipodeans* would risk anything to save it either.'

Touché, Benoit! He'd learned to argue in Australian in one easy lesson. A few moments later the man in the white apron ungraciously threw at us the thing that the French call *The Addition,* the Germans ominously call *The Reckoning* and Australians refer to as *The Damage.* The bill was going to be seriously big and I was nervous that Benoit was going to tell me he didn't have any money. Instead, he grabbed the small curled-up square of paper and pulled out a credit card.

'It is okay. I must invite you, because I *hate* my food so much.'

I feared I was going to like Benoit.

❖❖❖

IN MID-JUNE THERE was a grading session for the *mairie* French course, a month-long government-sponsored affair that started in July. I still hadn't received a *carte de séjour* (it was a prerequisite for the course), but the Préfecture de

Police had given me a curious piece of paper saying they would be prepared to give me a *carte de séjour*. But hadn't. The woman at the *mairie* registration table looked at this document, shook her head, sought more senior counsel and eventually said 'Okay.'

I was led into a room in the École Élementaire, or primary school, with all the other applicants whose names began with D, E or F. We had to complete a short exam. For me it was the first serious exam since leaving school. Or would have been if I'd taken the ones at school seriously. I had to complete sentences like 'It was raining so hard that . . . ' I couldn't remember the word for wet, which restricted my answer somewhat, so I ended up saying ' . . . that the world was like a bath'. Or thinking I had said it, notwithstanding that I was unable at that stage to use the past tense and was, in any case, only guessing what the first half of the sentence said. That set the tone. As I was trying to complete the grammar section, I noticed that the Spanish nun sitting next to me was looking across to see what I was writing. What was God thinking? Probably *choose a smarter one if you are going to copy, sister*.

A dictation passage was read out. The teacher and some of the examinees started laughing at something within the text that was obviously a joke. I knew I was in trouble. Still, I avoided the beginners class, which was my intention, and was told I would be in a class called *Faux Debutants*, which is a polite way of saying 'a minuscule fraction better than completely useless'.

As I walked out of the grounds a voice followed me. 'Mr Tony, Mr Tony.' It was a Polish guy, the loud one I had heard speaking English, Spanish and perhaps also Russian to various people in the courtyard, as well as what seemed like wild, unconventional French. He was thin and tall with lank sandy hair, a long face and a scratchy beard he played with incessantly. I knew he was Polish because before the exam we all had to explain (in French, of course) where we were from.

'I have met an Australian before, Mr Tony, *il était de* Canberra,' the Pole said to me now in heavily accented, English-pocked French. Or was it French-pocked English? He had long arms and legs and his whole body seemed to jerk rhythmically with frenetic nervous energy. His blond fringe swayed like a grass skirt on his forehead. It exhausted me to even be near him.

'One *jour*,' he went on. 'I'm going to go to there, Mr Tony, to *l'Australie*, when I have *l'argent*.'

I continued walking down rue d'Alesia toward the *métro*, making little attempt to slow for conversation. The arched windows and blond bricks of the school were on my right. On my left, the Polish guy and the traffic were locked in a tussle to see who could be the loudest. 'Oh, good,' I replied, not sure what I could add, and hoping he'd turn the volume down a little. I kept walking but didn't leave him behind.

He was still with me as I crossed the rue de la Tombe Issoire, a road where Henry Miller once lived, as I strode past the locksmith and *Coiffeur* and retirement home and *Auto École* and bistro and *Immoblier* and *Boulangerie* and *Triperie*. It was seven or eight minutes, one of the longer walks you can take in Paris without hitting a *métro*. Fortunately, the heavy coverage of trees on either side of the road provided some shelter from the heat.

'Mr Tony, Mr Tony.' He kept talking as we went past Alesia Fleurs with its plants and buckets of flowers spilling onto the street and more piled up in the window boxes above. No, it wasn't talking, it was yelling.'You will be in my class *ensemble* with me for the lessons in next month. You must *parler à moi* everything Australian.'

To the soundtrack of chattering buses and horns and screaming motorcycles and the Polish guy, I turned into the hugely busy Avenue du General Leclerc, with its bistros and brasseries and, at last, reached the Alesia *métro*.'Everything Australian,' I whispered, theatrically trying to bring the volume down.'Of course, everything Australian. But right now, I've got a train to catch.'

And that was my first conversation with Tadeusz, the man who would become my most unlikely muse. But all that was in a strange, unimagined future. Right now he was merely embarrassing me by talking so loudly and so badly on a crowded street. The fact that I didn't know anyone in that street didn't matter.You don't do things like that.

8

Chopping and Changing

Beauhurst, the large area just north of the central business district, once provided the locale for the New Independent Assembly building and the Undermann Senate (and is today the site of the Municipal Council Chambers). It was always intended to be the civil administration district. A.O. Wheeler – who planned much of the modern city – had the foresight to set aside in his original plans a large 'governmental' area. He designated the site 'Beauhurst' on his original map, claiming that the name was derived from Beaurus, the Greek God of Administrative Services.

✣ ✣ ✣

I lifted the glass and sipped the dark red liquid and suddenly I was back in modern times. More than that, suddenly I was sitting around with friends in Sydney, seeing colours all a little more vividly, being touched by a different sort of sun. All it took was some wine. Not just any wine, and not necessarily better wine than the local stuff. But it was Australian wine. One of those huge, boisterous, earthy South Australian shirazes that would have been difficult to find in France, and priced beyond belief. Tonight, it was free, and unlimited.

There had been an advertisement in *FUSAC* magazine about a function at the Australian Embassy to highlight Australian wines. The ad appeared on the day of the nuclear announcement. Free entry, all comers welcome. So I went along and spent a few hours in a huge white foyer in a building near the Eiffel Tower, drinking free wine and blabbing on to Australians, New Zealanders and other Colonials. There weren't any French there, except for Sandrine, who I had taken with me and was an honorary Australian anyway. I supposed that the French didn't think they needed foreign wine. Or didn't like us at the moment. Or hadn't seen the ad, since the event was, it seemed, only advertised in the English-language press.

As I walked around the room – or at least between the serving counter and the area where most people were standing, talking and gulping, I overheard twenty conversations, almost all containing the phrase 'nuclear testing'. One exception was Sandrine, who was talking to a red-headed Australian woman about finish and texture and palate and, almost uniquely, treating the event as an opportunity to taste wine rather than just knock it back. Another exception was a middle-aged South African woman with a Paul Robeson-deep voice who was talking not about potential nuclear annihilation but about herself.

'I think I hold a record for completing the most French courses without acquiring any of the language,' she said half to me and half to a Canadian man who had earlier suggested the French should do their nuclear testing in 'Queerbec'.

'The *mairie* course is particularly bad,' the South African woman added as she upended another amply filled glass of chardonnay. 'And it's full of really weird people.'

This wasn't news I particularly wanted to hear. My *mairie* course started in two weeks.

'But your first language is Afrikaans, isn't it?' I ventured, picking up on her Dutch-style inflections. 'Your English is pretty damn good and I thought each language was a bit easier than the one before.'

'Not French. It's impossible. That, or God has decided I shouldn't be allowed to speak in French.'

'So what brings you to Paris?' I asked.

'I'm writing a novel,' she said. 'Isn't everyone? And you?'

I looked down at the deep purple tinge of my shiraz. 'Ah, just having a . . . well, just a holiday, I guess you could say.'

An Australian man in a dark business suit joined our group. 'Paul,' he announced, enthusiastically lifting his glass and making eye contact with each of us. 'Hope you are all enjoying our little evening. Some lovely wines.'

'So what's happening?' I asked, assuming Paul From Officialdom probably had better sources of information than a black and white television broadcasting in a language I didn't understand.

'Well if you've been scanning the wire services, you'll know the French Consulate in Western Australia was burnt down this morning.' His face shifted into a half-smile. 'It's not even near the Pacific.'

'Who did it?' I asked.

'No indication yet. But, knowing this mob,' he sighed, figuratively looking around all of France, 'they probably did it themselves.'

✣✣✣

FROM THE TIME OF Chirac's atomic announcement, all things literary began to deteriorate. Furthermore, Melanie's thumping, whimpering and wailing had proved merely a warm-up, and every second day I found myself sitting at my computer, hands clasped over the keyboard, waiting for the noise to stop, quietly cursing the interruption.

Melanie's apartment had only one window, while mine had two, so it must have been markedly smaller. Yet at times it sounded as if there was a three-ring circus being performed within. Through wafer-thin walls designed for maids, who were rarely there because they were too busy working, the most common sound was that of a girl squealing and yelling, or yelping then sobbing.

One day, as I tried to find the words to show how Roy Wheeler's famed ability to acquire, to outmanoeuvre, to do business with friends and sworn enemies was evolving into his sole reason for being, a distant phone rang. I heard Melanie snatch the handpiece violently from its holder and rapidly say *blehr, blehr, blehr* (I still couldn't make out dialogue spoken more quickly than that on my instruction tape and I don't think she was saying 'Excuse me, could you please tell me the way to the railway station?'). She then spat out '*au revoir*' five or six times, each louder and more shrill than before, slammed the phone down, slammed her front door, thumped her way down the stairs to the lift, then slammed its door so loudly I could feel the vibration from my desk. After about five minutes, Melanie returned to her apartment just as noisily, arriving in time to answer the phone again and go through the exact same cycle.

It happened four or five times in a row. Maybe her

mother had asked if I lived alone because she thought that I might need protection. Either way, the words were no longer flowing in the city-state of Undermoon Bay.

I had to see Melanie, if only to find out whether she had horns and fangs or if she dressed in leather and chains and Nazi insignia. But right now I didn't have the courage to knock on her door. I returned to James Joyce's Big Holiday Cryptic instead. We were amid a long funeral scene, told largely through stream of consciousness and it didn't cheer me up.

❖❖❖

AT OUR SECOND MEETING Benoit again talked at high volume about many subjects, but mostly France and the French.

'We are very proud of our country and of our culture,' he said as he leaned back on a woven cane café chair that was clearly protesting. 'We have everything here: the food, the art, the sun, the snow, the language, the life. We don't emigrate.'

Benoit proudly and very loudly declared, 'I love my food', and by then I knew enough about France to realise this wouldn't normally be considered a declaration of gluttony, as it would from an Englishman or Australian. To most French people such a statement would mean 'I love to eat small portions of varied and exotically delicate food.' On the evidence so far, to Benoit it meant 'I love to eat enormous portions of varied and exotically delicate food – and anything else that is available.' Again I nursed an espresso, while Benoit ordered a *sandwich au jambon* and a large *chocolat chaud* and stridently explained his theories on the difference between the French and Anglo-Saxon mentalities.

'We are Latin,' he said, again patting his chest with his open hand in between words and *croques-monsieurs*. 'We like to yell. We like to push in. The *anglosaxons* are, let us say, reserved and don't like to make a scandal. But we French people don't think highly of the person who gets given a bad seat in a restaurant and doesn't argue until they give him a better one.

'And the French are not – I don't know the word in English – *pudique*. We all know that President Mitterrand had illegitimate children and many mistresses. We know about these things but we don't care. It is not like in England where everything is in the newspaper. To us, things like these mean that Mitterrand is really living. He is not just an administrator and nothing more.

'It is not like in the United States, where if the president has a mistress this makes a scandal because she might have the numbers of the atomic codes. *Non, non, non.*'

I wondered in a quiet Anglo-Saxon way if Benoit had been sent by the French Department of Cultural Stereotype Reinforcement.

Although a conversation with Benoit was like being involved in a minor motor vehicle accident, he was great entertainment and we began to meet regularly. And he proved as patient as Isabelle in correcting my deeply flawed French.

Like many of his compatriots, Benoit loved the term *les pays anglosaxons*. The expression literally means the Anglo-Saxon countries, but is generally used in reference to the USA and England, and their vicious conspiracy to suppress higher, which is to say French, culture. It is normally delivered with a scowl. Or, better still, with the combination of a concertinaed nose, pouted lips and a resounding farting noise.

The French still struggle with America; on one hand they talk about the special relationship born of La Fayette's efforts during the War of Independence, on the other hand they take it upon themselves to stand up on behalf of the world against American cultural imperialism. It could be argued that it is not the concept of cultural imperialism that France objects to, it's the success the Americans have with it. France, after all, floods the world with Alliances Françaises and does everything it can to export the French way of life.

In the popular French mind, Australia was held as a quirky, minor offender in the Anglo-Saxon conspiracy. It was a desert with kangaroos hopping around big red rocks, after all. Much too cute to be harmful. Until the nuclear announcement, that was.

✣✣✣

I'd been learning French by myself for two months now and was already prepared to completely discount anyone's claims to have learnt a language in six weeks or even three months. I had worked very hard on my French but hadn't even scratched the surface; Benoit had been learning English on and off for twelve years and, although good, still had work to do. One afternoon in the Parc Monceau, he was discussing his choices in health insurance as a student, '. . . and this is a type of accident protection,' he told me, 'but it doesn't cover us if we need hospitality.'

As I corrected him, I reflected that even if I knew all the grammar (a monumental task in itself), I'd still need to recognise a few thousand words to read a French newspaper or have a conversation containing any light, shade or health insurance benefit comparisons. And even then there are hundreds of exceptions in spelling, pronunciation and everything else. And countless idiomatic expressions without which I'd never understand or be understood. Such as telling someone to 'mind his own onions' when he stuck his nose into my business.

If someone was threatening me, would it ever come naturally to snarl back 'I'm not the type of wood we make flutes out of'? And how did the French end up using the word *person* for 'no-one'?

✣ ✣ ✣

JUNE 16 WAS BLOOMSDAY, exactly 101 years since the day on which *Ulysses* is set. I considered celebrating by roaming the city, Leopold-like, talking gibberish. Or flailing myself for my inability to make sense of a masterpiece. Instead I wrote, worked on my French, and read yet more of JAAJ's big book. Leopold was now in a newspaper office and the chapter was full of headlines.

UNPUBLISHED NOVELIST STILL DOESN'T
QUITE GET IT

Later in the day I went for a walk, down the rue des Francs-Bourgeois, past boutiques, through arched walkways lined with rows of packed restaurants and cafés, and into the Place des Vosges. This is the perfect Parisian square, built in the early 1600s with king and queen pavilions at opposite ends and beautiful lawns, fountains, sculptured trees and wide white gravel walkways in between. And it is the perfect place to sit and devour history books and the novels from 'American Paris' of the 1920s and early 1930s.

There were probably a couple of hundred people spread through the park, a few of them even sitting on the grass. I sat on a bench near a row of trees that looked like boxes on stilts, breathed in the verdant lushness as children played nearby, and began re-reading Henry Miller's *Tropic of Capricorn*. I started slowly working my way through the text, every so often staring up at the charcoal slate roofs sloping above red and blond bricks, at the rows of perfectly patterned windows, tiny railings and flower boxes, all hidden away from the chaos of motorised Paris. I loved Miller, even though he could be hopelessly repetitious, wildly inconsistent and probably wouldn't recognise a plot if one lassoed him and branded the words *beginning, middle* and *end* on his forehead. As far as I could tell, Miller only ever wrote two truly great books. I was planning to re-read both: *Tropic of Cancer* (set in Paris) and the later *Tropic of Capricorn*, which covers Miller's early years in the United States.

Miller was already thirty-eight when he arrived in Paris – even older than I was. He renounced materialism – or at least refused to take a paying job – and would soon experience, in his own words, 'every humiliation, degradation, poverty [and] starvation'. Miller didn't spend time compiling lists of character attributes and place-names, or creating chronologies and character timelines. He just threw it on the page in a surge of raw emotion, writing in nothing but the first person and setting himself the task of recording all that is omitted from books. Miller was an artist, and on rereading him I feared I was merely a technician. And he never seemed to ask the questions I asked far too often: 'What does this sentence say about me?' and 'What will my mum think?'

Although the *Tropics* are both rants – plain dumb in some parts and little more than crude pornography in others – they are also rich with amusing, wise, and highly emotive sections and some snatches, so to speak, of sheer brilliance. And, to amuse and depress and encourage the likes of me, Miller provided advice to the budding writer that: 'One must give up everything and not do anything else but write . . . one must write and write and write, even if everybody in the world advises you against it, even if nobody believes in you. Perhaps one does it just because nobody believes.'

Some of Miller's later work was produced for a dirty book publisher at a dollar a page. It's a trap for new players; fresh from my first reading of *Tropic of Cancer* many years earlier, a friend loaned me another one of Henry's Paris books which started with said author doing over a thirteen-year-old and her mother *ensemble*, in a style unlikely to be short-listed for any literary award. But from the jaunty, engaging first line of *Tropic of Cancer*, in which the narrator says he has no money, no resources and no hopes but is 'the happiest man alive', you know that at its best Miller's voice is simply like no other.

Miller's fellow writer, free spirit and adulterous lover, Anaïs Nin, called him a man 'whom life makes drunk'. Nin paid to publish Miller's first book with money borrowed from another lover, her psychiatrist. Cool or what?

After about forty-five minutes I switched from Miller to

book two of the three-volume *Penguin History of France*. An hour later I was still sitting in this perfect Parisian park ploughing through events that often happened close by fifty, eighty and more years ago and trying to build up the courage to make a further switch: to *Ulysses*.

Soon I was drowning in another stream of consciousness, as Bloom wandered about among the poor people of Dublin. A stroll through the underworld, I guessed. On page 228 there was majestic detail as Bloom licked his teeth and found something green. Spinach perhaps.

That was it for Bloomsday, but I did try to celebrate a different *jour* five days later: Music Day. Every busker in town is encouraged to let it rip, everyone with a stereo cranks it up to full blast and every church, shopping centre and other institution hosts live music. I went to several small concerts and tried to see a huge Music Day extravaganza in the open air of Place de la République. James Brown was playing but it was so crowded I could only loiter at the edges where the wind blew the sound around and the living legend appeared not quite legendary, and not altogether living.

And what was I thinking of as I watched the King of Funk in the City of Light? The city-state of Undermoon Bay, of course. By this time I had produced, through alternating bouts of gusto, elation and despondence, about 40,000 words. I knew the number because, as a former freelance journalist, I couldn't help but run a word check at the end of every day, work out how much that many words would be worth if sold at the standard rate, then cry. If I totalled up all the words I had to discard along the way, or had written up purely as background, I could have earned enough to run my own nuclear test program.

The volume of words I had produced was the good news. The bad was that most of them were pretty rough. Worse, though, it was becoming obvious the frame I was trying to hang my ideas on wouldn't allow me to deal with anything in detail, or to properly develop any of the characters. The 'history' sections didn't allow me to include living dialogue, except by the not-entirely-convincing method of presenting preserved newspaper interviews with the principal characters.

I didn't have a plot so much as a series of incidents, gripes and grudges. And it was starting to show.

There were many times when I wondered about the sanity of someone who threw in a real job for this flight of fancy. At such moments I seriously doubted my mission, I fiercely questioned my abilities. I thought of Greg, a mate back in Sydney who could sing like an angel and play impossible guitar passages that seemed to require fifteen fingers. I thought of my friend Paula, who could read nuclear brain scans and make decisions that saved people's lives. I reflected on aid workers who were risking everything to secure fresh water and medical supplies in the former Yugoslavia.

All I could do was write, and anyone could do that. You simply needed paper. My project seemed so shallow, silly and conceited. I felt I should have been working in Sydney suburbia, meeting a mortgage, raising kids, talking with other parents about school fees and the best local restaurants. I should have been normal.

On other matters, all remained much as before, and just as hot. When Paris is above thirty degrees, it's still and suffocating. The small white rocks that cover the ground in parks and some pavements cheer the place in low light, but on a hot summer's day the sun bounces off them with such intensity it is painful. And by June the city was starting to fill with damn tourists. Even more Americans, Germans, Italians, Brits and Japanese, it seemed, than they had in America, Germany, Italy, Britain and Japan. Their banter and camera-clicking seemed to drown out even the noise of a big city. Like the real Parisians I started looking at the map and planning an escape.

9

Of Madness and Mustangs

THE COMPETING AROMAS OF *sawn timber, tar, creosote, and freshly dug earth hang in the burning air. The racket of chisels, saws and labourers' curses overwhelms the crackle of birds and insects that provides the area's usual aural background. The footpath is blocked by an overloaded dray, piled with newly cut lengths of gum. 'Can we walk through here?' Louisa meekly asks one of the workmen.*

The large, shirtless man lifts his cap to the redhead and slowly runs his eyes up and down her length. 'Lovey, with your looks you can walk anywhere you damn well please.'

Louisa blushes, her mother-in-law, Rosemary, returns a stare that makes the workman fall silent and his companions look away. The new city is taking shape. More than a dozen beautifully constructed mansions have already been completed along High Street. Groups of small shops are receiving their final touches. There is a guest hotel, even a French-style restaurant.

'I wanted to be part of it all,' Rosemary says. 'It seems so unfair.'

'Why can't you be part of it?'

'I'm eighty-two years old. My body is falling apart and I'm a woman. Aren't they reasons enough? I was determined to give Alistair the space to establish himself and I've woken up one morning to realise that I am not needed. It's all behind me. It's a bitter thing to know you don't have a future. Can you imagine it?'

Louisa toys with uplifting replies; it would be worse to have done nothing in the past, everyone is sure that the grand lady has plenty of fight in her yet. *She instead bites her bottom lip. Rosemary does not want to be consoled. And, anyway, Louisa can feel the army of her own fears and disappointments massing around her. She is in no mood to console.*

✤✤✤

IF I WAS GOING to write about Undermoon Bay, I had to know the last detail. Maybe I didn't really need to assemble weather tables but it seemed to help and there were times I thought Undermoon Bay was building up into a living, breathing place. At other times, when Lawrence Jones's lack of ambition or Simone Wheeler's depression returned to trouble me, or my brain started to split in two with the strain of telling J.H. Wheeler's earlier deeds in parallel with the later stories, I'd have to check the mail again.

When noon arrived each day, I'd go for long walks. Initially it was to see Paris. Now I was hoping it would bring inspiration about early twentieth-century Australia. Unfortunately, it wasn't a great time to walk. There were tourists everywhere and the beggars of Paris had cancelled all leave. Everyone had a fresh tactic. A woman who looked like a test pilot for a pharmaceutical company came up and told a long story from behind dark glasses about how she had been ripped off in an international deal with the Disney Corporation and just needed a few francs until the court case was heard; deaf-mutes foisted badges or other knickknacks upon me and hung close until I paid for them (or refused to). People rattled cups under my nose. A tiny Arabic woman in a yashmak handed across a scrap of paper which seemed to say 'I can't speak French and need your help'. There was comparatively little I could have done, except tell her that *être* is as irregular as irregular verbs come and the historic past tense is a prick of a thing.

Near the Trocadero, there was always a squad of very forceful black men. They insisted as they blocked your path that your valuable donation – no, that's not enough – was going absolutely directly to the children of genocide-affected Rwanda.

At *métro* stations you could always bank on there being crews of buskers and drunks, plus of course the more literally legless and sellers of 'homeless' magazines.

Once on the train, there were the seat-to-seat carriage beggars, more buskers, the ten-year-old gypsy children with the darting eyes who went straight for pockets and purses, and the hunchbacks and out-of-work artists with their pronouncements of hardship and appearance to match. A healthy-looking blond-haired man near the Pompidou Centre had a sign that said: *Aidez-moi, je suis Finlandais*. Help me, I am Finnish.

Everyone wanted something and they seemed to speak as many languages as it took to ask for it. One day, as I returned by *métro* from a long walk, I felt like standing at the end of a carriage and making my own announcement:

'Listen, everybody, I'm an Australian in Paris and I'm horrified to find that the exchange rate is extremely unfavourable – worse than 3.5 to one – and that it sometimes costs me fifteen or twenty francs to buy a single coffee at a pavement café, and my book is not going as well as I had hoped, and I'm struggling with the language and aside from all that, I seem to be the only person within the entire *métro* system who actually puts a ticket into the barrier machine instead of jumping over it. So let the Lord help those who don't bother me!'

Aside from all that, summer in Paris involved long queues and premium prices. I was assured that in August the city would become a ghost town as all the locals left for their holidays. But in the meantime, I started to think: Paris for the Parisians! Except even that wasn't quite right, because I was thinking only of good, quiet, honest Parisians. Like me, for example. I didn't want those who threw their rubbish on the ground, and I didn't want the ones who took their dogs into shops and cafés and heaped expensive food upon them. I didn't want those who thought the Pacific should be a nuclear test site, and I didn't want the beggars, home-grown or not.

❖❖❖

AT THE END OF JUNE, the truly bizarre Presidential Amnesty was voted into law. Bizarre, that is, to the rest of the world. It happens in France every time a new president is elected. Prison sentences of three months or less are quashed, as are parking fines, speeding fines and other driving penalties. It is a sort of 'thanks for voting for me' from the new president and people had been planning ahead. The magazine *Auto-Plus* had been advising its readers to quit paying parking tickets in the run-up to the election. According to one road safety organisation report, average speeds rose noticeably before the election. It estimated the amnesty had cost up to 500 extra lives.

My month-long French course – three hours at a time, five afternoons a week – finally began, but did so during *une canicule* or heatwave. The temperature reached thirty-six one day. That would feel hot in any Australian city but it was simply stifling in Paris, where there was no air movement, minimal shade, huge areas of bitumen and concrete, and almost no air-conditioning.

As I sweated in the classroom every afternoon, it became evident that the Faux Debutant level was far too advanced for me, even though I knew scores of grammatical rules and hundreds of words. Somehow I was completely missing the key that allowed me to put pretty well any of them together with confidence. Still, I reasoned, it had to come. In the meantime, the French course allowed me to meet interesting people, and talk to them in English. In the corridor outside our classroom a Japanese girl named Yoko told me how she had lived in London, then moved to India, where she worked in a duty free shop at Calcutta Airport with an Australian girl named Sharon. Yoko had become upset when Sharon announced she was going home to die.

'It took me a long time to get used to your Australian accent,' Yoko explained to me. 'Not *to die*. To*day*.'

In class I sat next to a vegetarian Israeli masseuse, who now spoke Hebrew and English, but grew up speaking Romanian at home. Her parents left Romania in the 1930s. 'It was a very good time to leave Romania,' she said, implying there had at some point been a bad one. There was also a Cambodian, a Filipino, a couple of Koreans, two Chinese, a Sri Lankan, *beaucoup d'Espagnols*, an Italian, a Pole – *the* Pole – and students of several other nationalities. An American accountant named Tom had lived in Paris for ten years and knew even less about the French language than I did. He lived in an apartment in an American Government compound where all his needs were catered for – in English. He was being sent home for good in another month. So why was he learning French?

'I can't go back to my friends in Washington,' he explained, 'and tell them I can't speak the language after so many years in the place.'

My French school was rather like a real school, with the clever kids showing off, and people talking when they should be listening, and things being explained while everyone nodded knowingly yet didn't have a clue what was being said. The two things that unified the class were that everyone seemed to speak English, no matter where they were from, and everyone seemed to have it in for the French. Many were planning to leave the country at the first opportunity or deeply regretted that their jobs (or in more cases the jobs of their spouses) were forcing them to stay. Each firmly insisted that it was their own group – the Chinese, Arabs, Israelis or whoever – that the French despised the most and were rudest to.

The young Jordanian in the class, Matt, came up during a coffee break and smiled, revealing what looked like a complete set of gold teeth. 'You are American?' he asked in a warm and quite beautiful speaking voice.

'No, I'm Australi–'

'I want to go to America, not Australia.' He smiled again – yes, the teeth were pretty well all gold – and made eye contact so direct it was almost unnerving. He moved even closer and spoke in a low voice. 'But four times they have not given me a visa. Four times!'

'Why did –?'

'But that,' he continued, 'was before I married a French woman. I am again applying for the visa.'

'But –'

'I don't even like America,' he added in a low tone.

'Then –'

'No, I don't like America at all. I like Mustang. Fastback version.'

Matt planned to fly to LA, buy two Mustangs, arrange the shipping and fly straight out again. 'I have a cousin in Jordanian customs who can help me with duty. It is 300 per cent for everyone else. I will be able to resell one car for big profit and keep other one for free and still have . . .' He rubbed his fingers against his thumbs. 'I tell my wife we can then live in Jordan. We can't afford Mustang here.'

The next day Matt called me 'my Australian friend' and added that he had really enjoyed our conversation. I might have enjoyed it too, if I'd been involved. 'But watch out,' Matt said, almost pushing me out of the corridor into a side room, 'here comes the Polish guy. He talks over the top of everyone.'

Matt may have lobbed his stones out of a glass house, but they were well aimed. Whenever the class took a break, and sometimes when it was in progress, the Pole, Tadeusz, would call out 'Mr Tony' from the seat behind and play with his tiny beard as he talked at a million miles in a mix of idiosyncratic English and what – if I had been able to understand it – was almost certainly equally idiosyncratic French. Whenever any other European language was mentioned, Tadeusz would say something like 'I *parle* a little of *zat* language, you know,' then rattle off a sentence that sounded like a blend of Piedmontese and dolphin echolocation.

He walked up to me in the courtyard during a break in that first week as I reviewed my notes on the *passé compose*.

'My Canberra friend calls me Tazza,' he said as he bounced around, his black eyes fixed on me, lest I tried to escape his conversational grip. 'We Polish people say my name *Tow-day-oosh*,' he added in a piece of exaggerated over-pronunciation before throwing up his hands in a very French-Polish-Czech-English-American way. 'But Tadeusz is a silly name for the English speakers. *Trop difficile*. So I want for you to call me Tazza too.'

I didn't intend to call him anything. One to avoid, I had decided.

✣✣✣

ON MANY JULY AFTERNOONS and nights – and even some mornings – the heat and still air would force me to leave the apartment. I would walk around the streets of Paris, slaloming around things that various barking rats had judged excess to their bodily requirements, trying to sort out my characters. Despite the sultry conditions and the summer crowds, the city threw endless surprises and delights at me, such as filling the ancient Place Vendôme, the home of the Ritz Hotel and the most expensive jewellery and cosmetic shops, with massive Dalí statues. There was a woman made up of drawers, an elephant with the legs of a grasshopper and melted clocks on leafless trees, all in huge bronze relief.

On another walk I looked with envy at people in cafés and restaurants eating, drinking, smoking, talking, or being simply and uninhibitedly lost in a newspaper at a table far out onto the footpath. They mostly had money, which I didn't. At least not enough to do what they were doing as anything other than a rare treat. But more importantly, they were there to enjoy themselves, to soak up every drop of this amazing city. They hadn't screwed it up by setting themselves the ridiculous task of creating from the ether a plausible series of circumstances that would enable Undermoon Bay to escape Federation. They didn't have to work out Lawrence Jones's bizarrely complicated family tree, they weren't wandering the streets assembling time-lines in their heads and despairing they'd never successfully resolve the sexual tension between Roy Wheeler's wife, Simone, and the notorious wheeler-dealer Henry J. Smith.

These people chewing their langoustines and oysters and sipping their wine weren't stupid enough to try to make the history of a place that never existed leap off the page. Bastards!

If I had been a character in an old French film, I would have stormed into a bar, cigarette in hand, and snapped at the barman to bring *un cognac*. I would have sculled it down and marched out without talking to anyone. Instead, I walked home without stopping. And like Boxer, the trusty and doomed horse in Orwell's *Animal Farm*, I said 'I must work harder.'

✣✣✣

UNDERMOON BAY'S FAVOURITE WRITER, Lance Branch, was known as 'the poet', a term that would only ever be applied in Australia (or its Undermoon Bay microcosm) with lashings of cynicism. Not so in France, where such a title would be great honour. At times I believed things were not working for me because I was not being enough of a poet. A French poet. Arthur Rimbaud said that the true poet had to force upon himself a systematic derangement of the senses. He must endure all forms of love, suffering and madness, he must escape the suffocation of conventional society by a course of self-flagellation and self-degradation. By this measure, I was clearly not making enough sacrifice. Or having enough fun.

Isabelle had mentioned Rimbaud. She had taken it upon herself to deliver me reading lists of French classics as we sat in cafés. 'You need to read Rabelais, Racine, Rousseau and Baudelaire. And of course Rimbaud and Verlaine, preferably in the original.'

I nodded at her suggestions, and avoided mentioning my difficulties reading Joyce in the original.

'There is so much,' she said, her dark eyes sparkling with a rare hint of enthusiasm, 'and I am so jealous of you, Anthony, because it all lies before you.'

I'd love to be able to say that, spurred on by this entreaty, I soon read all of Rimbaud, but he remained just one of a long list of French writers whose name I could identify as famous, but that was it. Ditto Rabelais, Racine, Rousseau, Baudelaire, Balzac and Victor Hugo, who apparently wrote more than soulless, forgettable musicals.

Rimbaud's quote could have applied equally to Paul Verlaine, Rimbaud's one-time 'special friend'. Verlaine too was a poet who never had to go up to the mirror, have a good hard look at himself, and say 'I should have tried the systematic derangement of the senses approach.' All any great Australian writer seemed to do to get the creative juices flowing was to drink a lot and a bit more. And I wasn't even doing that. But Paul Verlaine got that challenging drinking-too-much stage down pat by the time he was seventeen. He was soon writing sonnets of lesbian love, had poems set to music by Debussy, wrote the sublimely beautiful *Chanson d'Automne* at just twenty-two years of age, married a sixteen-year-old in 1870, flirted with the Paris Commune, ran off with the seventeen-year-old Arthur Rimbaud (but not before trying to strangle the young wife and setting her hair on fire), consumed fantastic quantities of absinthe and hashish, then shot Rimbaud in a drunken bar-room stoush.

It was a promising start, but there was more to come. Verlaine went to prison, converted to Catholicism, went back on the drink, had various further homosexual encounters, rediscovered his previous weakness for female prostitutes and, among all this, found time to write some of the most beautiful verse in the French language and two books of erotic poetry considered so obscene they were suppressed until well after World War II. Even in France.

When Paul Verlaine died at fifty-two, he was not an outcast like Oscar Wilde. He was a highly respected figure throughout France. That was the standard of the competition. And I was going into the tournament unseeded.

It wasn't just Verlaine.

'I don't know how anyone could start writing anything

before they have read Emile Zola,' Isabelle wondered out loud. I could only think in response that Zola, presumably, also started writing before he had read Zola. And the simple fact is that you just can't read everything, or see everything, or systematically derange your senses, endure all forms of love, suffering and madness and still meet rent and turn up to French conversation exchanges on time.

✣✣✣

IT WAS THE DAY English-speakers know as Bastille Day and the French call simply *quatorze juillet,* or July 14. After a morning's writing I walked down my local main road, the Avenue de la Grande Armée, towards my local internationally famous monument, the Arc de Triomphe, to see another enormous military parade.

The 1940 experience might have turned the French off tanks rumbling down the Avenue des Champs Elysées but, no. A few hundred men on horses and thousands of marching men in elaborate uniforms were followed by a hundred or more tanks scuttering across the cobblestones that peek through the bitumen. Years ago, bitumen was placed over the cobblestones of most Parisian streets, partly to quieten the noise of tyres passing over them during the daily Paris Grand Prix, and partly to thwart the periodic French custom of pulling the stones out of the street and trying to use them to bring down the government. The last expression of this exciting national pastime was the student-led uprising of 1968, but you never knew when it might happen again. The surprise today though was not insurrection. It was the sight of so many students lining up behind their radioactive president. Benoit had told me that his university – Pantheon-Assas, or Paris II – had groups of right-wing student agitators patrolling the campus and menacing anyone wearing left-leaning badges or tee-shirts. Who has ever heard of right-wing, pro-nuclear university students? What sort of weird country lurked behind this veil of sophistication and normality?

Standing around the world's most chaotic roundabout – the ten lanes or so that ring the Arc de Triomphe – I made it to within a dozen or so paces of *Monsieur le Diable,* standing upright in the leading Jeep-style army vehicle. I resisted the temptation to say anything rude, if only because the densely packed crowd around me was madly cheering the man, no doubt pleased that nuclear testing in the Pacific was going to show the world that France was once again a force to be taken seriously. The man next to me had no such restraints. He ranted, he raved, he ranted some more. He was forty-something, with a train ticket safety-pinned to his shirt and green colouring on one side of his hair; exactly the sort of dribbling loon who always seems to be able to make his way through any size crowd at any public event in order to stand right next to me. His harangue, almost none of which I understood, appeared to be directed at the world in general rather than President Chirac. And at the end of it he turned to me and loudly announced 100 or so times something that sounded like the French for 'Charles de Gaulle was my father'. Congratulations, mate.

As the president climbed out of his vehicle carrying a folded flag he was puffing out his chest and struggling to contain an 'I always told you so' smile aimed directly at his former classmates and the girl who turned him down at the high-school dance. The crowd, except me and the occasional green-haired man with a train ticket pinned to his chest, was cheering Chirac with an enthusiasm almost equal to the enthusiasm with which Chirac was lapping it all up. Every triffid has its day.

Afterwards, I headed towards the *quatorze juillet* concert and fireworks/light show next to the Eiffel Tower, starring Jean-Michel Jarre of *Oxygen* fame. But the crowd was so great – supposedly a million people – that I had even less success than with James Brown. Instead I wandered back down streets filled with shady-looking teenagers throwing bungers. It was like a war zone. Something exploded right near my ankle and my eardrum rang all the way home.

A few days later, an eighty-year-old imam named Abdelbaki Sahraoui, one of the founders of the Algerian Islamic Salvation Front, was killed in Paris by members of another Algerian group, the GIA (*Groupe Islamique Armée*). Sahraoui's sin, apparently, was moderation. He had publicly condemned terrorist acts by Algerian Islamic groups. Although it wasn't obvious at the time, the assassination would soon have a major effect on everyone in Paris. And on my writing.

10

The Pole that Didn't Count

The Hideous Bluff National Park is one of the area's most popular retreats, its beaches and picnic areas reached by Hidgins Track from Aqua Street in Gadda Gadda Gadda (itself often noted for the rapid-fire local pronunciation of the three words in three different ways: GARda-Gadda-GuDAR). It is believed the bluff was named after the local aboriginals' pronunciation of the name of an early European settler, David Hidgins, which sounded more like Hideous than Hidgins. Declared in 1880, the Hideous Bluff National Park is the habitat of an estimated 1000 species of plants and 400 different types of animals and birds. With landscapes ranging from open woodland to temperate rainforest, the area contains seven ocean beaches, three rivers and is home to the large and uniquely colourful Undermann Banksia shrubs. It is proudly claimed as the oldest east-facing ocean-lined national park of more than 50,000 hectares in the Southern Hemisphere.

✣ ✣ ✣

'Mr Tony, Mr Tony.' After each French class I would briskly walk away and, as I muttered excuses about having to rush somewhere or other, Tadeusz would keep talking just as he had on the day of our first conversation. His apartment, he'd told me, was near our class. Fortunately, it was in the opposite direction to my *métro* station. Unfortunately, such a geographic detail didn't stop Tadeusz following me. Sometimes as I descended the steps to the station I'd look back to see that he was still talking. He seemed unable to take a hint.

'I have *acheté* a *boite* of cassettes on *phonetiques*,' he explained one day. 'They are *designé* for the English speakers to make their French pronunciation right. I will borrow you to them.'

I didn't think a lot more about Tadeusz's kind offer to loan me to a box of cassettes. Not until the next day, at least, when he announced that after class we were going to his apartment to pick them up. 'And I will be *fairing* the coffee for you on my *machine nouvelle*.'

I'm not sure why I agreed to go, but I did. Maybe it was that 'Tazza' didn't offer a choice, or that I knew my pronunciation was appalling and that these tapes might help. I followed him through the front door and up the steps in the late afternoon heat. Then up more steps. And, good grief, could there be yet more? We were headed for a maid's quarters in the roof of a building with no lift. The tread of every tightly winding step was small and slippery and narrower on the inside than the outside. It was all feeling a little Dr Petiot, I thought, even if the bait was a little less than a life-saving journey out of the country. 'Before you can use the tapes you need an inoculation,' I imagined Tadeusz saying as I followed him up the stairs. 'But *tout est bien*, I am a doctor in Poland.'

While I carefully watched my footing, Tadeusz almost flew up the stairs, not just talking the whole way but at one stage uninhibitedly warbling something like 'Beautiful women are my life, my mornings, my noons, my starry, starry nights . . .'

'You may not believe me,' he told me as we finally arrived at the summit, 'but I learned my *anglais* with songs like this.'

I believed him unequivocally. By now I was sweating and out of breath but still managed a hearty exhalation as Tadeusz threw back the door to his apartment. 'Struth,' I found myself saying, 'I can't believe how small it is.'

It wasn't the most polite way to comment on someone's home, but when the door was opened I felt I needed to step back not forward. I needed to give the things inside a little more room.

'It is eleven square metres,' said Tadeusz matter-of-factly. 'It costs me and my woman 2200 francs a month.'

Those dimensions made it about a quarter the size of my apartment though more than half the cost. It was as cramped as a very small caravan. And since Tadeusz had told me his woman was a student – it sounded rude in English but was understandable as the French use the term *ma femme* for 'wife' and 'woman' – it must have also been a phenomenal strain on finances. Most of the furniture was under the bed, which was at eye-level and reached by a ladder. This ladder seemed to start in the shower, which was at one end of the bed and built into a moulded plastic bubble. Every other smidgeon of real estate was filled with a huge collection of books in English, French, Polish, Russian, Spanish and one or two other languages that Tadeusz spoke, no doubt with the same speed and lack of inhibition he applied to French and English. And there was a new coffee machine sitting up on a small bench, reflecting light.

'We call this our big apartment,' Tadeusz explained with what I first thought was irony. When the coffee machine produced a loud beep, he filled a small plug with ground coffee and continued.

'The *appartement* before this one was nine and a half square metres, and in *les banlieues* . . . the outside Paris.' He looked at me with a grin. 'I moved everything here by *le métro*. The desk, the mattress, twelve big *boites* of books.'

Yes, this apartment was still a little small, Tadeusz admitted as he passed me a freshly made – and possibly lethal – espresso and I contemplated where in the flat he could possibly fit a soundproof chamber. 'But it is only twelve kilometres from my work, and I can take my *bicyclette* which is cheap*lier* than *le métro*.'

I sat on a short stool under the bed with my elbows pressed tightly to my body. I drank the coffee and surmised the reason Tazza was larger than life when he left these four walls: he needed to be considerably smaller than life within them. Inside he seemed quieter, shorter, more gentle in his movements. And unlike Matt the Jordanian, who was very talkative but not very listenative, Tadeusz asked questions and waited for answers.

His work, it transpired, involved manning a stall at 'the markets', somewhere outside Paris. It was a few hours each morning, seven days a week. He hoped it would become full-time, or at least more hours on fewer days. After finishing at the markets, Tadeusz would ride back the 12 kilometres to his house, then walk to our French class. He also did what he called little *boulots* (odd jobs) some evenings – 'but not this evening, this evening is my holiday off'. Three nights a week he biked a further ten kilometres in a different direction to attend a free evening course in English.

'I love my life in Paris,' Tadeusz said with what was suspiciously close to a winning smile.

It was hard to divine the full story because of his thick accent and propensity to jump between languages, but it seemed that three years earlier Tadeusz had been working on his parents' farm in the north of Poland. He didn't get on with his father, so left for Paris with a bus fare and a tourist visa and slept in parks until he found a squat in a soon-to-be-demolished building.

'After Poland has become free of the Soviets there was *beaucoup* corruption,' he explained, throwing in some other words that I didn't understand and which may have come from a different planet. 'Many criminals bought their way out of jail and bought the new *passeportes*. Many went to Paris, where they stole on the local Polish community.' Tadeusz said he was robbed of everything by such people four times, though he didn't explain how. Meanwhile, he learned Spanish at the public libraries because he had met some Spanish girls with whom he had some *aventures*, and he gained enough French to be able to secure a job at the markets working for an American woman who was 'crazy' and didn't pay him.

Perhaps disarmed by Taduesz's candour I admitted what I had told no-one else in the French class: that I was writing a novel.

'I think this is *la meilleure*, the best talent,' he said. 'To know so much more about life than the rest of us.'

I wished he hadn't put it like that.

❖❖❖

IT WAS HARD TO push the problems with *Undermoon Bay* out of mind when I was trying to concentrate on learning French. Potential failure was staring at me from every dark corner as I sat at thirty-four, just as I had at fourteen, in a stinking hot classroom with the words of the teacher going straight through me.

At least the teacher wasn't a nun or brother. She was named Cecile and was in her late twenties. Cecile was one of those thin, dark-eyed, thoroughly attractive French women with buckets of style and the ability to speak excellent English, and probably German and Spanish as well. Didn't seem able to smile, but sometimes I expect too much.

Stephen Dedalus, meanwhile, was making himself busy with twicreaking analysis, before corantoeing off. If not obvious read my usual portion of joyce. distracted at times very dense. car horn blaring outside sun hits edge of desk writer runs fingers on cool underside. feel hostility to jamesaugustinealoysiusjoyce must moderate, shows lack of culture. he genius, rest literary dirt beneath his feet best book ever. bits written in paris, published here 1922 much controversy lift door slams another car horn blows outside have sore toe middle one on left foot does it have a name perhaps just middle toe. itching for days maybe agenbite of inwit. Men working on apartment below as i try to write great hits of the hammer and the whole place is shaking and i'd quite like to go down and kill kill kill nothing quite as annoying as a hammer with its irregular rhythms when you've got a headache, torture. O, groatsworth of fleshcase, dissolute eardrums, *tableau*! more noise from melanie like she is being whipped or doing the whipping. i think of the rats of paris, all different types hiding in tiny corners of buildings tadeusz is another, invisible to the big people of the city can run back into his hole, had to for years with no paperwork. nervous will meet melanie in corridor could be like petiot police will say didn't you notice anything? yes the way melanie spits out *non* and *au revoir* really puts the wind up me. maybe headache exacerbated by not eating think there's still some of that baguette left – baguette, baguette i must not forget (if it's not a song played at the gaiety theatre it should be) – O sticking key on the compaq as i worry if own book already lost cause. self esteem takes battering on bad days. O jesus scared at times. very scared not living the life. not my characters. me. as i read rare sound of talking lifting up from courtyard understand bits now in paris nearly three months enormous effort on language nowhere near proficiency promised on back of packet. some writing days good but *undermoonbay* dragging, writer bashes hand on table and repeats stupid little mantra now 50,000 words in but suspects hopelessly, desperately, depressingly bogged down with complexities of plot and structure. suddenly joyce writing in viceregal official language then all characters in a pub nothing seems clear. Going to watch the finale of the tour de france down champs elysées next week, thinking of that when should be concentrating on bestbookeverwritten. snatches of songs in pub. Sirens perhaps, maybe it's just me daydream sequences, more song snatches, french, latin, more noise from woman next door. would have her in wildest fantasies.

biting, screaming, slamming against furniture. can't happen scared anyway too much henrymiller. maybe I should cheat. melanie is a book better than anything i could dream up. perish the thought. self loathing. will not cheat. oh, writer's block A poison for which there is no anecdote.

✣✣✣

I HAD BOOKED TO go to Prague in three weeks. It was a short break in a cheap and exciting city. It provided a date to aim for, a milestone to work towards. If I could just keep plugging away until then, trying to meet my word target, maybe the trip would recharge my batteries. Maybe a fresh read on my return would give me the insight that would make the disparate elements of *Undermoon Bay* finally make sense. There seemed to be so much to do to turn it into anything even heading in a direction with which I was happy. But today, at least, was a day on which I thought bits of it were good. Perhaps even great.

When you have a successful morning's writing, and I had many during that summer, you feel charged with life. Or at the very least, to use Victor Hugo's famous phrase, *Less Miserable*.

When the words flow Paris is a city of impossibly beautiful women, of magnificent food and unlimited architectural wonders. When they don't, the whole of the so-called City of Light is just a tiny, badly ventilated, cheaply furnished apartment where you are condemned to stare at a computer screen and rework something that doesn't really need reworking and hope that the phone will ring, or that you will hear the concierge padding along the corridor dropping mail on the doormat. Almost anything except Melanie shoulder-charging her sideboard. Something had to give, and it soon would.

❖❖❖

IT WAS THE THIRD day in a row. Cyclone Melanie's noises were piercing the wall in various combinations and at various rhythms and my work was painfully slow. One of the many weird things about my neighbour was that I never heard any other voices coming from her room. Just Melanie and whatever extreme emotion she had chosen to adopt for the day.

I was now trying to flesh out Simone Wheeler, to make her more than the flat, convenient character I feared she was. But soon after 11 a.m. a particularly rowdy scene commenced next door, complete with lots of sounds that couldn't possibly have been made with vocal chords. I couldn't concentrate on anything else, so I did something I had only seen done in films and bad sitcoms. I picked up a wineglass from the cupboard, put the business end against the wall and rested my ear on the base. It was not so much out of perversion (after all, I couldn't understand enough French to comprehend what she was on about) as to find out whether there really was anyone else there, whether a crime was being committed, or whether Melanie was trying to eat her way into my apartment. What I could hear through the glass on the wall was only slightly more detailed than what I could hear without it, probably because the walls were so thin, but for a moment or two I thought I could hear a second voice.

I was starting to think that I was becoming obsessed with my female neighbour like the man in the Smokie song who lived next door to Alice for twenty-four years and didn't get around to asking why she was leaving. Except Melanie may not have been leaving. She might have been going to stay, to annoy and intrigue forever. And when Melanie was in action it was impossible to do very much else but listen. And to be just a little afraid.

Sitting there with my empty wineglass, I couldn't work out whether she was happy or sad, debating politics with a mute, reciting poetry, practising for a play, engaging in dynamic meditation, selling phone sex or deciding where to stick what in and how far. I had to meet Melanie. I decided I was going to knock on her door, if not today, definitely tomorrow. And if not tomorrow, perhaps when I got back from Prague.

✣ ✣ ✣

THE HEAT BROKE TEMPORARILY. Dirty black drops of rain fell all over the city. Loulou suggested we meet at her place rather than a park. I took the *métro* to Les Gobelins, near the Chinese *quartier*, to find Loulou in a room not much bigger than Tazza's but darker and more depressing. There were piles of other people's washing on every flat surface and bowls of cat food on the uneven floorboards.

'I mind a woman's cat for three days a week and do people's ironing,' Loulou explained. It just paid for her food, university fees and rent in this subsidised apartment block.

Loulou's Paris apartment block was owned by the government of Madagascar and it seemed to be run rather like the government ran Madagascar. The toilets were overflowing, the common areas were never cleaned and the building manager wore expensive clothes and drove a big new Rover.

A small television phased in and out of focus, and in and out of colour, as it screened a dubbed American soap opera. Loulou caught me looking at the rows of books on a small shelf above the television. Every one was a Duo or Harlequin romance novel, in French.

'I buy them second-hand, the price is very interesting . . . almost nothing,' she slowly explained with a tilt of her head and overly broad smile. 'I know I shouldn't waste my time. But I read these and watch the daytime television.'

Loulou pulled a small photo album from a box on the bed. 'Today I want to show you some modern buildings in Tananarive. I don't want you to not like *le Madagascar,* to think it is primitive.'

A small photo fell to the ground. It was of a group of people standing in front of what looked like a fibro shed. Loulou picked it up, looked at it, pointed to the woman on the left and smiled. 'And this is my sister who is *décédé.*'

That means dead, doesn't it? I thought.

She handed me the photo. 'Tell me about your sister,' I said.

'My younger sister, yes? She was having a baby but the hospital was on strike. She died.'

Loulou said this in a tone that made it clear to me such things were sad but unremarkable. And she still wanted to show me the modern buildings.

❖❖❖

THE PROBLEMS WITH *UNDERMOON Bay* continued. I repeated my mantra and told myself that, with one mighty bound, Tarzan would burst free. But, alas, the crocodiles kept snapping at the heels, the natives kept raining down their arrows and the rope was fraying. At times despondency set in, sometimes a horrible blackness, a firm belief that the success or otherwise of my book would equate to no less than a referendum conducted among the Australian people as to my worth as a human being.

I could have started drinking to excess or imbibing powders or dealing with this in a more poetic way. But I remained a creature of routine with no other solution than to get up at the same time each morning and face the screen. Sometimes I found myself reflecting how Henry Miller really did spend a huge amount of time whoring and getting fabulously trashed in fabulously low dives. Hemingway filled his life with the same things as his writing – wars, plane crashes and violent sport – and grabbed a new wife for each phase of his literary career. Orwell took up a gun to defend what he most truly believed in and nearly lost his life as a result. If anyone eventually produces my biography it will say 'most of the time, he wrote'.

I found another way of temporarily escaping *Undermoon Bay* before noon with a clear conscience. I called it research. I would sit at my desk, flicking through a museum catalogue or guidebook and assuring myself that I was not whiling away writing time but delving for inspiration. Sometimes it was true, and with such inspiration, I wrote long tracts on Undermoon Bay architecture and rail systems and geology. And there were other times . . .

On what might have been the hottest morning of the year I was strolling through the Musée d'Orsay, page by page. The side-hinged balcony windows of my apartment were open but not a skerrick of new air was coming in. There was a knock on the door and, although I wouldn't have admitted it, I would have been grateful for almost any interruption, except perhaps someone selling something.

It was someone selling something: a man flogging calendars and diaries to raise money for *les handicappes*. It was only the repeated use of the phrase *les handicappes* and the unmistakable demeanour of a man looking for money that enabled me to work out that much. '*Non*,' I said. It was one word. Just one word spoken in as good French as I could muster, yet the man immediately switched to English. My French pronunciation was clearly going nowhere, my novel was going nowhere, and neither was the man with the calendars.

'I'm working,' I said, blatantly misrepresenting the situation. I slammed the door and returned to the Musée d'Orsay catalogue, still fuming, and decided novel writing was a stupid idea. I looked at a photo of the painting *Arearea* by Paul Gauguin. His approach was a much better option. Completely renounced Western civilisation, moved from France to Polynesia, lay on the beach, made love to lots of local women, did about the right amount of work and didn't have to deal with a whole lot of competition: the only Impressionist-influenced Breton painter in Hiva Oa.

No petty squabbles over funding, no bitching about rival cliques, no office politics, no Melanie crashing into his side wall or whipping and book throwing and dog barking and wailing (though if there were, he would have at least met her by now . . . and painted her naked). And there were no Grand Salons to have to shock and send into righteous uproar. Just lots of sun and sand and luscious, jump-on-able females. Oh, and the clap, which made him tortured, disfigured and suicidal, then dead at fifty-four. Can't have everything.

I was starting to think I was working in the wrong genre. The French bought more comic books than novels while the Loulous of this world read dozens of romances a year but no literary fiction. I had once heard a radio interview with a man from Mills & Boon. He said they were always looking for new authors and, by fiction standards, paid very highly.

'So why don't you just stop complaining and cash in,' I now said to myself with a laugh. 'It might enable you to stay longer in Paris, anyway, so you can still paint your masterpiece.'

'Yeah sure,' I replied, immediately realising that if talking to yourself is a sign you are going mad, having a conversation just might be the confirmation. Anyway, Hemingway would have rather starved than sold out. Then again, I thought, Hemingway was never really going to starve. In his Paris memoir he said that hunger was good discipline and that his fervent belief in his own talent made poverty bearable. But he forgot to tell his readers about his wife Hadley's recent $8000 inheritance and $3000-a-year trust fund at a time when an apartment like theirs cost just $18 a month. Ernest wasn't bagging pigeons in the Jardin du Luxembourg to ward off starvation; he and Hadley had a housekeeper/cook and regularly zipped off for ski holidays in Switzerland and bullfights in Spain. And this from a man who once wrote to F. Scott Fitzgerald: 'All you need is to write truly and not care what the fate of it is.'

None of this of course was strictly relevant, because I wasn't in real or imagined danger of starving either. But somehow or other it helped sway the decision that I needed to dash off a romantic novel. I'm not sure how to explain it.

Call it cabin fever, or a crazy notion that somehow writing the slight and the superficial could fund the deep and the meaningful. Just don't say it was merely an excuse to get away from *Undermoon Bay* at a time when I hated the sight of it.

Anyway, it couldn't be that hard or take that long. I had never believed the story that Mills & Boons were all written by retired army captains. Even if they were, the sheer number of new titles meant they must often be looking for new army captains, and I could always lie about my service record. For research purposes I bought two Mills & Boon books at W.H. Smith, the outrageously pricey English language bookshop on rue de Rivoli. One was so badly written I couldn't believe it. It was set in South Africa and was full of lines like 'the girls sat around and talked about fashion'. The other was set in New Zealand and was surprisingly well crafted, though it reeked of all the cynicism I was about to apply to *Mansions Of Glory* by Antoinette Davina.

11

The Bomb

Julia Thompson stood at the base of the giant stairway. Her small, pale right hand rested on the wide hardwood balustrade. Her soft, heart-shaped face stared in awe at the intricately constructed glass and steel ceiling so far above.

She paused for a moment to soak up the ambience of the slate-lined foyer with its towering atrium, and to enjoy the dense coolness provided by the rows of massive terracotta pots, each containing a tree-sized fern. At that moment the sun left the last of the clouds behind and a shaft of light burst into the foyer. The newfound sunshine did more than bring the foyer alive. It added fire to Julia's long auburn hair and injected extra depth into her almond eyes.

Bathed in the light and warmth, Julia reflected that this scene was like one from any of the movies that had soaked up her lonely teenage years. Of course, if it had been a movie, the girl might have been a little more obviously pretty and the light blue dress that Julia was wearing might have been a little closer fitting. And the scene – one supposes – would have been set in New York or Paris rather than Sydney, Australia.

And most importantly, the girl would have felt totally at home in the lavish surroundings, brushing past prized artworks with careless abandon and throwing herself into the foyer's vast and sumptuous leather armchairs with a blasé air that Julia could never confidently muster. But the house – this vast and elegant three storeys of steel, glass, slate and native hardwoods – could not be improved on by Hollywood. Neither, for that matter, could the view of what looked like a thousand yachts, each throwing its sails against the sky in a ballet around the white fans of the Sydney Opera House.

✣✣✣

THE WRITER TEMPORARILY KNOWN as Antoinette Davina sat around one evening with a notepad and a glass of wine and plotted it all out. Julia Thompson was a twenty-five-year-old journalist on *Lovely Homes and Beautiful Gardens*. Although she was on another run-of-the-mill assignment, it didn't stop her daydreaming about what it might be like to wake each morning in such a house, to sit on any of the massive cantilevered balconies and read for hours on end, to feel the sea-breezes on her face and experience the legendary 'southerly busters' shake and cool the hills around the harbour at the end of a hot summer's day. Antoinette Davina would have liked to have felt one herself in the midst of this fearsome French heat.

Julia's reveries were periodically interrupted by Veronica Vreland, who was leading Julia and her photographer from room to room. Veronica was determined to use every surface texture, water feature and skylight as an excuse to deliver a monologue about herself, her dreams, her plans and the architectural contribution to the northern Sydney skyline that her fiancé – the media magnate Ross Farrington – was generously and selflessly making with this new house. Farrington himself would soon carry his athletic frame down that giant staircase, his dark brown leather deck-shoes squeaking on the polished surfaces, the muscles in his long, tanned legs rippling . . .

He would immediately, subtly, masterfully, etcetera-ly demonstrate that he was not happy with his fiancée Veronica taking it upon herself to put his new house in a magazine. And, *golly gee*, within a few pages Julia would discover that the launching of a takeover bid for the Image Magazine Group by Zentre Corporation could soon make Farrington the owner of *Lovely Homes and Beautiful Gardens*. On any day in the magazine office, Julia could be subject to his intense and unnerving stare and a tone which, on that fateful first meeting, she couldn't help but think of as arrogant.

The plot was utter flummery and it was all great fun at first. But *Mansions of Glory* required more structure and discipline than I bargained on and started eating up precious time. After just a few long days at the computer I was itching to jump back to *Undermoon Bay*. Once the initial buzz had disappeared I had to justify my change of direction by telling myself that writing anything is good practice because there are clear and precise ways of writing, no matter how inane the subject, and everything needs a structure. Even bad things are available in good versions. But that didn't change the fact I had set out to storm the literary world and was sitting in a small flat writing romantic fiction so light and wafty it was likely to slip out between the gaps in the keyboard and dissipate into the atmosphere.

After completing the introductory chapter and a synopsis of the rest of the book, I packed it in an envelope and sent it off to Mills & Boon in London. I immediately returned to more serious labours, but would now await each day's mail even more anxiously. I could stay longer in Paris if *Mansions of Glory* earned some decent money. And nobody need ever know.

❖❖❖

I WAS BACK WRESTLING with *Undermoon Bay* on yet another stinker in July, as my trip to Prague – my escape – drew slowly closer. As always, the television was blinking away in the background. A sudden drama caught my attention and I stopped writing. A series of news flashes showed images of people being pulled out of the St Michel station in stretchers. There had apparently been an explosion in the heart of the Latin Quarter. A field hospital was being set up in front of nearby Notre-Dame cathedral and soon helicopters were ferrying the wounded out of the area. I kept hearing the words *quatres morts* and *les Algeriens* mentioned. My language skills had progressed sufficiently to know that *quatres morts* suggested four dead and *Algerien* was French for 'second-class citizen', except when scoring goals for the French soccer team. Perhaps one of the many militant Algerian organisations had claimed responsibility, or perhaps they were going to receive the blame anyway.

Very soon Jacques Chirac was on the scene. The reports were saying 100 injured, many seriously. By the end of the day they were saying 200 injured, as well as four killed outright. The bomb had been a crude homemade job using a barbecue gas canister. It had been hidden under a seat and detonated in a tightly packed carriage before the doors opened at the station. The GIA seemed to be responsible. It was protesting against France's support for the interim Algerian government, a secular administration that had seized power after a flirtation with elections looked like producing the wrong result.

Within little more than a day the streets were filled with 3000 sinister looking *CRS* special police with berets and dark military-style clothing. Soon the government launched the ominous sounding Vigi-Pirate anti-terrorism program and there were soldiers with machine guns prowling the train stations.

The next time I hopped onto a *métro*, I started to imagine what an explosion would be like. Would I even know there had been one? Would I wake up in hospital to find there was less of me? Could you run from an explosion, would ducking under a seat help? It was nerve-racking and I'd look up and down the long, human-filled metal box and sense that most others were feeling exactly the same way. They too were scanning the aisles and looking under the seats trying to see if there was a 'suspect package'. Okay, seven killed – that was the latest figure – in a city of seven million. The odds looked good; there were more than 300 train stations in Paris and it would be really bad luck to be at the wrong one. But there was a tenseness in the air, with constant bomb alerts across the city. The buses became much more crowded, though there was no reason they should be safer.

To add to the anxiety, *la canicule* continued, with the temperature occasionally scraping the underside of forty degrees. Soon after the bomb, all garbage bins in the *métro* were sealed and the *CRS* men in the black overalls rifled through any bag you were carrying into a *métro* station. The big shops installed metal detectors. There was a widespread belief the St Michel bomb was to be the start of a long campaign. And the coming weekend was the busiest of the year for public transport: the annual *Grand Départ*. Parisians would be leaving *en masse* for their summer holidays.

There were security guards and metal detectors for the last few days of our French course too. Although my attention may have been compromised, as the lessons progressed I began to feel I was coming to terms a little more with the French, their language, their lifestyle and their red tape. But still very little of the French I was cramming into my head was coming out my mouth. Sure, I could read more signs and advertisements, and didn't need to look up things in the dictionary every ten seconds while reading a book aimed at a five-year-old. Every fifteen to twenty seconds now sufficed. By contrast, everything in Tadeusz's head came flying straight out. There was no filter between his brain and his mouth. Sometimes I wished I had his lack of inhibition, that I could just walk into a shop and have a go. But I was always too nervous.

After the course finished, Tadeusz rang to say he was so busy he couldn't talk for long. This was a prelude to him talking for long. 'I am very tired today,' he explained, 'because I was all last night hardly working. But can I *visite*?'

'Yes, but not *au matin*,' I replied. Not quite talking French was obviously catching. 'I will be working then.'

I convinced myself I was just being polite, really I wasn't annoyed to hear from him. Tadeusz's unpredictability provided a welcome foil to the heavily structured life I was living, the rigid format I knew my days had to follow if my mission were to succeed. It was also true that Tazza's life experience couldn't be more different from mine and he was a character waiting to be clamped between hard covers. I started to wonder whether it was possible to weave a Polish guy into *Undermoon Bay* – or maybe even *Mansions Of Glory*.

She stole a furtive glance as the lean, tanned Tadeusz strode out to join them on the sun-drenched veranda. His piercing dark eyes darted around the gathering, his lean limbs moved frenetically, his talking accelerated with every step. She wondered if he'd just freebased a crate of those high-caffeine energy drinks.

Maybe not. But I'd wryly decided that when I finally, reluctantly produced a career memoir – *The Path to My Nobel Prize* – I should claim Tadeusz's apartment as my own. 'Those twenty-one flights of narrow, slippery stairs were good discipline,' I would write. 'A fervent belief in my own talent made living in 11.5 square metres bearable. And the parks were always full of pigeons.'

✣✣✣

'I HAVE HEARD RUMOURS,' said Sandrine, 'that bombs are being found right across Paris. People say the information is being suppressed in the interest of public order.'

I asked Benoit if it was possible that the GIA was just calibrating its equipment so it could computer-simulate future terrorist actions.

'I don't think so,' he said.

✣✣✣

I WAS HAVING THE last few stabs at *Undermoon Bay* before packing my bag for Prague. I was going seriously cold on writing faux history and had decided there were two possible explanations why it wasn't working. The first was that I didn't have the experience or skill to do it; the second was that real events have a gravity that fictional ones almost never can. If you know it is true, reading that 10,000 people died in a battle will move your senses even if described with little skill, and will do so a great deal more if described well. When real people are dying in real wars the tragedy is instantly and undeniably tragic, the humour is automatically bittersweet, the efforts of certain people are incontrovertibly heroic. And when you wheel in a character like Julius Caesar or Abraham Lincoln, you don't need to spend thousands of words building him up. He is a star from the moment he hits the page. Nobody can create a character like that in a make-believe world. Can they? Please tell me they can't.

Tadeusz arrived with two large bottles of apple cider under one arm and held out a brown paper bag when I opened the door.

'It is *boudin,*' he beamed as he scratched his small beard and clumsily made his way inside. '*Boudin*: I think you say blood pudding sausage. Now I have another extra job with *un boucher*. I cut it up for us now.'

He was wearing an elaborate blue and yellow shirt, creased as if it had come straight out of the box, fashionable long shorts and bright white running shoes with what looked like spirit levels in the soles. He made his way directly to my table, hurriedly cleared a space next to the computer, pulled out a Swiss Army knife and started to cut into the small white sausages as if they were alive and likely to fight back.

'I bring things for you because I always like to speak English and *voir* my *bon ami.*' Tadeusz paused in his sausage massacre to lift his wrist and twist it in my direction. 'See, I have a new watch, it is Citizen with Eco-Drive *pouvoir*, very new from Japan, and my wife is in now in Brittany.'

I was not sure what the connection between these things was or whether the punchline meant his wife had left him. Indeed, I had no idea when Tadeusz ever did see his wife.

'Nice watch, Tazza,' I said. 'You've really warmed to consumerism, haven't you?'

'*Peut-être*. I am seeing this light-power watch and just had to *acheter* it. I say to *ma femme*, "In communist time we Polish are sad because we do not have anything, but now we Polish are sad because we do not have everything."'

Today's main subject was self-indulgent American writers who called themselves radical but were really traditional, and English magazines that were concerned with whether people were homosexual or not.

'What could it possibly matter,' Tadeusz said stridently. 'I have *rencontré* the friends who are the homosexuals and it wasn't important a bit.'

The extent to which it wasn't important a bit was highlighted by the extent to which Tadeusz kept returning to it. He then charged on about Polish writers and how the country never had any freedom and so they all had to leave the country to write the truth and so anywhere you went you would find Polish writers and artists associated with the cause of freedom. And some of them were homosexual too.

He pulled a CD out of his bag. 'You have a player? This is very new . . . my favourite Polish *chanteur*.'

'No,' I responded, pointing at the small Panasonic. 'It only plays tapes.'

'I will have to *chante* it for you myself.'

I looked hard at Tazza's face and realised he was joking.

✣ ✣ ✣

LEOPOLD BLOOM WAS LOOKING at whores on the way back from the pub. Or in his mind. One section of *Ulysses* started in the first person but by the next page had transformed into a sales contract. Soon Bloom turned into 'Barney Kiernan's', and met a person described as 'the citizen'. He rubbed his hand in his eye. That was the clue and I caught it. Bloom is the outsider. The citizen is the Cyclops, and an anti-Semite to boot. Maybe it just takes a few hundred pages to get into the swing of Joyce. Hey, it's not a tabloid newspaper story, it doesn't have to get you in with the first sentence. The language then turned all cosmic, perhaps because someone in the pub thought they'd seen Paddy Dignam and we all knew Dignam was dead.

Joyce boasted that if Dublin was destroyed it could be rebuilt brick by brick from the pages of *Ulysses*. I, for one, would struggle to find my way around such a rebuilt city. But at least I was slowly becoming orientated. I thought.

✣ ✣ ✣

HEMINGWAY WROTE OF HIS DAYS hanging about in the cafés of Paris with his pencils and notebook. I used the cafés mainly for conversation exchanges and, unlike Papa, I rarely discussed horse-racing tips or cycling results with the waiters.

Nor would I yell for a dozen freshly shucked *portugaises* and a carafe of some rare and authoritative dry white wine I had discovered on a game fishing trip off the Riviera. Sometimes Isabelle and I were on such a tight budget we would find ourselves in a Quik store, a sort of quasi-McDonald's not mentioned by Hemingway, but which served the cheapest hot black liquid in Paris.

It seemed a shame. If you want the very thing that makes Paris such a great place – the ambience of a Parisian café as much as the coffee itself – you have to go to a traditional tables on the footpath café and talk about artists such as Rimbaud, along with all forms of love, suffering and madness, right there among a crowd discussing similarly weighty things. Quik didn't quite provide such an atmosphere, though it was air-conditioned.

While Isabelle concentrated on other people's novels, Benoit was the most insistent in asking about mine. (Loulou's questions centred around such things as whether I could write a letter on her behalf to show how good her English was, so she could apply for a job as a nanny in Canada.)

'We French,' Benoit stressed as the walls of the café vibrated, 'prize writers and other intellectuals very highly.'

'I'm flattered you think writers are intellectuals,' I responded. I had eventually told him in very general terms about my cerebral novel – produced without compromise etc. – and left out the bits about compromise etc. I couldn't tell him about the Mills & Boon, of course. But what if I couldn't finish *Undermoon Bay*? What sort of fraud would I come across as? What else could I do with my life? I started to think I would be condemned to writing other things, such as Mills & Boon romances, even one chapter of which became damn tedious once the amusing novelty of doing it had passed. And which, I might add, still hadn't elicited an excited response from the publisher. Or any other type of response. And it had been a good week or two now.

❖❖❖

THE TEMPERATURE REMAINED IN the mid-thirties and the heat was setting off burglar alarms as I contemplated what I could do if I failed to make a mark with fiction.

Maybe, I thought blackly, I could reinvent myself as one of those self-help authors who apply new terms to the blindingly obvious and manage to convince the masses they have successfully distilled the secret of life into 200 large-type pages. Or I could spit out management texts speaking in fridge-magnet grabs about throwing away the past in order to show full respect to the future. Or I could write marketing dribble, encouraging people to pay over the odds for things they don't need. Or I could go back to technical writing. It would all be more profitable than fiction, I was sure. But then it was all journalism of one sort or another. No, never again . . .

The *Grand Départ* occurred with unprecedented security, and without incident. The shutters were now down on many buildings, and the sign *Fermature Annuelle* was up. The parking meters were turned off and parts of the city – the non-tourist parts – looked almost deserted. The front pages of the newspapers showed the faces of three Algerian men the French police believed could help them in their inquiries. There was a reward of one million francs for information.

If the level of security in Paris had been impressive before, it was now simply amazing. The police were out in unprecedented numbers. It was a particularly nerve-racking time for anyone born in North Africa – that increased the chances of being stopped and questioned by about 3000 per cent – and also for the *sans papiers*, that army of people living in Paris without a legitimate visa, passport or *carte de séjour*. From talking to people in the French course, it seemed that half the people they knew were in the country illegally, either overstaying visas or having slipped in through Italy or some other place more lax with border controls. Others were tenuously keeping within the law by taking ever more courses to extend their student visas, or by getting the train to a border. There they would have their passport stamped by another country, or apply for a new visa.

It wasn't just the wealthy who had decamped. There were hardly any beggars. Even the brown-paper man had disappeared. I hoped someone had tightened his string, put a postage stamp on one of his corners and sent him to the south of France, and that he was now sunning himself on a beach. But I suspected otherwise.

Closer to home, I had realised that my novel was going to work only if I could make it about people who appeared thoroughly authentic and developed in the context of an exciting and well-rounded story. I could no longer see how the hell I could achieve that in a false history book covering two centuries, so I'd started rewriting many of the history bits in the style of a conventional novel, putting the emphasis on description, dialogue and something at least a little closer to a conventionl plot. I was still aiming to use lots of breakout boxes around this more conventional narrative, and to have constantly changing perspectives (in time and viewpoint) to mimic different camera angles. But for all the effort, there was a sense of gloom about it. Maybe I had just worn myself out. Maybe I was wasting my time anyway.

The terrorist bomb had largely pushed the proposed nuclear tests off the front pages and into second item on the television news. Still, various people found time and ready media access to launch tirades against opponents of France's legitimate right to do whatever it damn well pleased wherever it damn well wanted. For a nation that wished the world to believe they didn't give a fig what other countries thought, France was still spending a lot of time discussing the protests in Australia, how Peugeots were being vandalised on Sydney and Melbourne streets, and how businesses were taking Gallic words out of their names.

Australians let Britain conduct tests above ground in South Australia, people repeated in print, television interviews and conversations. Yet, those same hypocrites, racists and *anglosaxons* (add scowl, hand signal and farting noise here) were getting high and mighty when France tried to do testing below its own sacred earth, the French *département* of Tahiti. And Australia sells uranium to France. So what right has it got to complain about nuclear tests?

❖ ❖ ❖

BENOIT ARRIVED AT MY apartment late one afternoon with a gift: a Claude François tape containing, among other things, a French version of the Peter Allen song 'I Go to

Rio'. I had earlier watched a television documentary about this wide-lapelled, flare-wearing 1970s singer with a haircut strangely reminiscent of Benoit's. The French were very proud that his song 'Comme d'Habitude' was later changed and rendered in English as 'My Way'. Adding to the Claude François legend was an inglorious end: he was electrocuted in the late 1970s when trying to repair a light-switch while sitting in the bath. I had raised the subject soon after I saw the program, expecting Benoit would also consider François a figure of fun.

'I sorry if you saw a show and didn't like him, but the songs of Claude François are very good to dance to,' he proclaimed instead, leaving me with the unlikely image of Benoit dancing. Of more interest, Benoit said that it wasn't a light-switch that Monsieur François was trying to turn on. 'We say among ourselves that he was using some sort of, this is a word I don't know in English, *un vibrateur*.'

Although there was no real evidence to support this theory, I was prepared to take it as gospel. Aside from the fact that it was told to me by a real French person, I was trained on the tabloids and knew the maxims: (a) never give anybody the benefit of the doubt, particularly a celebrity; (b) a nasty rumour is always held to be true unless superseded by an even nastier one; and (c) any source is a reliable source if it says something more appealing, interesting or exciting than the alternative.

Claude François, however, was now in the background and Benoit was talking earnestly as I quietly prayed that Melanie wasn't about to put on a scene. 'The Australians are making the anti-nuclear protest an attack on the French people. It is a stand the *anglosaxons* would never take against the Chinese, even though they have just exploded their own nuclear device.'

'But our expectations of France,' I responded, 'are higher than those of a government that puts political prisoners to work in toxic chemical plants and uses tanks to make its students go further.'

I worried that any gravity in what I was saying was being undercut by the sound of maracas and Claude François singing *'Je vais à Rio . . . de Janeiro'*. 'And if the English were doing what the French were planning to do,' I added, 'they would get an even harder time from the Australians. It's just hard to imagine any First-World country other than France doing it so plainly in the face of world public opinion.'

Mine sounded like a valid argument but I knew Benoit was at least partly right. I had spent a minor fortune on the latest copy of *The Bulletin* from Australia and I knew that many Australians who took it upon themselves to be outraged at the slightest hint of a racist comment were now running around telling anyone who would listen that the French were a bunch of arrogant frog bastards.

12

A Prague Awakening

THE WHINE OF UNCONTROLLED masculine sobbing pierced the clay and mortar and brought neighbours into the fenced front yard of the Jones estate. Misery had quickly overtaken shock.

Martin Jones hadn't bothered to insert his cuff-links or brush his hair. He was oblivious to the gathering, and to the flowers and friends surrounding him. The covenant with the divine had been broken. Wasn't banishment and seven years hard labour enough? Wasn't such suffering to be credited against the next generation? Of all the whaling boats they were now operating with greater and greater safety, why was that the one that had to go to the bottom? Why hadn't he, as chairman, over-ruled this stupid insistence on not having a support boat during the chase?

What had he done to deserve the loss of both sons?

After the drowning, Martin Jones kept thinking 'I wish it could have been me instead'. He deeply meant it. But to even voice the thought sounded so pointless.

'Caroline pleaded with you,' said Margaret. 'Our daughter-in-law pleaded with you, and you ignored her.' Margaret Jones felt guilty even as she said the words. But somebody had to be punished.

❖ ❖ ❖

WHEN MILOS FORMAN FILMED *Amadeus* in 1984 he needed only to remove the cars from the streets of Prague to recreate old-world Vienna. I spent the first full day walking around the city with a crazy half-smile, and filled with a huge escapist buzz. I walked for eight or nine hours through magnificent Baroque streets unsullied by McDonald's and Coca-Cola advertisements, down narrow cobblestone lanes that had changed little in hundreds of years.

The roofs were red, just like Sydney's. But I felt light years from the modern world. And, more importantly, light years from *Undermoon Bay*. Every building in the city centre was either under scaffolding or recently restored. And it was all being done to the highest standard. If these people had had any money in the 1950s and 1960s everything would have been ruined. The city was once overlooked by the world's biggest statue of Stalin but the communist government never got around to 'improving' the buildings. I walked across the ornate, fourteenth-century Charles Bridge, once the only crossing over the Vltava river, and looked at a beautiful old building covered in frescos of ostriches. According to the *Eyewitness Guide*, a couple of hundred years earlier it had been the site of a highly prosperous business owned by one James Fux. It sold feathers and other ostrich products. I was leaning against a suitably ornate railing contemplating a business named 'James Fux Ostriches', when an entirely cylindrical German man tapped me on the shoulder and asked if I could photograph him, his equally cylindrical wife and the Charles Bridge. He gave me a full five-minute explanation on how the camera worked. Fill-in flash, main flash, auto focus, zoom, date function . . .

'What if I just push the button?'

'Zat vill be fine too. It has an automatic program you know.'

Later I went to a photo exhibition about the Nazi occupation, followed by the place in the Czech Republic that most fascinated me: the Orthodox Cathedral of the Saints Cyril and Methodius. Years earlier I had seen *The Heydrich Terror*, a documentary that took my breath away. It told the story of how in 1942 members of the Czech Resistance had been parachuted in by the RAF to assassinate Nazi strongman and official 'protector of Czechoslovakia' Reinhard Heydrich.

A former fencing champion and Gestapo chief, Heydrich was considered a shining example of Aryan manhood and the Nazis gave him two separate state funerals. After the wholesale torture and slaughter of suspected sympathisers to the parachutist's cause, the Nazis tracked down Heydrich's assassins to the crypt of the Orthodox Cathedral of the Saints Cyril and Methodius. A pitched battle saw 600 German troops fight it out against just seven parachutists. Miraculously, the Czechs held the Germans at bay for several hours while trying to tunnel out through the sewers, and while also thwarting Nazi attempts to flood the crypt. Eventually the German troops triumphed and the parachutists shot themselves rather than be taken into custody.

In what the SS considered a 'measured response', it murdered 5000 people, including most of the officials of the church and the entire population of two nearby towns incorrectly believed to have assisted the parachutists. It also stepped up the liquidation of the Czech Jews, so that Hitler could complete his bizarre plan to turn the Jewish quarter of Prague – still intact today – into a museum showing the 'Depravity of the Extinct Jewish Race'.

The top level of the Orthodox Cathedral of the Saints Cyril and Methodius had been restored but the crypt was much as it had been then, apart from containing a photographic exhibition of the events of 1942, prepared and donated by the British War Museum. Everywhere I looked there were bullet holes and I could see where the parachutists had tried so desperately to break into the sewerage system.

Prague was meant to be a complete break, and for a short while it was. But I soon found that, instead of walking around Paris trying to tie up my plot points and breathe life into my characters, I was walking around Prague trying to tie up my plot points and breathe life into my characters.

My opus and its severely tangled web of people and events couldn't be evaded just by changing cities. It was soon at the forefront of my mind again. I was fixating on nineteenth-century Australasia rather than the architectural magnificence around me, and I was no longer sure what I was trying to achieve, how I was going to achieve it or, in my darkest moments, how I could have been so deluded to have set off on such an ambitious path.

The story of the parachutists – rather like Petiot's serial killings in my own street, or anything to do with the occupation of Paris, or the deportment of the French Jews or even a crude gas bottle bomb blowing apart commuters – was yet another reminder of the slightness of my stupid little project, my pathetic pretension, my folly.

Of course books don't all need to be about huge, history

shaping events. But they need to be about something important, and I wasn't sure any longer I was writing about anything worth writing about. I walked beside the trolley bus track on the banks of the Vltava and ruminated under a perfectly blue Czech sky. What is any novelist trying to achieve? Is it to draw attention to pleasing or interesting paradoxes, to entertain, to be funny, to make people think, to merely record events or perceptions of events, to provide a framework for glib observations, to create a riddle or puzzle, to find God or change the world? Is it a need to just write in the same way as a guitarist can't stop strumming, or an alternative to Catholic confession in a secular age? Is it about leaving something worthwhile and permanent, or highlighting life's quirks such as why the old and ugly man behind the ticket counter who has just been extremely rude and unhelpful to me will become all sweetness and light to the pretty twenty-two-year-old woman following behind? He knows and she knows he will get absolutely nothing out of it, so logically he should be even ruder as a result. But it never works out like that.

Hemingway mistrusted adjectives. He wanted to remove the presence of the author and lay raw action on the page so the reader would experience it verbatim. Fitzgerald strove to distil the poetic essence of the Jazz Age, which he was sure was richer, faster and more extravagant than any era that could possibly follow. Orwell believed words could bring down the capitalist system and help replace it with something fairer. Joyce wanted to smash the conventions of literature and reinvent all the rules of writing. Miller rooted around and didn't want to tell only his mates. Exactly what I was trying to do, I was no longer sure.

A visit to Franz Kafka's house, now a museum, didn't cheer me up. What a misery the author of *The Trial* and *The Castle* was. Would have disappointed everyone including himself if he didn't have an early and dismal death. Fortunately the story has a fitting ending: he did head back to the pavilion early, having failed to get most of his writing published in his lifetime, or to have lightened up.

Why did he bother? Why was I bothering? Fortunately, temporary relief from such big questions was available by the glass from any of several nearby beer halls. And soon I was one of ten or twelve people sitting at the end of a long, wide trestle table in a dark and large dome-roofed cellar. A couple of old blokes leaned against the bar. A trio of middle-aged, beret-wearing Czechs sat opposite me, flicking through a collection of charcoal sketches and casually discussing the artworks' nuances. Or the football, I couldn't tell.

The blackboard listed Guinness, Kronenbourg and Murphy's. But they were three or four times the price of the local stuff, called *pivo* and available in light and dark shades. I opted for *pivo* in light and then dark shades at two-thirds of not very much a glass, plus a plate of klobàsy sausages and bread dumplings and gherkins. The sounds of an oompah-pah band gently drifted in from the Old Town Square. I looked up at a giant stuffed ape propped on a ledge below the curved, brick ceiling and as I sipped the *pivo* I felt like asking this massive hairy primate how a project that started so well could have slumped so quickly, so dramatically, so far. And whether it was possible that after so much planning, so much hard work and such high hopes, I might return home a failure.

A thirtyish woman with short, wavy, jet-black hair was seated on the same bench as me, a little further along the table. She was smoking a cigarette and reading a book, though I couldn't make out what language it was written in. She was drinking a pint of Guinness, which suggested she might be a foreigner, and I couldn't help but notice she was both pretty and cerebral-looking. I felt I needed my copy of *Ulysses*, and ideally a pair of glasses at least as thick as hers and some loose tobacco and cigarette papers.

I had nothing to smoke and I had left Joyce back in Paris, with the bookmark placed almost exactly halfway through the text. The scene before my departure took place at Sandymount Beach, with the writing style imitating that of a romantic novel, a genre with which I was now well familiar. Our Dublin ad salesman was admiring a young woman sitting on the sand. With his head filled with thoughts of what he could do to the pretty young Gerty MacDowell, Bloom put his hand in his pocket and spent several paragraphs doing what some cruel people might argue Joyce had himself been doing for 450 pages. Not me, though. I was determined to dig, to study, to understand. And of course to finish the bally thing on my return.

After another *pivo* I leaned over and quite obviously read the spine of the woman's book: *Prozac Nation.* I'd never heard of it. A few moments later we were talking.

'It's Annie,' she introduced herself, leaning back and rolling her right hand through the air as she spoke. 'I'm a film-maker.'

Annie had intense eyes behind dark-framed, slit-like glasses and a strong American accent. Her voice sounded compressed, like a disclaimer at the end of a radio commercial where fifty words are fitted into three seconds. 'But I know that sounds incredibly pretentious, so I don't normally tell people.'

'I'm sure that's the case,' the *pivo* and I replied, 'but with us having known each other for so long . . .'

She looked over the top of her glasses, pursed her lips and tightened her grip on the Guinness.

'So what's the book like?' I asked. The tenseness in her face diminished a little and she lifted *Prozac Nation* and waved it around.

'It's like, so full-on. So, so full-on.' As a literary review, it didn't tell me a lot. She sipped her black ale so subtly the level didn't change, then reached to the ashtray to pick up a cigarette that was now fifty per cent ash cylinder. I noticed her fingernails were painted sky blue and that she had a small tattoo of a seahorse between her thumb and index finger.

'I'm making a film, like, a short film, like, twenty-two minutes, at the moment,' she continued, talking so fast there was the hint of a minor sonic boom trailing each word. 'It's about a young Czech girl who is, like, on the edge of despair with the changes around her.

'You're probably thinking, "What, changes like western film-makers arriving?"' she added with what might have been a laugh. I *was* thinking something exactly like that. 'But,' she continued, 'there's, like, a lot of other shit going down.'

Prozac Nation, now resting on the table between us, was subtitled 'Young and Depressed in America'. A winning phrase, I thought. Pity the Czech parachutists didn't have a copy to read in the crypt. They could have learned how bad life can get when Daddy won't let you drive his Merc and you can't get the right type of cocaine.

Having apologised in advance for any perceived pretentiousness, Annie then quoted a string of obscure films and books, the titles of which were generally lost in the *pivo* bubbles. Her habit of joining every phrase with 'like' could have been really annoying. If, like, she weren't pretty. I just had to see the new film by Yimou Zhang. Or was it Zhang Yimou? 'It's the funniest Chinese film ever,' Annie assured me in rapidfire terms.

To my enormous credit, I responded to all her pseudo-intellectual posturing by being incisive and doubly down-to-earth. Er, not quite. I lobbed back a whole lot of amber-fuelled clap-trap about the art of writing. I blurted out literary concepts that I wasn't even sure were literary concepts. They might have been medical terms or the names of building materials. Annie looked at me wide-eyed. She was either stunned by my ability to, like, soar way above her mind-space, or she was mentally constructing the blithering idiot character that would finally make her new script work. The barman wandered back to ask if we wanted anything more. We did. He brought another Guinness and another *pivo* then went back to leaning against the wall, flicking through a Czech–English dictionary.

'I've always believed,' I continued, 'that if I worked hard enough and long enough and cast everything else aside, I could achieve something worthwhile in Paris, something innovative and powerful.' I still believed it too. I had to believe it; there was no Plan B.

'J'ai habité à Paris,' Annie said. 'It was a few years ago that

I lived there but I enjoyed it. I can see what you mean. And it's a very easy language to learn compared with Czech . . . you know there was another bomb there?'

'What, since the one at St Michel?'

'Yes, at the Place d'Étoile.'

I didn't know whether to be more shocked by someone thinking French was easy to learn, or by the idea of a bomb around the corner from my apartment. 'Hell, another one? Was anyone killed this time?'

'Not sure. I just heard, like, a radio report and it was in very fast Czech.'

I was unsettled for a while, but Annie and I kept drinking and talking for what must have been hours, using ever longer words to describe ever hazier conceits. I told her about the scariness of the earlier bomb and she mentioned the evilness of Chirac and I mentioned the evilness of prime minister Juppé and we both agreed on the evilness of all their predecessors and all their successors and I was pleased to hear she hadn't read any Joyce which gave me some sort of half-cocked upper hand and we continued to drink *pivo* and Guinness and gabber. At some point, a group of travelling minstrels in medieval dress marched into the beer hall and sang Czech classics, such as 'That's Amore', while everyone clapped and sang along and put coins in their floppy, upturned hats. There was more *pivo* and more Guinness – or perhaps the same Guinness – and a local couple talked to us for a while and some of the conversation was in Czech but it seemed to make perfect sense and Annie was becoming prettier and prettier and towards the end of it, I realised I had discovered what I was here for, what we were all here for. I had discovered the very meaning of life. Better still, the literary solution that would relaunch and reinvigorate my writing had suddenly materialised. The world regained proportion, and I was hugely keen to return to Paris and my keyboard, where there would be no more delays.

Eventually phone numbers were exchanged – she had to 'like, get back to a person', she said – and I walked across the chequerboard pattern of the Old Town Square not remembering what Annie looked like, exactly what I had said to her as the evening had progressed, or from which direction I had walked to get to the beer hall in the first place. Worse, by the morning I'd completely forgotten what the meaning of life was. Did it matter? Maybe not. Perhaps it was enough that it was there; that for one brief, brilliant, beer-soaked, ludicrously happy moment everything had made perfect sense. And the thing I did manage to remember was much more important: the solution to my literary stalemate.

❖❖❖

I WAS BACK AT MY desk in rue le Sueur and glad of it. The blank screen no longer scared me. Even Melanie could no longer distract me. I thought.

The reality of The Great Work was that a drastic solution was needed. Even in the unlikely event of Mills & Boon funding me to stay longer in Paris, that would only be a slightly surreal sideshow. I hadn't come here to write pulp and I needed to feel I was making progress. Serious progress with a serious work. And right now!

The second truth was that the bombs in Paris had shocked me, as had many other things on this trip including the poverty in St Petersburg and the strange, sick obsession in the US with the trial of O.J. Simpson, the black football star accused of murdering his white wife. A reported ninety-five million Americans had watched the car chase that preceded his arrest. In California and then the East Coast I watched in disbelief as the trial was screened everywhere with a sportscast-style commentary.

In Prague another matter came to mind: the death of a friend a few years earlier. That death – the only close friend I had ever lost – was something I had never properly dealt with in my mind. I just worked harder, and pushed the full impact away. With a break from *Undermoon Bay* and the wisdom that can come only after several *pivos* in a dome-roofed cavern with 'That's Amore' playing, it all started eating away at me. It was time to act.

13

Letters to Hercules

Dear Craig, Well here I am, in Californ-i-a. Wavering between complete shock and total anaesthesia. Please excuse me starting on first name terms, but in the time it took me to get from Sydney to LA, I decided that we are friends. You just do not know it. It is not necessarily logical, I admit, and it may be something to do with my state of mind and my level of imbibing on the plane. But it is the conclusion I have reached.

You do not remember who I am, do you? Just another customer on the way to the airport, I expect. You gave me your card, but you probably spend all day giving out your card, and you tried to sell me Amway or whatever it was, but you probably try that one on every mug on the back seat. I may have told you I was interested in being a reseller, in taking my first step towards millionaire-dom. I do not remember. But as with most people who tell you that, my real answer is no. Not in the slightest. I do not intend to ever return to Australia, and your network is probably not set up for a Culver City, LA, office.

Another thing you need to know is that I am not writing to tell you only about myself. I have another mission. A much more important one. And I have chosen you as my man. Why you? Maybe it was the way you smiled that loopy grin at me, maybe it was the fact that you actually knew your way around Sydney and did not try to charge me extra for a suitcase that you had not even helped load. Maybe it was the warmth of your voice, the first that did not cut straight through me in weeks. The way you said 'catchya soon, mate' when I hopped out, and 'too easy' when I turned back and asked for a receipt.

Maybe the name on your business card was important. It sounds so strong, where I feel so brittle. There is another possibility too. Maybe I am getting secret pleasure from bombarding a salesman with information when he cannot get me back. But I think not. I come in peace, though with no return address. And what is the mission? I have not entirely sorted it out in my own mind. But there is a story I have to tell. An important story. To someone. And it is going to be you.

❖ ❖ ❖

The title of *Letters to Hercules* may have been vaguely inspired by *Ulysses* – 'yes, Mr Interviewer, now that you come to mention it, Joyce was one of my big influences' – though I never picked it at the time. The concept was much simpler, or started that way. The framework had come to me while American Annie's voice sprinted along: a man named Peter Franklin wakes up one morning to realise he doesn't want to do his job anymore. A huge jolt in his private life suddenly makes it blindingly obvious that being a freelance computer marketing support consultant is the most pointless pursuit in the entire world. Furthermore, every single thing about Pete's wife, Maria, annoys him, and not for any reason that is necessarily her fault.

Everything else annoys him too. Absolutely everything. So Pete skips work, walks into a travel agent and purchases a plane ticket much like the one I bought, which allows him to stop in the US and various other places en route to France. His last real conversation in Australia is with the taxi-driver who drives him to the airport. Pete spends the early part of his flight availing himself of Qantas's free alcohol and staring at the man's business card, which has raised lettering saying 'Hercules Consulting'.

Instead of taking up the exciting business opportunity this card supposedly presents, Pete instead decides to use his last point of contact, the unlikely named Craig Hercules, as therapy. He resolves to send the man a series of letters explaining the failure of his marriage, his job, his life, and the real circumstances that have seen him leave his homeland. These raw and angry explanations will be intertwined with the here and now of Pete's travels, plus a series of flashbacks to an earlier, happier time. Armed with anonymity, Pete will finally try to deal with unresolved feelings about a close friendship and the apparent suicide that ended it.

It had finally become clear that my attempt to master *Undermoon Bay* had thoroughly broken down over that long, hot summer. I had lasted just three months from go to woe. I had left for Prague hoping I'd never see the manuscript again, secretly praying for my building to burn down while I was away, thereby providing me with a noble way out.

However, I hadn't given up, I assured myself. The new work was merely an exercise in structure and characterisation and I would soon return to *Undermoon Bay* with renewed vigour and improved technique. I also vowed that in this second attempt at my first 'real' novel, I wouldn't create such a rod with nails in it for my own back. This time I would observe the most boringly basic rule of authordom: write about what you know. I would also adhere to a lesser known but equally important literary rule: don't write your first novel from fourteen different viewpoints while skipping between eras and tenses and writing styles. And it was working. My writing was powering along with a force and speed unknown since the early days of my arrival.

Though I told myself *Letters to Hercules* was merely an exercise in breaking writer's block, I knew it was more than that. It was to do with the need to record things. Most people I know can never quite understand what it is like to be born with the hard-wired, inbuilt need to put everything down in words, to feel like something hasn't really happened to you unless you have written about it. Being blessed or cursed with the writing gene means having things spinning around your head all day and feeling an inexplicable need to commit them to paper or hard-drive before they disappear. It means being so conceited as to think your thoughts are worthy enough to preserve; it means accumulating reams of notes on every size of paper, ripping things out of the newspaper; leaving markers in all manner of books with scribbled notes and page references; constantly wrestling to capture a feeling, an idea or mood in words. And there was this major, major thing in my life that I hadn't written about, at least not successfully. I had once tried, but it had made me too sad and too angry.

The flashbacks in *Letters* started with a terrible

phone-call, much like one I had received from my friend's uncle. I had known the friend from the last years of primary school and since then we had shared houses, trips, mad ideas and ridiculous ambitions. At the end of school I was quiet, fearful and shy, and he loud, fearless and funny. He was a machine of perpetual commotion. He knew more about almost any subject than you could believe possible. He had an instant reply for anything and it was never the one you expected. ('Thanks for doing nothing,' I once snapped at him when he had promised to help but disappeared at the crucial moment. 'It was the least I could do,' he answered instantaneously.) He had a mind he could have turned to almost anything but which he eventually turned to nothing because, tragically, he became increasingly troubled as we stumbled through our twenties. As I started to find my feet, the ground slid away below his. It was a very slow process and I'm not sure when I admitted to myself he was no longer the person he had been. I could only hope something would change, some unseen spark would rectify whatever it was that had gone wrong.

Then one week he was sleeping on my couch and spending most of the day in tears or blanked out on prescription drugs. The next week he didn't exist. It was the saddest time of my life and even now it hurts me to think about it. But, isolated, insulated and desperately scratching for inspiration, I did more than that in Paris – I *wrote* about it.

In *Letters to Hercules* Peter Franklin receives the phone call. The uncle slurs and sobs into the phone that Patrick, 'or Ronald, as you call him', has passed away. He is in shock at first, but some time later Peter is crying helplessly on Maria's shoulder. Nothing will stop these huge, wailing waves of tears that are heaving up through him from the bottom of his stomach and choking him because he can't get enough air back in. And Maria is holding him with her entire being. Nothing in the world will make her let go. And he knows full-well that she would willingly pull out one of her own teeth if it could possibly reduce his suffering.

One difference between the real story and the fake was that, six weeks after the phone call, Peter Franklin was out the door without so much as a goodbye. I stayed and buried myself in my job, my home life and whatever fiction project I was working on at the time.

✣ ✣ ✣

I HADN'T GIVEN UP on my plan to knock on Melanie's door. There was enough tension in the air to make it seem less daunting. 'So how about these bombs, hey?' I could say. Well, maybe not. But how to best approach it? Should I wait for a noisy incident and knock on her door with a concerned 'Are you all right'? Or was it better to make my move when her room was very quiet, so there wouldn't be the subtext of 'I am here because I fear you have been violated by a rhinoceros'?

I decided on the 'when it was quiet' approach, partly because when it was completely quiet there was a better chance she wouldn't be there. I walked up to Melanie's door, stood square to it and lifted my knuckle as my heart raced. Suddenly I was hurled back a dozen or more years to the thing I liked least about working on the newsbeat of a tabloid newspaper: the death-knock. The test of who was going to be a great reporter in that environment was determined by the death-knock, that cold call on the family that had just lost a son to a shark, or the widow of the businessman who had topped himself after being arrested on kiddy-fiddling charges. I had plenty of death-knock experience because I spent nine months on the midnight-to-dawn stint, known as the graveyard shift because of the type of assignments it usually involved.

MYSTERY BODY FOUND IN CREEK
TODDLER TWINS PERISH IN HOUSE FIRE
BEAUTY QUEEN IN HIGH SPEED CRASH – PHOTO

On one occasion I was cruising the streets with a driver and photographer in one of the fleet of white Commodore sedans that News Limited had fitted out to look like undercover police cars. It was about 5.30 a.m. We were looking for news. We were always looking for news, but it was a quiet night. No bodies – mystery or otherwise – in any creek, no two-year-old twins playing with matches in weatherboard houses and every beauty queen (a tabloid term for 'bank clerk who once applied to be a Parramatta Eels cheerleader') had managed to miss the telegraph poles. Suddenly the car's clunky two-way came to life. It was Carlos, the early morning chief of staff.

'Hey, mate,' he bellowed, 'they've just found that missing twenty-year-old at the bottom of The Gap. We've managed to score her boyfriend's address. Bash on the door, mate, and see what he thinks about it.'

Carlos was what some people still nostalgically call an 'old school journo', which is to say a workaholic drunkard with ex-wives and a gambling problem. In the office Carlos was all flailing arms, profanities and phone throwing. He was like a threshing machine, though without the people skills. And at his request I was now sitting outside a terraced house in Surry Hills, just south of the city centre, with the task of waking up a man I didn't know and asking him about something he didn't yet know: that his girlfriend was lying cold, still and broken on the rocks at the bottom of Sydney's most famous suicide spot. I asked the snapper to stay in the car, so we 'don't spook the guy', then walked to the house.

'Carlos,' I said, returning to the radio, 'I've just banged on the door, mate, but nothing. Not a thing.'

'Well thump it harder, you stupid prick,' was the response. 'Bash the bejesus out of it. Mate, this could be news to you, but we've got a paper to get out.'

My story about the door wasn't a complete lie. I really had knocked on the door – mate, *maaate* – but, equally, I could have hit it harder. It was just that some inner urge, I think it's the one called human decency, took control of my hand. At roughly the same moment my clenched fist produced the lightest taps it could, I realised I didn't want to be a newshound anymore.

Some other reporters loved the challenge of death-knocking and flourished, but I wanted to write such stories no more than I wanted to read them. And now, all these years later, I was back with my fist raised and my breath shortening. This one was for me, not Rupert Murdoch. But I was just as nervous. There was someone whispering inside the apartment. Sure, it could have been a radio or television but it also could have been her. I knocked four times. The strikes on the wood weren't hammer blows, but then again they weren't super-soft 'the love of your life's at the bottom of an 80-metre cliff, just wondering what you think of that' knocks either. I could detect the floorboards vibrate. Somebody must be walking towards the door. The spy-hole darkened a little. Perhaps. I waited. And waited. Nothing. I quickly decamped to my apartment and closed the door so carefully I couldn't hear the wood touch the jamb.

❖❖❖

THE TENSION IN PARIS continued, and with good reason. Every second *métro* seemed to be delayed due to a 'suspect package', and the city was crawling with even more men in black with even bigger machine-guns. The bomb at the Place d'Etoile, the one Annie had heard about in Prague, had injured rather than killed. Soon after my return, a bomb was placed next to the TGV high-speed train line. A triggering system was supposed to set it off when the Paris–Lyon train shot past at 300 kilometres per hour. Fortunately, the driver spotted something odd up ahead and stopped in time.

Vigilance of the people is the best defence. But they become slack. The day after the San Michel bombing everyone was looking under the seats and scanning the platforms for anything irregular and looking askance at anyone even slightly suspicious (read: even slightly Algerian). But soon everything returned to something approaching normality. Sure, an area of a *métro* station would often be roped off and everything would stop while security forces looked, for example, at a sports bag left alone on the platform. But on one occasion I saw the men in black spend several minutes examining a bag at a distance before one of them shrugged his shoulders, walked up and opened it. He found someone's lunch. Which he took.

Other times I'd see four or five *CRS* police walk into one train carriage, rather than go into four or five separate carriages and have no-one to talk to.

Soon the situation was transformed from one of fear to one of irritation. The delays and double-checks annoyed, and I started having thoughts like: *wouldn't Suspect Package be a good name for a rock band?* I walked to the Bibliothèque Trocadéro and the entire Avenue Foch was teeming with police. Traffic was stopped and there was a general feeling of something ominous in the air. Hang the danger, I wanted to cross the street. Which I did by cutting through various police barricades.

While bombs were going off in Paris, France was advancing its plans to continue the Cold War unilaterally. Late one night I made the trip down to the corner to push wine bottles through the slot in a public recycling bin. When I got there, I thought, why am I doing this? What difference to the overall environment is this pathetic contribution going to make in the face of eight nuclear ka-booms? To add to the aggravation, I was losing count of how many times I saw 100-year-old photos in the French press, showing Australian aborigines being led around in chains. Sorry, did I miss the connection?

14

Slimming Cream

Do you remember me . . . what I look like? Would it ring any bells if I said that I am however many centimetres make five foot ten? That I have dark hair and blue eyes and perfectly straight teeth thanks to five embarrassing teenage years with metal strips across my pearly whites? Probably not. But what might make you remember me is that I was the one who left you with the large black fountain pen with the white blotch on the cap.

'Like Sydney?' I think you asked me that as I sat dazed in the back of your cab. It is a typical question, I suppose. The need to make conversation, to seem like something other than an automatic pilot. Or for you, a prelude to the subject of multi-level marketing. Understandable. Hey, I should know, I was in a different branch of the same business. The same daft business.

If you had asked me that question about Sydney a couple of years ago, maybe even a couple of months ago, I would have said yes. I would have said it was the most beautiful city in the world. That a fireball Sydney sunset is without equal. But then it happened. My worst nightmares suddenly all came true and the city became unliveable. It was like every bad thing in every dark hole had risen flood-like, in a swelling, malevolent mass, for no other reason than to drown me in its misery.

And if you had asked me if I liked myself a couple of months ago, I would probably have also given you an enthusiastic answer. I was Mister Bigshot. Mister Eighty-Dollars-An-Hour, up-front please, and you can pick up the entertainment bill too. I was guaranteed to have the crispest, most tailored shirt in any meeting and to emit the most expensive squeaks of Italian leather footwear as I walked into the room. Look no further to see the must-have tie design for this week. When a signature was required, you could count on me to have the most sparkling gold nib on the most elaborate Montblanc fountain pen. It took a death to make me realise what a contemptible life that was.

I had intended to burn every bridge. Then I realised that I need a link or thread, no matter how thin. They say that love is only love if you give it away. But there is nothing much you can do with self-hatred but keep it. And eventually it will eat you up.

Leaving that souvenir with you – 'it is okay, use this to write the receipt' – was no accident. I had no need of the receipt, I wanted to get rid of the pen. It was the last bit of the old me to be jettisoned before I jumped on the plane. Look after it. That model cost me $890, duty free. No, that does not mean it is worth $890, it just cost that much – and there were idiots stupid enough to pay it. Idiots like the man I was. I think I will have to stop this letter. But you will hear from me again. Keep well. Drive carefully. Sell lots. Yours, Peter Franklin.

✣ ✣ ✣

IN PETER FRANKLIN'S UNSOLICITED letters he promised (or threatened) to 'start the story at the very beginning', to empty himself of the memories that were haunting him, of earlier days and of his friend Ronald. These stories of the past were to be mixed with the misery Peter was finding and the futile and harmful relationships he was entering into in the place to which he first escaped, California. As the plot progressed he would flee again, across the States to New York, then to Russia, the UK and a Paris blighted by terrorist bombs, unbearable heat and rowdy protests. Not to mention a shrieking girl next door whom the narrator always misses seeing but is sure is trying to eat her way into his apartment.

My second attempt to doorknock Melanie was no less harrowing. Again I knocked hard, but not too hard, again I was not quite sure what to follow with after saying 'Hi, I'm Tony from next door . . . your mother suggested saying hello, but I've been a bit busy, what with writing a book, doing French courses and holding a wine glass up to the wall.' Again, there was no-one home, or no-one in a position to answer the door. Was this a good thing? Hard to say. Now that Melanie was slated for the book, I wasn't sure whether she would work better as a mystery woman or whether, on meeting, her role would change completely.

Meanwhile, I don't think my learning-another-language-by-television-osmosis idea was actually doing as much good as I had hoped. But having the box on gave me the chance to regularly catch the ravishing, ever-so-French Emmanuelle Gaume, who presented the only weekday morning music video show. It was on M6, a station that also allowed me to discover that as well as the France where adults sit around in smoky cafés and discuss being and nothingness, and children study philosophy in primary school, there is an unsmoky, café-free, shallow-thinking France packed with an entirely different type of being and nothingness. It was when Ms Gaume and her flimsy but forgivable video show finished that the parallel, Sartre-free France came to the fore. It was then that the home shopping show started.

Today the terribly sincere male presenter was again staring straight at the camera, spruiking Creme Maigre, just one of many wonder products in his armoury. I could almost do the spiel by heart as I sat typing. I had heard it scores of times before. Lack of variety, after all, was the spice of M6 life. And the national obsession with cellulite – not that anyone much seemed to have it – provided a particularly profitable avenue. I looked around at the television to see a woman who carried about as much fat as a racing bicycle pasting the so-called thinning cream on her thighs and calves. She then wrapped her pole-like legs in cling wrap, reclined in a chair and pretended to read a magazine.

My wandering brain tried to work out if I could have a death-knock scene in *Letters to Hercules*. But with Peter being a computer marketing support consultant, it was going to be hard to arrange. I turned around again and looked at the small, black and white screen. Another gaunt woman, this one in a bikini, was being covered with little patches of plaster wired to some sort of machine that was guaranteed to make her lose weight. Or would, if she had any weight. The whole device cost only 445 francs and if I rang straight away I would receive a minuscule tub of skin cream. *Gratuitment!*

I next looked up during a newsbreak showing shocking images of carnage in Bosnia. It was dealt with in less than thirty seconds and I couldn't help but think that M6 wasn't taking seriously the biggest war in Europe since Hitler walked the earth. When I saw the blue-helmeted soldiers turning up in white tanks, I couldn't believe the UN was taking it seriously either. Elsewhere the reporting was relentless and at times it was hard not to think: *I've had enough, it's too complicated, let them sort it out themselves.* Nonetheless, the things Chirac was saying on the subject, and the actions of France, were shining lights, at least by the dismal standards that characterised the rest of the Western European response. More French peacekeepers had been killed in the deconstructing of Yugoslavia than troops from all other Western European countries combined, but Chirac said France was staying there to get the job done. I was left in that dreadful intellectual bind that occurs when someone you intensely dislike says and does things with which you wholeheartedly agree.

On other matters, all was pretty much the same in France. It remained amazingly difficult to communicate. When people came up in the street and asked a question while I was daydreaming in English, I couldn't say a single word. Not even '*Je ne parle pas le Français.*' So much had gone into my head, yet so little seemed to be coming out. I lacked the skill, but perhaps more importantly, I lacked the confidence. There were days when I felt speaking French was completely impossible.

I couldn't understand ninety per cent of the things said in a documentary about the legendary Parisian photographer Robert Doisneau. They might as well have been speaking another language. Fortunately, those amazing images of Paris in the thirties, forties, and fifties – the kiss at the Hôtel de Ville, the *garçon* carrying two bottles of wine, the schoolboys and factory workers and washerwomen – hardly needed words anyway. A world of charm and simple pleasures in black and white.

✣✣✣

When I was younger I could have avoided putting vast amounts of work into things that turned out to be dead-ends if I had first asked a simple question: 'What am I trying to achieve here?'. With *Letters to Hercules* I was older and wiser and asked the question loud and often. Alas, I never gave myself a precise answer, though I knew at its heart was the need to capture in words the nature of a lost time, a lost friend and a bond that had been so important. To write a proper biography of my friend's all-too-short life might have been a better starting point and it was something I had once considered. But it meant talking to too many people I didn't like or didn't trust. And it probably meant finding out things I didn't really want to know. It also, by necessity, would have put me in the story, and I didn't want to be in my friend's story. So I chose the *Letters to Hercules* format.

More than anything, *Letters to Hercules* was born of frustration. Frustration at *Undermoon Bay*, frustration at learning French, frustration at the bureaucracy, frustration at trying to understand Joyce or understand why anyone would want to plant bombs in a peaceful city or restart nuclear testing. And almost every aggravation and irritation was channelled and amplified through the increasingly lonely, despondent and misanthropic Peter Franklin.

'I did not make computers, design computers, program computers or even sell computers,' Pete wrote to Herc once he had arrived in Paris. 'No, I was a freelance contractor to an organisation which provided marketing support to computer importers. So do you think it was the people who actually did things – the builders, designers, programmers and sellers – who got wined and dined to within an inch of their lives? No sir! It was the folks like me, treated like royalty by advertising companies and any other gooses who thought . . . well, I'm not quite sure what they thought.

'At times I felt like a parasite. But when I listened to most of my colleagues, I realised the computer manufacturers were the parasites, hanging as they do off the backs of freelance marketing consultants.

'On days like today I look at the people walking on the street here and they could be the same people I saw in LA or New York. They walk past like automatons and I wonder why the bugger any single one of them could be bothered to help keep the electricity system functioning or the plumbing working or doing anything else which keeps the wheels turning. Let alone feed the starving or plan for the future. Or design software or plan nuclear tests. I could not even build up the enthusiasm to be the virus in the machine. Let it all go to waste.'

Peter's wife Maria was sweet and harmless. Sure, she had domineering Italian parents whose ideas were locked in the late 1950s, when they arrived in Australia. The job of impressing them with material success was delegated to Peter while Maria worked in a supermarket and daydreamt of kitchen makeovers. On weekends she dragged Pete out to open-for-inspections to look at houses they couldn't possibly afford. Then again, Maria had more common sense than Peter and after the horrible news she couldn't have done more to help. He paid her back by leaving her with a whole lot of stylish but worthless furniture, a shelf of stupid management books she would never even consider reading, a stack of compact discs she hated, most of his clothes, an exercise bike in pieces clogging up the hallway, a real bicycle in the dust-covered spare room and a 1983 Saab 900 parked on the street outside. The car was rather like Pete: flash on the outside but falling apart.

'What will she do?' Peter wrote in one of his more drunken and mournful moments. 'She might throw it all out, Herc, or dump it on the street or on my poor mother's impeccable lawn. She might set it alight or – who knows – leave it intact and dust it each week like a shrine. And when the history of the world comes to be written, or even the history of our city, or of our street, or of our house, who will honestly give a stuff what happened to all those things, or what happened to me, or to her, or to the tiny sparks that once flew between us?'

✣✣✣

I was living in the most fabulous city and realising a dream. I was enjoying the company of the people I met and revelling in the huge appreciation of art and photography and films and books to be found everywhere. I could feel my world and my life experience expanding, yet every morning I would fire up the laptop and become the hapless and vitriolic Peter Franklin, who was stumbling from one disaster to another, treating women badly, and drinking far too much while venomously disowning every aspect of his previous life and serially dumping on people, even those who had supported him at his lowest moments. At times Peter Franklin was so lonely he would talk to himself, but so depressed and filled with self-revulsion he refused to listen.

Day by day *Letters to Hercules* became darker and nastier. I became worried that my laptop would deliberately sever a vital wire or throw itself out the window.

'So how is your book going, Anthony?' Isabelle asked one afternoon as we sat near the Museum of Natural History in the Jardin des Plants. Her clipped tones and the slow, serious, shaking of her head that followed placed impossible expectations on me.

'You know I don't really talk about my secret project,' I replied. 'But I will say that I was struggling for a while, but now think it is going well again.'

Of course I couldn't tell Isabelle I had abandoned one book and started another. Or that I was now writing about the here, the now, the ordinary, the grubby, the unpoetic. I could only fudge it and wonder what would happen when she finally read it. At that point, she and Sandrine and Benoit and everyone else would sound like the neighbours interviewed after the quiet suburban man has been revealed to be a homicidal axeman who stir-fries his victims.

'But he seemed such a nice guy.'

'Quiet. Very quiet. Never caused anyone a moment's bother.'

'Can't believe it. He was always friendly. Had him over to my house once. I shudder now just thinking about it.'

I asked myself why I was writing like this. Why was there

another me between certain hours? Was I trying to hide behind fiction to say things not just about 'Ronald' but about my life too? Was I a coward? Had I become a complete hypocrite, considering my holier-than-thou starting point? They were cutting questions, but I chose to ignore them, despite the fact I had asked them myself, so could hardly pretend to have not heard. Anyway, some people thought about such questions too much. I needed to get on with things. And get on with things I did.

An attempt was made to atone, nonetheless. It was an odd one in retrospect; despite everything, including the Préfecture's de Police's shenanigans to deny him a *carte de séjour*, I had Peter Franklin slowly falling in love with the city. On his behalf I spent a day writing down all the things that he was prepared to admit to Hercules that he liked because 'singing the praises of this place is so much more fulfilling than spruiking the merits of a whole lot of boxes of chips and motherboards'.

Pete raved, just as easily as I could have raved, about the age-old twisted streets of the Marais, next to the Seine. The almost perfect symmetrical beauty of squares such as Place des Vosges. Baron Haussmann's Paris, created on behalf of Napoleon III, with its sense of space: the wide boulevards, the huge parks, the monstrous buildings which somehow avoid giving the place the feeling of emptiness such scale might create somewhere else. The lining up of the various landmarks such as the Luxor obelisk at Concord and the Arc de Triomphe, providing a balance that defined the city. The big, round, dark-green Morris columns on street corners carrying posters for theatre plays and musical *spectacles*. The older phone boxes and *pissoirs*. And

Revolutionary Paris, with the spectre of the guillotine hanging over so many landmarks.

The rue de Rivoli with its rows of shops under awnings. The amazing wine shops, or *caves*, all over the city, a delight even for those who can afford only to pick at the edges, with hundreds of types of wines and Champagnes and aperitifs and digestifs. The *boulangeries* with their choice of breads and brioches and *pains au chocolat* and *croissants* and cakes and flans and rolls and *tartes*. The seafood restaurants with their preparation areas out on the footpath and their trays of lobsters and langoustines and massive oysters and mussels and periwinkles and God knows what those other things are . . . gonads of Loch Ness monster?

The aromatic *fromageries*, their windows filled with countless varieties of cheese. Racks of little cylinders of soft yellow, or mustard gold cheeses, covered in ash or mould or black paste or grey grains of who-can-guess-what. Or those with varicose veins of blue or green, or wrapped in fussily designed paper, or packed in fancy boxes. Discs of Gruyère de Comté as big as truck wheels. Cheeses as hard as rocks and as soft as whipped cream, as white and shiny as snow or as dark and rough as charcoal.

And, above all, those amazing cafés.

'You have no idea, Herc, how much I wish that I could sit and discuss something, anything, with Ronald in one of these cafés. Or just watch him and listen to him. He would probably be loudly telling me why the French are such a bunch of fools, or questioning why more resistance workers marched in the Liberation Parades after the war than ever bothered the Germans. "The Frogs?", he would growl. "In their sissy uniforms and Pierre Cardin tanks . . . "

'Or he would be talking over the top of me and not listening to a word. That was the later Ronald. He would irritate me, and load me with his problems, which most of the time I would dismiss as not being problems at all, as if the fact they were only in his mind made them less dangerous. And no doubt he would whinge and whine and repeat himself. But it would still be him and I would be happy. I would just sit there smiling, filled with joy to know he was among us. And I would sleep soundly at night, instead of drifting through that horrible half-world with that one hackneyed phrase turning over and over again. "I should have done more."'

There is another Paris too: that of the ultra-rich with its restaurants and private shops and clubs. The grand hotels, with their astonishing façades and foyers and impossibly painstaking and expensive menus posted out the front, and the uniformed men in the doorways who give you a glance that says 'Piss off. Don't even look. You can't afford it.' It was not Pete's Paris, nor mine. Just as there was another Paris of beggars, and gypsies and poor Arabs.

'In the Bois de Boulogne, Herc, I can walk for hours or sit beside a lake and read, or write the long letters I have been sending you. There are times when Paris seems exactly where I should be. At other times I wish I was a million miles away rather than simply on the other side of the world. But most of the time I am just so lonely. I think of what I have lost, I think about what I have thrown away. I start wishing I was opening a bottle of wine with Ronald. The younger, vital, funny, healthy Ronald. Or walking alone along a deserted, never-ending Queensland beach. Or even sitting in the soft afternoon sun with Maria, running my hand though her curly black hair, my fingertips across her soft olive skin, pretending everything was the way it once was. If it ever really was the way it once was.

'More often though, I wish I was dead. Stone cold dead. With no forwarding address.'

15

Stretching the False

Dear Craig, Bet you did not think there would be a second letter, let alone a fourth, or a fifth or a sixteenth. Probably reckoned the first was a one-off from a drugged or disturbed nong. Showed it to the wife, said 'what do you make of this?' as she uncrinkled the tightly folded, cramped pages. Maybe you showed it to some of the customers sitting above the squealing back axle of your clapped-out Falcon. Posed the same question. Good way to get their attention before moving into the Amway.

Did you tell them what I have told you? How I walked out on my wife and my clients and my indoor soccer team? How I am hugely guilty over having no guilt? I should be crammed with remorse. I am better than this . . . but I do not feel that way. Not one bit. I just feel numb. And you are welcome to tell anyone who is the slightest bit interested.

✣✣✣

Jasper. Those two syllables will always send a shiver down my spine. Jasper, whose biggest mistake in life, other than not changing his name, was to say: 'Have you got room in the car for me?'

When all the noise stopped everyone said they were

fine, except for Simon, the drama merchant, who reckoned he had broken his back but of course it was just bruised. Jasper said he was just feeling a bit dizzy and needed to go for a walk. Ninety minutes later he was dead.

Being the driver, I spent the first few weeks looking and feeling like my life was at an end. It seemed that the only noble way out was to go and shoot myself. Everybody at Jasper's funeral stared. Unlike Simon, I had no dignifying wheelchair or neck-brace, I had not even cut myself on the broken glass. But I had Ronald with me, and I will never forget him standing behind me and grabbing my shoulder with a vice-like grip. To steady me and reassure me. He had not even been there on that god-awful night, but by holding my shoulder so tightly he was saying 'It has happened to the two of us, and the two of us will get over it.'

It was Ronald who talked to me for hours after the crash and did his utmost to convince me that these things happen in the great NSW Jackpot Lottery of life. And that is that. He had been Jasper's friend too, but he refused to blame me. He said Jasper did not have his seatbelt on properly and everyone else did. So he hit his temple on the edge of the window frame. And the only reason we had the accident in the first place was because a drunk went through a red light.

All those months later it was Ronald who sat with me right through the inquest, who calmed me down before I had to give evidence. 'It is finished now,' he said when the verdict came through. 'There is no need to be in mourning all your life.'

* * *

'VERY BUSY, VERY TIRED. But I have made good with the markets.' From someone else this may have been a reference to La Bourse, Paris's stock exchange. But it was Tazza who was speaking and he was referring to the fruit-and-veg stall where he still worked for the American woman who was crazy.

'I now I have *quelque* things for you to see,' Tazza said over the phone. Within twenty minutes he was at the door, carrying a large bag of cakes from a Polish bakery he had discovered in the Marais. He was also carrying a helmet and a pair of large leather gloves.

'I have bought *une moto*,' Tazza announced proudly as he made for the cupboards to grab plates and forks, 'and you must come for a ride with me.'

'Congratulations,' I said, avoiding the terrifying subject of being on anything movable controlled by Tazza.

'I am *decidé* that I am sick to pedal my *bicyclette* to work now when it is nearly thirty degrees when I am up at 5 a.m., then in the afternoon from work to class when it now forty,' he said. 'I am lazy, no?'

'No, no, *pas du tout*.' If Tazza came around any more I was sure I'd start slipping in Russian words too. 'Good on you. You deserve a break, you deserve *une moto*bike.'

I was genuinely happy for Tadeusz but I knew that, in the eyes of many French people, those from Eastern Europe and Northern Africa would never be seen as anything but scrounging, bludging, pilfering, sponging, good-for-nothing, culture-free leeches who were dragging the country down. We ate the cakes, we drank instant coffee and the sheer aura of enthusiasm surrounding Tadeusz dragged me down the stairs, to the lift and into the courtyard where he had parked his new motorcycle, no doubt breaching every house rule. He walked around it – more a motor scooter than a motorcycle, I thought, and certainly not new – and pulled a second helmet from under the seat. Then he turned to me and ran his hands over it like a barrel girl introducing a prize. 'And what do you think a *moto* like this will cost?'

Probably both our lives, I thought as I climbed on the back. 'No idea. A wild guess: 15,000 francs?'

'*Non,* I *acheté* this one for 10,000,' was his excited reply.

'That's great, er, competitive shopping.' I was nervously ranting. I stared at the back of his bright orange helmet and shuddered a little more as he flicked the switch and brought the engine to life. There followed a ride through the busiest parts of Paris, and a complete lap of the Pompidou Centre including the paved areas that I was sure were pedestrian only.

My chauffeur and tour guide rode with roughly the same speed and precision he employed when talking. With two fairly big blokes aboard, the tiny machine was screaming its mechanical head off to keep up the breathless clip Tazza demanded of it. The view to either side of the helmet in front looked like a snippet from a low budget car chase film, with a heavily accented tourist commentary shouted over the soundtrack.

'This is the best building *à Paris,*' Tazza yelled, his entire body revolving so he could point to what I regarded as not just the ugliest building, but the one I'd least like to have to keep clean. 'The Centre Pompidou is *la meilleure,* the best, because from in there you can't see the Centre Pompidou.'

He threw the bike sideways into a little street – or

walkway. A group of Asian tourists parted like a school of fish in the presence of a noisy, two-headed, erratically swerving shark. My elbow collided heavily with someone's camera. 'Shit, Tazza. How about I point out the interesting buildings and you watch where we are going?'

From then on I ignored anything he said and just looked at the back of his helmet. When we finally returned to the apartment and it was clear I had survived, Tadeusz's voice started registering again. As I rubbed my elbow he told me how much more he now wanted to go to Australia. He also tried to secure a commitment from me that I would go to Poland for a holiday. It was so beautiful, and much *cheaplier* than Paris.

'You should go with me. I go in *l'autobus*. It is thirty-six hours but not expensive and they utilise Mercedes type. Good *et confortable*.'

'We'll see,' I said, meaning no.

✣✣✣

From Isabelle I had previously learned that *bastion* was one of those very rare words in the French language that ended in '*tion*' but was feminine, while *l'amour* (love) and *l'orgue* (an organ of the musical variety) were equally rare in that they were masculine in the singular but feminine in the plural.

And on this day I learned from Loulou that you had to speak English if you hoped to find the right husband. Back in her small, sunless room, with somebody else's cat pouncing around, and some other body's ironing piled high, Loulou tilted her head from side to side and smiled broadly as she explained that in Madagascar the French language is still used for business and in schools and universities, but people speak Malagasy at home. Before completing nearly five years of university study in Paris, Loulou had studied for four years in Madagascar. She also did a year's compulsory national service, though instead of working in the military, she was given the job of teaching English to schoolchildren in the capital, Tananarive.

'But I thought you didn't speak English before you came to France,' I said.

'No, I didn't. I had to read the book before each class. The students would ask me questions and I would have to tell them that I was only a chapter ahead of them and they would have to wait until later in the year to know difficult things like that.'

One reason Loulou was staying in France and learning English, she explained, was that she hoped to meet a Frenchman or, better still, an American – but not *un Americain noir* – who would want to marry her. But this was unlikely, she explained, because most Europeans and Americans preferred Europeans and Americans.

'I want to improve my race,' she said with her eyes scanning up and down her bare arms, 'by being more white.'

IT HAD BEEN A good year thus far for anniversaries and August provided the fiftieth year since the nuclear bombs hit Hiroshima and Nagasaki. There were no parades down the Champs Elysées for this one. As August became September the weather softened (August had been one of the hottest on record), but there were more bombs. Mad man-hunts were shown on the news and the level of security continued to mount. The Eiffel Tower was guarded by the French Foreign Legion.

Events such as these were woven into *Letters to Hercules*, as were the continuing O.J. Simpson trial, the brown-paper man, French bureaucracy, even the Asian woman who regularly lay in the Plaisance *métro* station next to an upturned hat. She had twisted claw-like things at the end of each leg that looked like the feet of some extinct bird of prey. There were strikes in Peter's Paris and, as time progressed, there would be bombs abroad too.

With the format in place, I was like the kid who discovered much too late that everyone else knew how to break into the lolly cupboard. They had been stuffing themselves silly for years while I munched, monk-like, on a SAO biscuit. The 'faction' genre was addictive. Pages of the past and present poured out and the dramatic tension was upped considerably by a game of cat and mouse. Maria was now determinedly on Pete's trail.

I still had five months left in Paris. It might just be enough.

16

Two Singers

As I write this, Herc, I am looking at a photo that I brought with me. It was taken at a party, about three years ago. Ronald was never a cigarette smoker, but he had a pompous predilection for a pipe, a device which required so many minutes of dicking around for every minute it was alight that Ronald argued he could still call himself a non-smoker. On this occasion, however, he had succeeded in producing a cloud of smog so thick that it confused my auto focus, leaving him a bit blurry. The effect gives his face a dreamlike quality which, in the very early days, is really how I thought of him: born older and wiser than the rest of us, almost god-like, hovering over every critical situation, looking at it in stern judgement. Isolated from the immediate, the person from whom a compliment was so much harder to earn, yet so much more valuable. He was the schoolboy who never cried, who never uttered the slightest complaint. But you knew it . . . you knew he was just quietly sitting back and taking it all in.

Jane is half out of the frame. Ronald has that slightly sagged look about his person. His head is cocked at an angle and he is resting it in one hand. The other hand is extended as if to brush away the photographer.

About 3.30 a.m., near the end of that last winter, he rang. I was very asleep and mumbled into the phone. Ronald was sniffling, struggling to catch his breath. 'Pete, I have been driving around all night. I am at the phonebox down the road. I am in a pretty bad way, could I come around?'

'Yes, I suppose so,' I yawned.

'No, Peter,' Maria snapped. 'Tell him to go away. We have got to go to work in a few hours.'

I could not send him away, even though I knew it was going to make the morning hell, and that this was the sort of encouragement that would make middle-of-the-night meetings an even more regular occurrence. And I am telling you this now, Herc, because these are the sort of scenes I had completely erased from my memory until I started writing to you.

His V8 rumbled up, and Ronald and I sat in the loungeroom and talked in ever smaller circles for an hour or more. He said (yet again) life was not worth living, which, as usual, I took as simply seeking attention. We had all been saying it in one way or another since the days when we sat around jawing on about the arms race, the appearance of the neutron bomb or the pointlessness of waiting seventy years to become soil fertiliser. Everything was the Department's fault, as always: Ronald's health, his financial circumstances and the split with Jane.

'The Department is not well organised enough to deliberately and maliciously cause difficulties,' I tried to explain. 'It is staffed by people like you.'

Ronald ignored the comment. He stared at me with glazed eyes, holding on to the arm of the chair tightly, as if he needed to stop shaking. The voice though was as strong and clear as always. He talked about the split as if it had happened yesterday, as if Jane was staying at her mother's due to a tiff. Not someone who had moved interstate without leaving any contact details. Someone who had not talked to him for two years.

'When they see my doctor's records and the report in which the occupational psychologist says my depression is specifically due to the treatment I have received at work,' he suddenly announced, 'the court will not be able to deny my right to compensation. But it should not come to that. The Department should settle out of court.'

Ronald left as first light arrived, happier, it seemed, to talk things out, even if they were the same things as always. Another day, another melodrama.

✣✣✣

THE *ANGLOSAXONS* LIKE to think that all French singers except Edith Piaf and Yves Montand (a sort of a Gallic Frank Sinatra) are bad, and tell themselves that the French don't understand pop music. Being of a generous bent, I was prepared to give my newly adopted nation the benefit of the considerable doubt. And I had convinced myself that learning a language would be more fun if I also studied song lyrics. I was finding the spoken word in things such as the television news to be a machine gun-like clatter of syllables with no clear start or end to each word. With the slower, more stressed pronunciation of the singer, the student of the language could receive the pronunciation as well as the actual words. So I trotted off to the library, borrowed a whole lot of cassettes – mostly quite a few years old – by people such as Michel Sardou, Roch Voisin, Laurent Voulzy, Sylvie Vartan and Alain Souchon.

Based on this evidence, I decided that the stereotype of the French not understanding pop music was solidly grounded in fact. The melodies were paint-by-numbers, the lyrics seemed lame even when you couldn't understand them, and they never quite fitted the music. But I worked through translating the songs word for word, trying to work out the grammar at the same time and improving my limited vocabulary. Although I called this my bad music therapy, I am prepared to admit that the music collections of most libraries around the world are actually a catalogue of what people don't want to listen to. Getting to the music that you like involves a lifelong filtering process. I had to listen to what I could get. Anyway, my bad music therapy did eventually lead me to a couple of French poets other than Rimbaud or Verlaine. They were both singers and songwriters, they were both dead and each would soon become a minor obsession. Even Peter Franklin fell under their charm.

They were Jacques Brel and Serge Gainsbourg. With Brel the appeal was his extraordinary songs for which there is no equivalent in English. In Serge's case it rested partly with his songs, and largely with his life. Serge rates as one of the world's truly odd people, on one hand an appalling and disgusting human being, on the other a sublime talent who did everything exactly his own way. But Gainsbourg was almost unknown in the English world, except via his song 'Je t'aime . . . moi non plus'. This three-minute simulated orgasm caused a huge controversy in France and England when released in the late 1960s and ended up as the theme to an ice-cream commercial in Australia in the 1990s. The title means 'I love you . . . me neither'. Gainsbourg said it was modelled after a quote by Salvador Dalí: 'Picasso is Spanish, me too. Picasso is a genius, me too. Picasso is a communist, me neither.'

French males wanting to hit the big-time as actors and singers have a big advantage if either old or unspeakably ugly. Ideally, they should be both. To say 'Serge was no oil painting' is not correct. He looked almost exactly like one of the portraits Picasso did towards the end. Serge had ears like open car doors, a nose shaped like a hoop and eyes that looked like they were just leaving. And he was always unshaven and often looked like he had been bashed up the night before in some seedy dive. Which was often the case.

It made the contrast provided by the delicate, highly melodic, jazz-tinged songs of his all the more fascinating. They included 'Le Poinçonneur des Lilas', about a man who punches the tickets at a Paris *métro* station and ruminates about topping himself because he is so sick of 'little holes, little holes, little holes', and the haunting 'I've Just Come to Say I'm Going'.

Serge died in 1991, having fuelled himself for most of his life on unfiltered Gitanes (eighty per day of the strongest versions on the market), various drugs and great amounts of alcohol. He selflessly took upon himself the task of offending all and sundry right up until the end, which came in his sixty-fourth year. This somewhat eccentric personal crusade included recording a duet called 'Lemon Incest' with his fifteen-year-old daughter, Charlotte. The film clip showed the pair in bed together.

In 1986 Serge found himself on a French chat show with a very young Whitney Houston and announced to the presenter: 'I'd like to fuck her.' The presenter, who had been translating Serge's French for Whitney's benefit, quickly and with no small measure of panic said, 'Whitney, er, he says he likes you very much.' This hasty damage-limitation strategy missed the point that Serge had switched to English to mouth his offending phrase.

The end was sad. The quality of his music deteriorated year by year and a film clip showing one of Serge's concerts from about 1990 is like watching a huge stadium concert given by the sort of man that lives in a *métro* station. Serge would mumble mad Franglaise lyrics, all the time having great trouble holding his head up straight, presumably as the result of long-term alcohol damage. But during the 1960s and 1970s, Serge recorded many beautiful songs with many beautiful actresses and female singers who incomprehensibly – and unjustly – found him absolutely irresistible. His looks were no deterrent to Bridget Bardot, Catherine Deneuve and his longest-term partner, the English gamine Jane Birkin.

Having fallen for Serge, I was well aware that I was equally a victim of falling for the 'whole package', so sought-after by publishers. Whenever I read a book I like, or hear a spectacular album, I immediately want to find out more about the person who created it. Separating the work from the life can be hard. Serge, for his part, was the complete artist: drank like a fish, smoked like a chimney, snorted like a pig and screwed like a Black & Decker impact driver.

Similarly, at the Musée d'Orsay the Van Gogh room was always the most crowded. No-one can look at Vincent's paintings without taking into account the madness, the missing ear, all that. Again, the whole package. How does one compete? Mind you, having your success posthumously must take some of the gloss off it. One time while visiting the Musée d'Orsay I slowly examined the prominent statue of Monsieur Bonaparte, entitled 'Napoleon rising to immortality'. It was rendered thirty years or so after his death. As egotistical, war-mongering, murderous, invading dictators go, the old NB has done better than most in the posterity stakes. But again, the full package. Only smaller.

If the average reader was also looking for the whole package I clearly wasn't one. I was just a bloke in a room writing.

✣✣✣

I WAS NOW ON the home straight with *Ulysses*. I had less than 200 pages to go and was still attacking it line by line with care and grim determination. It seemed to me that people had built empires with less effort and fewer changes of direction than shown in some of Joyce's single sentences. We were back in the time of knights, language-wise at least, then in a play, with Leopold Bloom and Stephen Dedalus and urchins and The Idiot and The Bawd and Mrs Breen and The Dark Mercury and The Honourable Mrs Mervyn Talboys and Shakespeare and even inanimate objects speaking (in several languages, of course). In one section Leopold is named Emperor of Ireland; elsewhere he and Stephen seem to be in a brothel, where the ghost of

Stephen's mother fronts, causing him more guilt. Stephen denies he killed her, thumps around a lot, gets very drunk, and is helped home by Bloom. After several large swathes of nautical history, there is a long dialogue between Bloom and Dedalus that is perhaps the most readable part of the book. How's that for confidence – putting the most accessible section 700-and-something pages in.

To keep the brain up to speed I was also working my way through the complete lyrics of Jacques Brel. Although not nearly such a controversial case as Serge Gainsbourg, Brel nonetheless smoked too much, drank too much, womanised a fair bit and fully complied with the ugly provisions of French entertainment law (as it applies to males). At something near the height of his fame, the gawky, buck-toothed Brel threw it all in to sail around the world with a girl named Madly. They eventually settled in French Polynesia's Hiva Oa, Gaugin-style. But Brel ended up with cigarette-induced cancer rather than the clap, recording the songs on his last album in single painful takes just before he died.

Like most famous French people (and most famous Australians), Jacques Brel was actually from somewhere else. In this case Belgium. He sang in what Sandrine assured me was such beautiful, poetic French that it was studied at schools and universities. When I first listened, it just sounded like a mess, and like most French lyrics never seemed to properly fit the music. Yet the more I studied Brel's *parôles*, the more the magic became apparent: the exotic imagery, the black humour, the frankness and the Frenchness (notwithstanding Brel's Belgianness). In 'Ne me quitte pas' the singer begs a woman not to leave him, all along the way making more and more extravagant and lyrical promises. He will bring her pearls of rain from countries that are completely dry, he will invent new and unspoken words that she will be able to understand perfectly. When his entreaties all fail, he asks for permission to merely follow behind, discretely and in silence, as 'the shadow of your shadow . . . the shadow of your dog'.

In 'Madeleine' a man waits each day, flowers in hand, for a girl who never arrives. The sheer good-natured optimism of the singer reveals he is quite happy to come back again the next day to wait again, even though everyone but he knows that she has no intention of ever showing up. 'Les Vieux' ('The Old People') is about a couple who have lived too long and cried too much and laughed too much and one day will 'sleep too long'. All the time the pendulum of the big clock in the hall keeps the beat and whispers 'I'm waiting for you'.

Unfortunately America's Rod McKuen, the self-proclaimed world's most popular poet, obtained the English translation rights to Brel's songs. 'Le Moribund' is a fascinatingly black song about death, spirituality and infidelity, with the dying, cuckolded narrator's sardonic chorus of 'I hope you all laugh and dance when you put me in the hole' became, in McKuen's hands, 'We had joy, we had fun, we had seasons in the sun.'

✣ ✣ ✣

Letters to Hercules continued to flow more smoothly than anything I had previously written. Soon I was glowing with the hubris that comes when writing is the most important thing in the world and you believe you have invented a completely new type of novel that will shock, amaze and excite. Forget Chirac, I was now the one puffing out my chest and smiling an 'I always told you so' smile aimed directly at my former classmates and the girl who turned me down at the high-school dance.

By this time the cast of the novel included a young Polish man who looked a little like he should be selling forged ration tickets in a B-grade movie. His name was Tadeusz, but that was for convenience because I couldn't think of any other Polish names. I could change it later with the search-and-replace function. There were versions of Isabelle and Benoit too, even Sandrine. And, all the while, the mysterious girl next door was banging harder and harder on the wall and having louder and more bizarre arguments with her silent visitors.

The writing-about-what-you know caper appeared to be the answer to my literary dilemma, and Peter telling Hercules of his past and how he came to meet Ronald would soon put him – perhaps inevitably – in the schoolyard.

17

A Bigger Bomb

BACK IN PRIMARY SCHOOL there were two brands of religion: Catholic and Public. I was the first, while Johannes next door went to a public school, and was therefore the second. Whenever my sister and I were around, Johannes and his three older brothers used to sing: 'Catholics, Catholics make me sick. Call the doctor! Quick! Quick! Quick!'

Despite our best attempts, nothing could be made to rhyme with 'Public'. It did not matter. God had chosen us. Or had we chosen Him? I cannot remember. But either way, Louise and I were going to heaven, and Johannes and his brothers were not.

Our Lady Of Dolours, in the southern suburbs of Brisbane, was very likely the most thoroughly regular school in Australia in the late 1960s. About eighty per cent of the heads were covered in blond hair (my dark brown locks being a very rare exception), and the closest we had to a foreigner was Rosemary, who went with her family to England for most of Second Class and came back with a slight accent. A broken home was unheard of, though the poles under Chris Smither's house were clearly rotting and the whole front verandah was covered in thick vines.

The fat boy, Brendon, was not even fat. But convention

– founded on Billy Bunter and Enid Blyton and the other relics of 1940s and 1950s England that filled our reading lists – said we should have a fat boy in the class. And so Brendon, who must have had about four spare pounds on his frame, won the role. The personification of evil was Karen, who stole chalk from the blackboard rails, copied from the girl next to her, wore glasses and had long, black, frizzy hair. She was beaten mercilessly by everyone in authority.

With polite neatness, my father chose to die right at the end of my final year at Our Lady Of Dolours. I can pin down just a handful of definite images: he was large and puffy and was going bald. He did not say a lot and what he did was delivered in short sharp stabs. These bursts of words would usually be followed by a huff and an exit stage right, him having issued what he considered to be an inarguable conclusion.

My dad had kept the family in debt by running his electrical repairs business badly and by collecting stamps and coins and books and gramophone records (never just 'records'). He also bought antiques and artwork and anything else that could be fitted into the study, the only room in the house where Louise and I were not allowed to go. It was filled with things that my father called 'investments' and my mother called 'inanities'. I assumed they were both financial terms.

My father hit me just once. It was when I ran through the house with a friend, tripped on the dining room rug and put my head through a glass cabinet full of rare and apparently valuable things. I was six or seven years old and I cut my ear slightly and nothing more. But when I had finished crying after the shock and the subsequent clouting, I had the feeling that my father would never talk to me ever again. I was wrong. He spoke to me several times during the next three or four years.

We arrived in Sydney at the start of 1971. Three of us, with some furniture, some clothes and next to no money. I was aged ten, and went into what was then called Fifth Class. It was a vast leap to Sydney and 'The Brothers' at Arncliffe, where there were real fat boys, real foreigners and real evil. Ronald was one of about 120 'new boys' but still stood out. He was shortish with a moon-face, blue eyes and a mop of the thickest, blackest hair I had seen. He had a mild Irish accent – which everyone made fun of – and hanging out of his back pocket there was always a big bundle of torn-out exercise book pages covered with closely spaced writing, all in capital letters.

His real name was Patrick but, in the convention of schoolyard names, Ronald was substituted because it seemed the least appropriate name anyone could think of. And once we started calling him that, he was that and could not be anything else.

Ronald looked out of place in a school uniform and was far too self-assured for his age. He used long words with a distinct scientific bent, talked a lot about old films and hated sport. For such reasons he was generally classed among the ranks of Italians, Greeks, fat boys, weaklings and those, like Harrison, who stank. He was the sort of person you avoided if you played football, competed in athletics and were generally gregarious. Like me.

✣ ✣ ✣

The story of Peter Franklin and Ronald continued to be relayed letter by letter from the Land of the Nuclear Deterrent. Then on September 5 it really happened: boom boom, white water, molten rock, international outrage and a glut of pre-fried fish. *Liberté*, *fraternité* and 50,000 tonnes of TNT.

I couldn't help feeling that Monsieur Chirac had achieved his aim of becoming an international household name. A global village idiot. But many people walking down Paris streets looked strangely proud.

Tadeusz, meanwhile, could now ride his motorcycle to my apartment in stolen moments between his various jobs and courses. He sometimes turned up unannounced, though always in the afternoons. I felt I should make an excuse, yet I always said 'come in'.

A couple of days after the first nuclear test, the television stations were regularly replaying a series of ugly brawls that had taken place in Papeete, Tahiti.

'Did you see these,' I said to Tadeusz as he walked through the front door. 'The French government kept telling us the residents of Tahiti were keen on the nuclear program because of the economic bounty the army technicians brought to the islands. But it looks suspiciously like they are pulping their city's facilities and belting up the police.'

'Bombs,' Tazza said, with a shake of his shoulders, a half smile and a scratch of his beard, as if the word alone said everything that needed to be said. It would take more than a few bombs in the Pacific, or even in Paris, to faze this Pole. But then he wasn't from somewhere as soft and safe as I was. Anyway, he was more interested in talking about his *new* new motorcycle.

'You must *voir* this one, Mr Tony. It is almost as good.'

Tadeusz had another motorcycle because the first had been stolen. Shortly after our ride around the Pompidou Centre, he had rung and mentioned it almost as an aside. Furthermore, some special deal he had done on the insurance, which involved claiming the bike was garaged outside Paris, proved to be less than a winning one. Crushed? No, here he was a short time later with a new machine – and a bottle of wine.

'It is from Georgia, the first country ever to make *le vin*,' Tazza said. 'We will celebrate my newest *moto*.'

'Georgian wine . . .' I lifted the bottle and tried to read the label. 'Is it any good?'

'Ah, Georgian wine,' Tazza sighed. He allowed himself a rare pause while I took a tentative sip. It was red like a Cab Sav, but sweet. I tried to find a polite way of saying it wasn't too flash.

'Georgian wine,' Tazza sighed again as he took a sip. 'We had it in Poland in Soviet times. It is *merde*.'

The way he spat out *merde* so forcefully and unexpectedly made me cough up what was already in my mouth. I reached for a paper towel as he continued. 'A customer at the *boucher* swaps it for sausages. It's not as good as a French wine – or the *vin Australien* we can take from Marks & Spencers at Boulevarde Haussmann – but it is Champagne if you use your imagination.'

I took another small sip. 'Does anyone have that good an imagination?'

'In *les temps* Soviet,' Tazza immediately replied, 'everybody had that good an imagination, *oui, oui, oui*. There was no choice.'

✣✣✣

THE NUCLEAR TESTING WASN'T the only downer. Although the people I met and came to know in Paris were extraordinarily friendly and helpful, many of the people I didn't weren't. I was walking past the obscenely expensive boutiques of Avenue Montaigne one afternoon on my way down to the Seine. A bejewelled, be-San-Tropez-tanned blonde drove straight across my path, nearly running me down in the course of illegally parking her Mercedes sports on the footpath. She leapt out and ran across to a shop without even a hint of contrition, or concern that I was by then standing with my foot raised, seriously considering kicking her car.

One Friday night around the time of the first *Essai Nuclaire,* I decided to resort to some good old fashioned escapism and see Peter Jackson's *Heavenly Creatures*. I walked down to the Avenue des Champs Elysées, where most *Versione Originale* films are screened (the 'VO' is the version with French subtitles, rather than the *doublé* version in which all the dialogue has been redubbed into French.)

When I finally arrived at the front of the long queue, a middle-aged couple rounded me up on the outside – one to the left, one to the right – then leaned over and handed a 200-franc note to the women serving. Just a typical piece of French queuing, and the woman behind the counter served them ahead of me without comment. I told the pushing couple, in *Versione Originale,* that it was rather impolite to behave in such a manner, though I didn't use those exact words. By the time I had finished my succinct character appraisal, they had already disappeared into the cinema.

I left without buying a ticket, kicking the ground as I walked up the world's most famous street, now bathed in a foggy yellow light. I bumped shoulders with the usual cast of pretenders and spruikers and noisy tourists and beggars, and stepped around various squishy objects expelled by coiffured hounds. I had rarely been homesick in all my time in Paris, but the city swelled up to overwhelm me. As I half-tripped over a pile of rubbish, it struck me that the way the French were happy to poop in their own nest meant they would never be concerned about the condition of a nest belonging to someone they didn't know on the other side of the world. And I was still fuming over the couple that had pushed in. I'll get over it, I tried to tell myself, but they'll spend their whole lives being dickheads. Sadly, such a prospect probably didn't bother them.

Thoughts towards my host nation became less and less charitable as I walked up towards the giant white arch and was nearly run over by two unhelmeted teenage hoons, hunched up on a tiny motor scooter and racing up and down the footpath to part the pedestrians in an endless game of chicken. It didn't help that I had near terminal flu. The French think they are so liberal selling wine in corner stores and beer at McDonald's – and even in some high school canteens. But try finding throat lozenges. Like many quirks of the French system, this is a monopoly of the pharmacists and to buy anything claiming to fix a sore throat cost a minimum of ten Australian dollars.

And there was the language. I still couldn't understand more than one word per sentence when the rubber-lipped newsreaders raced through the news. Sure, I was picking up more words in signs, newspaper headlines and children's books. But I knew that even if I came to grips with the future perfect and the past impractical and all those other ridiculous tenses and moods that made up this insanely complicated, multi-conjugationed headache of a language, I still had no chance of ever understanding it the way I understood English, let alone writing a book or even an article in it. Hell, at the moment I couldn't even use it to quickly fire an insult at pushers-in that was befitting the crime.

When I trudged up the last flight of stairs and walked through my front door the phone was ringing. It was Loulou, whose older sister had arrived in Paris with dubious paperwork. Loulou was talking in French slowly like I was an imbecile – which in French I knew I was – and I could understand only enough to know that she was asking me for money and using a high-pitched, sugary sweet voice I hadn't heard before. I could sense she was putting on the voice as much for her sister, who would have been there in the tiny flat with her. It was the last thing I needed on a day like today.

'Loulou,' I replied with my fingers resting on the plug next to the phone, 'I've just arrived and . . .'

At that point I did something I'd never done before. I reefed out the plug and cut off the call as if it had simply dropped out mid-sentence. I left the phone that way and resolved not to talk to Loulou ever again as I went and poured a large glass from the duty free bottle of Scotch that I bought at the airport and that had somehow survived all these months. Probably because I don't particularly like Scotch.

At a time like this, my view of Peter Franklin's view of the world was even less balanced. He was still furiously churning out his letters to Craig Hercules. His obsession with writing his letters was at least as strong as mine with writing the novel. He would spend hours every day, hoping that in the process of revisiting and recording diverse parts of his life, he could find some hidden truth that would make sense of his endless slide.

By this stage Peter had been successfully tracked down to Paris by Maria. The big meeting was approaching. And Peter was slowly warming to Tadeusz, whom he had met when both were reading the English papers at the Bibliothèque Trocadéro. Tadeusz had started talking to Peter at full volume, despite the sign saying '*Silence*'. He would later suggest Pete call him Tazza because Tadeusz was too hard. He lived in an apartment so small the only living space was under the raised bed.

Pete suspected his frantic multilingual Pole had made a Dorian Gray pact concerning his Citroën 2CV. It was a car on which every panel was a different colour, except for the bootlid, which wasn't any colour at all because it wasn't actually there. The hole was covered with a piece of home-cut canvas held on by wire. But Tazza looked more affluent and better groomed with every meeting.

Peter Franklin had also met a pretty American bohemian in a bar in Paris. She had just arrived from Prague. She was a novelist not a film-maker but, for the moment at least, still named Annie. Writing fiction, or talking incessantly about her plans to write it, wasn't the only thing Annie did. She was in the process of sleeping her way through the men of Europe as apparent research for a, like, book project.

Meanwhile, the parallel flashback story traced the development of the unlikely friendship between Peter and the late Patrick 'Ronald' Matterton. It followed Ronald's progression from eccentric but optimistic youth through one problem after another and into a disturbed and self-harming state. And it showed how the twisted negativity of the latter-day Ronald was now overtaking Peter.

'Live every day,' he remembered Ronald once saying, 'like the one before it was your last.'

On a day when I was down on France and my main character couldn't have been more down on himself, I wrote a scene where Peter Franklin found himself sitting opposite the person in the world he liked the least. And it wasn't Jacques Chirac or the middle-aged couple that had, by sheer coincidence, pushed in front of Pete in a shop.

'During the course of most days, Herc, I suddenly and for no apparent reason think of stupid things I did or said when I was young and have this fierce shiver run right through me. I do not know why this has started. Or accelerated. But the other night I completely excelled myself. I had (another) night of plastered deliberation, drinking fifteen-franc red wine, and I found myself sitting opposite myself at nineteen years of age. What a horrible concept. What a way to lower an evening that appeared to have nowhere left to fall. What a loathsome person sharing my table. In fact, what a loathsome pair.

'I seemed to be sitting at both ends of the table, and each version of me hated the other. Pete the Elder shivered with disgust at the sight, sound and ideas of his younger self. Pete the Younger was unsure of himself and filled with the conviction that the world hated him and failed to understand him and did not have the feelings he had, or the perception that he had. He explained that computers were going to take everyone's jobs, that socialism would bring people together.

'But Pete the Younger also shuddered with contempt and disbelief at what he would become. Disgustingly pragmatic. Old and boring and totally uninterested in the plight of the average worker. Embracing consumerism, embracing computers. Finding enjoyment in long walks and sampling different cheeses.

Put a gun in the middle of the table and there would have been a race to grab it and shoot the other. Blow away the past and the future.'

✣✣✣

THE WEEKEND OF 16–17 September was what the Parisians call *la rentrée*, the time when Paris comes out of its summer slumber and the schools, courts, and everything else reopen. Alberto, my landlord, made a guest appearance. 'I am back,' he said when I opened my door.

'I'm pleased to hear it. Welcome, er, back.' I didn't know Alberto had gone away. Just about my only contact with him was to hand a cheque with his name on it to the concierge each month.

'I just thought I would check everything was, eh, all right with you,' he said, standing on the landing but looking straight past me into the apartment. Was he afraid his extensive holdings were being wrecked, that I had sublet one of my two rooms, or was running the world's smallest sweatshop?

'Yes, fine. I'll let you know if there is a problem.' He didn't leave.

'So everything is okay.'

'Yes,' I replied with a shrug of my shoulders. I could sense there was something he wasn't telling me. 'Everything is okay. Except that there are bombs going off in Paris and the South Pacific.'

'Ah, yes, I am sorry about those. It is madness. But everything else is okay?'

'Yes, okay.'

'Okay.'

'Okay.'

I closed the door and wondered what that was all about. And then it dawned on me that someone may have thought the crashing, whimpering and sobbing was coming from my apartment. Suddenly I was surprised that it had taken Alberto so long to pay a visit. I turned slightly red.

✣✣✣

MELANIE'S MAN ARRIVED ON a Sunday – that was the injustice of it. It was the only morning I allowed myself to sleep in and, suddenly, I was awoken by the sound of an excessively Latin man banging on her door and pleading in an excessively Latin manner.

The episode started relatively quietly by the standards I had come to expect from next door, but within a short time she was shrieking and he was yelling and the door was wrenched back as far as the end of the security chain, then slammed, then rapped on with a firmly clenched male fist as a prelude to once again being opened as far as end of the security chain, then re-slammed.

I lay there, blanket pulled up to my chin. Eventually I rolled my head in the direction of the clock and hauled apart my eyelids: 7.14 a.m. Every so often the man would seem to leave, noisily pacing across the landing as far as the steps. But then he would turn around and tramp heavily back to her door, thump on it again and recommence his entreaties. His apparent lack of success eventually led to him crying huge, gulping tears on our communal floorboards.

Against this background of yelling and shrieking and banging and opening and closing and pacing and stamping and howling, I was now very much awake and speculating on whether I should walk out into the corridor and say *fermez la bouche*! Though if I did, he would probably immediately switch to English like everybody else.

Attack, defence or neutrality? The lead-up to World War I was being played out on a seventh floor landing and I was a very nervous Belgium. I decided to just lie there and wonder what sort of people these were and whether they actually enjoyed behaving like this. Was it all a courting game, or a rent-a-thrill arrangement, or a serenade from lover to lover as a prelude to the two of them living noisily ever after? Either way, I kept thinking: kick him out for crissakes! Or move in together and avoid ruining two households. But make sure it is somewhere bigger. And somewhere else.

At least this new development proved that Melanie didn't have all her arguments solo.

18

Questions and Answers

I do not know where you went to school, Herc, but be thankful if it was somewhere other than Martian Brothers. Of course it was not really Martian Brothers. The order that ran the school was formed by splinter groups from the Marist Brothers and the Christian Brothers. The order's official name was Cross Link, yet I rarely heard it referred to as anything other than that contraction of Marist and Christian. Even the Principal seemed to enjoy the nickname.

It was an all-boys school with 1200 pupils. The school yard was about as big as half a football field and was completely covered in skin-removing asphalt. Lunch was spent wolfing down bad food then playing touch football, hand-tennis or games such as Cockie Laura and brandings.

Cockie Laura was an anarchic chasings game that often required using bystanders as shields or missiles. Forty-five minutes of this on a summer day and there was even less than the normal after-lunch enthusiasm for anything academic.

Brandings was more savage, and hence much more popular. A player would throw a tennis ball against a wall and, when it bounced back, everyone else tried to catch it on the full. When someone was successful, he screamed 'Freeze' and was allowed a free throw at any of the motionless figures around him. There was no points scoring system, nor a winner. The only object was to cause as much pain as possible to the person you liked least or, failing that, the person who happened to be closest. A variation of the game cut out the 'Freeze' rule. When you caught the ball, you instantly had to 'brand' someone. The result of this in an over-crowded playground was that the ball would be caught by one player, and a split second later, the rest would mow down other students in their haste to get away. Or run behind innocent passers-by who then would cop a tennis ball in the face, guts or cods.

I had – and I suppose still have – a very competitive non-competitive nature. When I arrived at Martian Brothers Arncliffe, I knew I could not out-run, out-fight or out-argue everyone in the school or score more tries in Rugby League, which was then the only football played at most Sydney schools. So it was important to not be put on the spot. At Our Lady Of Dolours, by careful selection of my competition and plenty of artful excuses, I managed to convey the impression of being at least as good as everyone else at the things that were generally agreed to matter. This was the way to be well accepted. It was a much harder task at Martian Brothers because of the sheer volume of boys, the higher standard of skills and the insistence on spontaneous, absolutely compulsory sports competitions.

Ronald did not seem to give a bugger what anyone thought about him. He did not play Cockie Laura or brandings. On sports days he revelled in being fifty metres behind the pack in the 100 metres, or in crossing his arms at the moment someone passed the ball that would have put him in the clear with an overlap. He was completely up a different tree.

Ronald had seen from the start that the best way not to be beaten in competitions that are ultimately of no real importance, is not to compete on the same terms as everyone else. All I could see then, even if I was not ready to admit it, was that Ronald was smarter than the people making fun of him and a great deal more intriguing. He knew about wars that I had never heard of, he talked of music that was far more interesting than the demons and wizards heavy metal the class opinion leaders had declared the sole acceptable type, and he could fire back a reply to an insult that was indisputable simply because nobody could quite understand it.

'You look like a pooftah, Ronald, with that stupid haircut,' I heard Tim Thompson say in front of First Form one day before the teacher had arrived. 'And I hate pooftahs, I hate them with a passion.'

Thirteen-year-old Ronald pushed back the black fringe of the offending haircut and said in his soft Irish accent. 'The man doth protest too much.'

Tim Thompson looked at Ronald for a full minute, the wheels slowly turning, and then said 'Ah, get stuffed, you stupid dickhead.'

Of course 'Ah, get stuffed, you stupid dickhead' was popularly judged to have won the exchange because Tim was cool and Ronald wasn't. But Ronald did not turn away and he did not look bettered.

It was years before I understood what Ronald meant by his reply and where it came from. And I am sure Tim Thompson still does not have a clue. Still, Ronald was not someone you wanted to be seen talking to more than occasionally. Not if you wanted to stay on the right side of the divide. The playground rules, after all, were strict. But I did talk to Ronald at certain times, and at increasing length. In the years that followed I slowly moved a foot into a second camp.

✣✣✣

NO SOONER HAD I read Joyce's lines about a certain O'Callaghan, who was the habit of ostentatiously sporting a suit of brown paper, than my own brown-paper man made his *rentrée*. Equilibrium was restored. And it was in September that I finally conquered *Ulysses*. Around the 770s, I reached an oddly intriguing section in which a series of questions was put, and answers provided in ultra-formal, scientific language. It started with an interrogation about which route Bloom and Dedalus took home from their drunken scrape, but evolved into a series of mathematical calculations comparing the ages of the two men at various points of their lives. When Bloom turned on the tap to fill the kettle, Joyce followed the water stream back to Roundwood Reservoir and, via a series of questions and answers, entered into a discourse on subterranean aqueducts, relieving tanks, overflow weirs and hydrokinetic turgidity.

The Q & A section was a work of extraordinary scholarship and I enjoyed it immensely. I could imagine Joyce working for months on answers to the questions he had posed about astronomy, biology, physics, finance, linguistics and locksmithery. But I could also imagine that it would have been easier not to ask them.

In the 830s Joyce provided a formal balance sheet for 16 June 1904, recording the money Bloom spent on the pig's kidney and sheep's trotter, among other things. Now fully in the swing, I calculated the year of Leopold's birth, using the information that stated Bloom would be seventy in 1936. Then I started making even stranger calculations.

Q. So when, Mr Davis, was Leopold born?

A. On the dates provided within the Q & A section of *Ulysses*, it seems Leopold Bloom was born in 1866.

Q. Could this explain Leopold eating pork and not being circumcised?

A. Yes, it could. Joyce reveals that Bloom's father, Rudolph, converted to Christianity in 1865, the year before Leopold's birth.

Q. Is it true that in some ways Leopold still considered himself to be a Jew?

A. Yes. He says 'I am the last of my race.'

Q. If Bloom did indeed live until 1936, how many pages would be required for James Joyce to document seventy full years rather than just one day?

A. Assuming that *Leopold Bloom: The Complete Story* was set in the same size Plantin font as the 1992 Paladin edition of *Ulysses* and paginated in a similar way, and assuming that allowances were made for the leap years, it would take 23,853,968 pages.

Q. And how thick would the standard edition of *Leopold Bloom: The Complete Story* be?

A. If the complete work used the same paper stock as

the paperback example cited above (the book block of which has 933 pages of text and a spine width of 4.8 centimetres), the 23,853,968 pages of *The Complete Story* would make up a tome 122,721.38 centimetres thick. This equates to roughly 1.23 kilometres or three quarters of a mile. To this figure must be added the thickness of a flexible laminated cardboard cover, and four pages comprising indent information, a title page, a three-paragraph author biography and a list of other works by the same author. This would increase the overall bulk by a further 1.3 mm.

Q. Did the Q & A section continue past page 800, and what did it reveal beyond matters of astronomy, biology, physics, finance, linguistics and locksmithery?

A. It continued until page 870. Among more tangential things, it included a forensic examination of every element of the main character's make-up. It was unlike anything else I had experienced. Extraordinary, in fact. A completely different way of approaching characterisation.

Q. Did the reader feel any more warmly to Leopold as a result?

A. Alas no, despite the above. Nor did he feel he really knew Leopold's wife, Marion (Molly) Bloom. Nor did he care that Hugh E. (Blazes) Boylan had only recently known her.

Q. How can we be sure of this last detail?

A. On page 862, Bloom climbs into the matrimonial bed and feels the impression of a male occupant who was not him.

Q. How does he react?

A. Bloom's response is muted. We receive a list of Molly's previous lovers, real and/or imagined. They include

Simon Dedalus, the father of Stephen, plus the Lord Mayor of Dublin and a bootblack at the General Post Office.

Q. Does the book conclude with a challenging section?

A. Based on what you've heard so far, what would you reckon?

Q. Don't try that one, sunshine. I'm the one asking the questions.

A. Well then, 'ken oath it does: a sixty-page stream of consciousness from Molly. And whereas the previous streams of consciousness were graced with some punctuation, this reader is not sure he saw any full-stops at all in this one. It read like it had been edited by Tadeusz, after banging his head on the raised bed.

Q. What happens in it?

A. Molly revisits some experiences with previous lovers, and keeps returning to sex, via everything else including a foot fetish.

Q. What is the final phrase?

A. I've read that the grumpy old man who runs the Joyce Estate won't let anything be quoted. But it is something like 'Yes I will I said yes I Will yes'.

Q. What did the reader do upon completing the phrase something like 'Yes I will I said yes I Will yes'?

A. He walked out into the soft afternoon Paris sun.

Q. What did the reader think at that moment?

A. He felt disappointment he had finally made it to the end of *Ulysses* but had no Joyce scholar to discuss it with, and to tell him where he had gone wrong as a reader.

Q. Was that last comment code for 'where Joyce had gone wrong as a writer'?

A. They are your words, not mine.

Q. They still deserve a response.

A. Yes, possibly they are.

Q. Could the reader's difficulties with the work, and sometimes negative opinions of same, be influenced by problems with his own writing, and by a deep-down resentment that Joyce found international acceptance in a field that you, Mr Davis, have proved pretty damn bloody pathetic at, thus far?

A. They could. But I hope they aren't. There is so much to admire about Joyce, so much that the book is almost immaterial. He worked so hard for so long. His eyesight was deteriorating, he was in huge physical pain yet he displayed enormous endurance, determination and a strict adherence to his artistic vision, even when he lost his physical vision. And he deserves respect for his decision not to whore himself to Mills & Boon who, I should add, still haven't replied to me. And for ploughing on through eight difficult years to complete his book, rather than jumping into something else after just three months. I was not even an apprentice's assistant by comparison.

Q. So what exactly was the state of your so-called novel writing at this point?

A. Well, funny that you should ask, because it may have been all bleak but it wasn't all bad. I don't want you to think I won't be going back to *Undermoon Bay* but, in the meantime, it's all *Letters to Hercules*. And here the 'historic' scenes are coming up convincingly, I think. The passages set in the present are nothing if not dramatic and the diverse strands seem to be moving together in a way that I never looked like achieving with my first Paris project. Peter and Maria have exchanged messages via the American Express office near Opera Garnier; he ignored her at the start but her persistence has paid off. A face-to-face meeting is nigh.

Q. Yeah, great. I'm so happy for you. Let's return to Joyce. Surely, Mr Davis, you must make one concession: that in reading *Ulysses* slowly and thoroughly you may have planted a seed. At some point you may revisit *Ulysses*, or even its difficult cousin *Finnegan's Wake*, and at last understand why 'masterpiece' is the only appropriate description.

A. Stranger things have happened. Though not involving me.

✣✣✣

AS IF TO DRAW a line under another episode, a few days later I was sitting at my desk and typing away. Suddenly I thought *what was that noise?* It was no noise, that's what it was. The next day the lack of noise was even more pronounced, and by the end of the week it was deafening. Yes, Melanie had gone.

This robbed me of a denouement to my real-life story. But real life isn't fiction. In the latter, Melanie could have a face and a voice. Peter Franklin could meet her. He wouldn't even need to knock on her door. But first Pete had to fight to stay in the country because, at the moment he and Maria had finally arranged to meet, the French authorities had summoned him to the Préfecture de Police for an urgent meeting. Pete couldn't quite believe anything urgent could ever happen at the Préfecture de Police, but he strongly sensed he was to be given notice to quit France.

Just as Paris was a moral holiday, so was Pete. He could do anything, say anything and, hey, this was fiction. It wasn't me who was responsible for anything he did or said, anything he got wrong, or anything that was offensive.

'They are trying to kick me out, Herc! They should realise it is them who have behaved like pricks. I did not decide to conduct nuclear tests. I did not run away from the Germans, or collaborate with them, or turn in my Jewish neighbours. I did not beat the shit out of Algeria, or rape Madagascar or start the Vietnam War. I never sent people to blow up protesters in New Zealand and I never threw up a series of trade boycotts when they were arrested. And I am not obsessed with *The Grandeur of Pete.*

19

Parallel Lies

Here, Herc, is one incident from my father's life that I still clearly recall. How he came home with a painting that he had paid $400 for. I cannot remember what it was supposed to be of. But it was very modern: broad black lines, with flashes of blue and red and a pair of breasts and the curve of a hip somewhere in the mix. Even then, I knew that the modern and girly nature of the painting had doubled or tripled the size of the infringement my father had so obviously committed. Four hundred dollars was the price of a second-hand car. My mother was furious and the argument was very loud.

'What is so good about it?' she shouted. 'Well, tell me that.'

'I can't.'

'Then why the hell did you throw away $400 of our money?'

'It is a picture,' my father said with a snort, as if this declaration was entirely self-explanatory.

'I know it is a picture,' shrieked my mother, even more urgently. 'Tell me what is so good about it.'

'It is a bloody picture. How many times have I got to say it, woman?' my father spat out. 'If you could explain

it in words, the bloke would not have had to paint the bloody thing. And I would not have had to spend $400 buying it.'

After my father was killed in action (not in Vietnam but on Anzac Day on the road outside the pub in Spring Hill), none of his faith in collecting, or perhaps my mother's skill in disposing of what he had collected, supported his continual use of the term 'investment'. When I later asked my mother how much the $400 picture had fetched (it was only ever 'the $400 picture', it was never a painting and certainly never had a title or an artist's name attached to it), my mother said tersely, 'One hundred and twenty-five miserable dollars, and I was damn lucky to get that'.

I wish I knew more about the painting. Because when someone lives a life so pointless, it is more reassuring to believe my father was secretly deep or clever. And had not been taken in by an art dealer. I want to believe he had bought something that would now be worth millions.

✣ ✣ ✣

I WAS WITHOUT A *father, which sometimes made me feel different and special, but more often made me sad and a little ashamed. Our family had even less money than before, and I had no-one to take me to the football and war movies like other boys. But in Sixth Class I discovered the much more shameful circumstances at Ronald's house. He lived with an uncle and aunt. His parents were divorced. I had never met anyone before whose parents were divorced. It was something base and exotic. The sort of thing that happened overseas. Perhaps even at one or two public schools. But not at Martian Brothers.*

❖❖❖

THE MAN WAS LYING on his back near a bus-stop, completely surrounded by members of France's crack paratrooper squad, the *EPIGN*. The camera was rolling as twenty-four-year-old Khaled Kelkal raised what appeared to be a pistol. He was then shot eleven times.

The *EPIGN*, or *Escadron Parachutiste d'Intervention de la Gendarmarie Nationale,* had tracked Kelkal down to the small town of Maison Blanche in the mountains around Lyon. And just how determined they were to get him became apparent later, when it was revealed the sound-track of the TV footage had been doctored. Of the eleven shots pumped into Kelkal's body at Maison Blanche, only the last was fatal and, unbeknown to *telespectators,* it came after a voice from within the *EPIGN* ranks yelled 'finish him off, finish him off.'

Kelkal's Algerian parents had brought him to France as a child. He grew up in the poor suburbs of Lyon and was regularly arrested for petty crimes. When he was finally sentenced to jail as an adult, there were people waiting for him. Kelkal went into the clink a common thief and came out a fully fledged Islamic militant. French interior minister Jean-Louis Debré now insisted Kelkal had played a major role in all the recent bombings and that his fingerprints had been found on the bomb planted beside the Paris-Lyon TGV train. Debré said Kekal's death, teamed with the capture of another twenty-eight militants and raids seizing 44 kilograms of explosives, meant the French state had dealt a decisive blow to the bombers. France was now a much safer place.

Events a week later suggested otherwise. Just hours after Kelkal's funeral, another gas canister blew up, injuring sixteen Parisians. Again it was packed with screws and nails to provide extra shrapnel (a favourite *GIA* technique within Algeria, where tens of thousands of people had died in extremist attacks and government reprisals during the previous four years), and again the *métro* was targeted. The station hit was Maison Blanche, the name of the town near Lyon where the *EPIGN* had 'finished off' Kelkal.

With something over 50,000 regular police, special police and soldiers roaming the streets, Peter Franklin's main fear was being stopped and told to produce his paperwork, now out of date. He hadn't kept his meeting with the Prefecture, instead accepting the advice of an immigration expert: Tazza.

'It is okay, you just need to *disparaître* into the crowd for a period. They are not stopping *et* checking *les blancs*.'

Pete also had to deal with Youyou, a foreign student with whom he had had a brief and entirely self-serving relationship, and who didn't seem to understand the rules. She now kept ringing and asking to meet, or asking for money, always for her university course or because her sister, who had arrived on a tourist visa with the intention of overstaying, was ill. And Youyou made jokes that didn't quite seem like jokes about why Pete should marry her.

There was the loneliness too, a growing sense of being in a place he didn't really understand, and further self-loathing when comparing his misery with the optimism of a Pole who thought he was the king of the castle because, after months of cycling across Paris each morning and night and working 1000 hours a week at the markets, he had been able to buy a car that was so wretched that even looking at it would send all the characters in *Prozac Nation* into network therapy (oh yes, *Prozac Nation* was in there too, as Annie's handbook). And of course there was Maria, who had been far more effective than the gendarmerie in tracking down Peter Franklin.

The meeting between Maria and Peter was set up in a café: a small, terribly Parisian one, of course. There was a chaste kiss. It seemed to take forever to be served and Peter was tense and scared and guilty and couldn't make eye contact. He stared up at the thin strip of neon above the bar. He looked at its full orange glow reflecting in the rows of mirrors along the walls. He dropped his eyes down towards the small, green circular table that separated them, watching the light bounce off its chrome edging, reading again and again and again the folded card that said *Petit Déjeuner Simple 35F*. There was a burst of German from one corner, a burst of English from another and cigarette smoke everywhere.

Maria slowly twirled around her finger a strand of hair that fell on the right side of her face, a habit that had long annoyed Pete, but which he had never mentioned to her in all these years. She looked European – Latin – enough to fit in, yet somehow like a little girl a long way from home.

'It was everything,' he said, still looking down. 'Not just Ronald. It was the people I knew, the job I did, the life I led. Everything suddenly made me nauseous. I mean everything. Not just the expectations and pressures and skulduggery at work and frustrations and lack of sleep. But the colour of the paint on our house. The type of stitching used in the seats of the Saab. The smell of the city, the chip on the lip of my office tea-cup, the little bruises I always get because of my defective skin, the stupid everyday tasks like flossing bits of food from between the gaps in my back teeth and looking for a parking spot near the office.

'I remember sitting in our lounge-room on my own one night long after you had gone to bed, running through endless lists of things I could no longer stand: the daily newspapers, the little musical stings between the shows on television, the actual shows on television, everything on the radio, the sound of my mother's voice on the phone, the thought of my sister's lifestyle. The thought of my own job, despite me talking it up to anyone who would listen. And – I am sad to say – the sight of your face. Even though you were so good to me in my moment of crisis and deserved so much better.

'That was it. It was everything. I finally managed to put my finger on it, or to realise that my finger was not big enough.'

A young woman walked in. She was gently smiling to herself and clutching a brace of carry-bags emblazoned with the Galeries Lafayette logo. Peter looked at her with contempt and jealousy. She was here just to sit and enjoy a coffee. Why was it never that simple for him?

Infidelities were confessed: Maria's sole transgression with precision, Peter's more numerous lapses with vagueness and mumbling. Still, Peter couldn't or didn't want to conjure images of the store manager climbing over his wife. It seemed unreal, strangely unimportant. The longer they talked – the first plain English conversation he could remember for months – the more Pete found himself wanting to sink his head into Maria's chest and slink off home with her.

Pete heard how Maria's female workmates had rallied around her in the wake of her husband's departure, how Maria hadn't thrown out a single thing of his, how she had defended Peter even to her own parents and how she had been driven into other arms by loneliness and fear, but regretted it immediately. There were things not mentioned too, such as how she must have watched their savings diminish but had done nothing to stop Peter accessing their shared account. And how Maria, who had never been overseas before, had managed to stand up for herself in this city with none of the drama he had managed to bring upon himself.

'You have got it out of your system now, Peter. It is time to come home, to your home.' Maria was more reasonable than he had a right to expect, but she was not offering him anything new. Just forgiveness and more of the same.

Pete eventually said no. He was not heading back to Sydney, not straight away. He could only promise he would think through everything she had said. She would have to go home and wait for a decision. He knew it wasn't fair but he couldn't face people, he couldn't go back to his former job, his former life. And anyway, he explained, he had agreed to go to Prague with a friend named Tadeusz.

What Peter Franklin hadn't told Maria was that another friend, one named Annie, was also going to Prague. In fact, she had convinced Pete to go, and he – drawn to the cost advantages of a car – had persuaded Tadeusz. The three met in Tazza's street next to the 2CV with which the Faustian pact had so obviously been effected. Pete explained to his taxi-driver in Sydney that Tadeusz appeared in a stylish new summer suit and wearing the shiniest, most elaborate wristwatch Pete had ever seen. There was tension from the start. Before they were even out of the Paris suburbs, Annie began throwing her hands around and stabbing the air with her cigarette as she speedily pontificated on one subject after another.

'Meat products are produced in concentration camps, in death factories . . . yet the length of the human intestine clearly identifies the species as vegetarian . . . carnivores have much shorter guts because dead meat quickly rots and becomes poisonous to the system.

'But even if you do not look at it that way,' she said, throwing her dead cigarette out the window, 'an acre of land used for growing vegetables can feed three times more people than the same amount of land used for livestock.'

'We can feed even more *peuple,*' Tadeusz replied with scarcely a pause, 'when we use the same land for the *supermarché.*'

❖❖❖

THE BEATLES WERE HAVING a reunion of sorts. The remaining 'Threetles' re-dubbed a John Lennon demo recording to create 'Free As A Bird' and claimed it as a new and authentic Fab Four single. At the same time Queen produced a 'back from the grave' disc, threatening to initiate a chart battle between lead singers who were entirely dead. I didn't like it, but what right did I have to hold an opinion? I too was fiddling with history, rewriting events, reworking real people, interfering with the back catalogue of life. The defence I kept in the forefront of my mind was that *Letters to Hercules* might have started from a basically true standpoint, but I was moving further and further from the truth, as was the original intention. The irony was that I had been seduced by the advantages of writing about what I knew, then had made so many changes I didn't quite know what I knew anymore. And I had been seduced by the lure of simplicity yet found myself chopping and changing sequences and telling a story in flashback that was progressing at one rate, and a story in the present that was progressing at another.

❖❖❖

MY TIME IN PARIS was not one which made me particularly well acquainted with French restaurants. But when I felt extravagant, or tired of being frugal, I would sometimes ring Isabelle or Sandrine or Benoit and we'd make our way down the narrow cobblestone back streets of the Left Bank to find a small restaurant around rue Mouffetard, perhaps my favourite street in Paris. Rue Mouffetard is still technically in the Latin Quarter (so named because the students at the nearby Sorbonne University once learned, and often conversed, in Latin) but with less of the tourist crush of Saint Michel and the area around the Seine. The square at the top is called Place de la Contrescarpe and is actually a circle, ringed by cafés and restaurants, which in combination just cry *famous people wrote and painted and composed in this area*. A plaque on a nearby *maison* – 74 rue du Cardinal Lemoine – said 'Ernest Hemingway 1899–1961 lived here'. Under which someone had scrawled 'and Serge Martin

1974–19??'. At one point Joyce lived almost exactly across the road from Hemingway – at number 71.

Just before the second nuclear test I was on the Left Bank with Isabelle, looking for a suitably crowded, noisy, studenty place to eat.

'My father has sent me a letter,' Isabelle announced. I had already heard that he lived near the Spanish border and they didn't talk often. 'My favourite type of letter. One with money in it. And I have some other good news, so tonight I will invite you.'

'I'd be happier paying for myself. But let me choose the restaurant.'

As we walked down the hill from Place de la Contrescarpe, a middle-aged man with huge facial whiskers walked towards us. He stood out from the crowd because he was clutching the ears of a massive dead rabbit in one hand and had a large gun-shaped leather case in the other. Rue Mouffetard is probably 50 kilometres from the nearest place you could go hunting. But perhaps a menu called for freshly slaughtered bunny and the customer was getting nothing less. Amid such surrealness I casually chose any old back street. Except that it wasn't any old back street, it was rue du Pot de Fer which I had already visited several times on my walks. And I was looking for a restaurant as close as possible to number 6.

'*Non fumeur*,' I said to the waiter. Recent legislation had required all French restaurants to have a non-smoking section. But when we asked to be seated there, he lead us away from the action, up a set of stairs, and into a tiny, characterless, windowless room with two tables in it. 'Boof,' he said as he gestured to our table. Although 'boof' is a standard and common French exclamation, in this case it probably meant that I was a great boof for asking to be seated in the non-smoking area. The alternative to this scenario – which I had also experienced – was that the waiter would point through the smoky haze to a sole table with a *Defense de Fumeur* sign on it.

'I think, Anthony, I would prefer the smoke to the empty room,' said Isabelle.

'Me too.' We were led back to the front, now even more crowded than before. The world and his experimental-filmmaker-concubine was there.

'This is rue du Pot de Fer,' I explained as we were sent to a tiny table next to the wall. 'The street where George Orwell – or Eric Blair as he then was – lived when he moved to Paris to become a writer. He took a small room in a hotel just over there, full of dirt and bedbugs. I love Orwell's writing. When I was in Scotland a few months ago I hired a fishing boat to take me to the farmhouse on the Isle of Jura where he wrote *1984*. It was amazing . . . windswept, completely deserted.'

I realised I was sounding a little obsessive.

'I haven't read Orwell.' Isabelle's clear diction neatly sliced through the din. 'I see the word Orwellian in the English press. It means ominous and deceitful language, doesn't it? I've always thought of Orwell as a deceitful writer.'

My mouth went dry. Poor George, dead of consumption at forty-six and now being mauled by a short French woman.

'No, no, no. That couldn't be more wrong,' I insisted, a little too loudly. 'It is one of the great tragedies in literature that the name of the clearest thinking, most straightforward English writer of all is now used to symbolise the opposite. He opposed deceitful language, he opposed deceitful writing, and he did this by satirising it.'

'Oh, I shall look further into it,' Isabelle said, waving smoke away from her face and moving her chair slightly so a woman at the adjacent table could contort her way past. 'One shouldn't make judgements without going to the source.'

'You should read *1984* and *Animal Farm*, of course,' I blurted out, sounding suspiciously like Isabelle with her lists of French books, 'and also *Coming Up for Air*, which is lesser known and underrated. And *The Road to Wigan Pier*, but most of all the essays. Only George Orwell could write an essay that made you realise that a war in which women and children are bombed in their homes is better than one in which they aren't.'

She looked surprised. 'And why should that be?'

'Because then every member of the public is forced to make a decision about whether the war is worth pursuing. In the past the people of many countries have given their support to unjust and unnecessary wars because they sounded glamorous and no matter what happened, it wasn't going to affect them in their safe, warm homes.

'Anyway, as Orwell argued, why is it less tragic for an eighteen-year-old male conscript to die than anyone else?'

I had already consumed two or three glasses of carafe wine and wasn't sure I had captured the true cogency of Orwell's argument, but at least I had gone in to bat for him. Someone had to, particularly in his own street.

Isabelle hadn't produced her good news yet so I

continued on my Orwell ramble-logue. 'Orwell said that writing a book is like a long bout of some painful illness. That you would never undertake such a thing if not driven on by some demon that you can't resist or understand. He should have known, he typed out *1984* on that miserable cold island in Scotland while horribly sick with TB.

'And he left instructions that if he died before he got to the end, the manuscript was to be destroyed. He only just made it; we almost lost one of the most important books of ideas ever.'

Although I could talk about Orwell and I could talk about Joyce or Hemingway, I couldn't talk about the most important writing in my life – my own. I drifted into small talk. This doesn't mean the small talk was that small. After all, there were amazing things happening all around the city, country and world. But when you are engaged in such a solitary, all-consuming task as writing a Great Work that will outlive all other Great Works (except perhaps your own Later Greater Works), everything is small talk besides what you are doing, and everything that doesn't seem like small talk seems that way only because you can see a way that you may be able to cadge a scene or character or idea for your book.

'You saw the verdict in the O. J. Simpson trial?' I asked Isabelle. The acquittal had been shown on the late night news, unusual because the French hardly ever showed anything that was not French, unless it involved people who were French, were protesting against France, or setting fire to former French colonies.

'No, I have heard the name in the press perhaps, but I am not sure that I know anything more,' Isabelle replied.

Fair enough, it wasn't like O. J. Simpson was a character in seventeenth-century English literature. The US press had called it the trial of the century, which may have been an exaggeration, but news about it was constant everywhere else. I was now trying to speak French and it took forever to explain the story because I had to keep flicking through my pocket dictionary in the poor light, or say to Isabelle 'what's the word for trial?' or 'what's the word for jury?'. Saying words such as 'guilty' with a French accent didn't seem to make them French words. When it was too difficult or too noisy I just went straight into English.

In one language or the other I explained why it was such a big story in the USA. How Simpson was a football star, how he appeared in movies ('No, he wasn't an actor, he just appeared in movies'), how the case had divided the nation largely because his murdered wife was white.

'Oh,' said Isabelle. 'What colour is he?'

I shook my head in surprise. It was time to switch back to English. 'You said you had some other good news,' I said, though in the back of my mind was still the idea that I had sold short Orwell's essay. And that the Simpson jury should have been recruited in Paris.

'I have a new man,' Isabelle said. 'Or perhaps I should say: I have decided that I have a new man. I can't say more than that, but I am very excited.'

She showed this excitement in her inimitable way, by looking and sounding exactly the same as always.

✣ ✣ ✣

A FEW DAYS LATER I caught up with Sandrine in the 15th *arrondissement*, to the south of the Eiffel Tower. I waited for her in the early evening in a small square filled with flowers under a completely grey sky. I could feel a cool breeze sneaking in between the bottom of my jeans and the top of my socks. Winter was definitely on the way.

In front of me a little black boy, maybe two or three years old, was running up and down a set of stairs within a small children's playground and giggling contagiously. At Parc Monceau, and most other ultra-wealthy parts of town, the babies are white and the women who take them there to play are black. I wondered what Parisian children of all colours would do in the freezing months ahead. I went back to my copy of the *International Herald Tribune* and read about the latest French nuclear test.

It was still quite light at 6 p.m. when Sandrine arrived. She shared the government's apparent confidence regarding bombs on the home front. 'I think we have arrested the important ones now.' Her green eyes flashed with optimism. 'And the Interior Ministry now has 70,000 men under the Vigi-Pirate project.'

If Sandrine had any concerns, they were about the cutbacks Chirac and his prime minister, Alain Juppé, were planning. She was sure this would soon disrupt that thing so dear to every Parisian's heart: the *métro* schedule.

'Some say we are going to see enormous strikes,' Sandrine assured me, with the cheerful resignation of a Parisian in the face of shutdowns, blockades and protests. 'Everything will be chaos.'

'Anyway,' she added, 'I hope it will all work out. And if we are to photograph the new lights on the *Tour Eiffel*, we should leave now.'

Sandrine was going to photograph the lights, not me.

But I was more than happy to take the walk to see them. And there are some towers you never tire of.

✣✣✣

IN MID-OCTOBER ANOTHER gas bottle filled with explosives and screws was detonated on a train moving from St Michel to Orsay Station on the Left Bank. The doors were closed, concentrating the impact. One man had to have both legs amputated on the spot but, miraculously, no-one was killed outright. At the end of October the French exploded another device of their own, a 60-kiloton bomb under Mururoa Atoll. A few days later I started my second government-run French course. A more intense affair than the first, it was scheduled to last a three full months.

My new teacher was small and dark-haired and looked like Edith Piaf. She became very excited about a lot of things, which meant that we were always sidetracked and rarely finished anything we started. But Madame Perrault was pleasant, spoke clearly and tried hard, even if she had a habit of snapping shut her book at the precise moment the second hand touched 4.00 p.m.

Again, there was a generous assortment of eccentrics. When Madame Perrault was complaining about how the French language was being corrupted by English (the Anglo-Saxon conspiracy, of course), the young woman named Sarah who sat in the row behind me said under her breath: 'Well if not for us Anglo-Saxon countries, lovey, your language would be German, wouldn't it?'

Another *anglaise*, Anne, was most notable for her fruity voice, Himalayan bust-line and shrill demands. 'Why can't you just explain it in English?' Anne demanded of Madame

Perrault whenever she couldn't understand something. Which was often.

This course would take me up until early February, at which point my plane ticket was fated to expire and my literary trust fund (which is to say as much of my own money as I would trust myself with to fund my literary project), would be pretty well depleted. I felt the end of my time in France was approaching at a speed considerably over the legal limit. By then I just had to have *Letters to Hercules* finished; I was increasingly tense about the prospect of returning home with two unfinished novels.

20

A Dream

Tazza spends most of his time chasing women. We have plenty of old buildings in Poland, seems to be his angle. The tourist areas of Prague are so small you are always running into each other. Every time Annie and I see him, he is with at least one girl and – on one memorable occasion – was sitting in a café with about three or four stunners, all of them cocking their heads to one side as he blabbered on in what could have been Spanish. Yesterday he brought two women into the beer hall where I was writing letters and Annie was reading Victimhood For Beginners *or some such rubbish. And we were both, of course, drinking.*

'Dobranoc,' *Tazza said. 'This is Polish for "good night" because my friend I think that the last trolley bus for our hotel will leave soonly.'*

'Sure, we'll head off,' I replied without a lot of enthusiasm for getting up or moving. 'And glad to see you are not going home empty-handed.'

'No, non,*' Tazza replied forcefully. He moved up close and conspiratorial. 'I do not make the screwing with them as I am a marry man.'*

'A marry man? What, like one of Robin Hood's marry men?'

'I am not sure. But my wife and I are – en Français *we say* – fidèle. *I like to talk and be with the pretty girls but will leave on my alone. Yes, always on my alone. I am like the man in the song "Beautiful Women Are My Life". Ha ha ha.'*

'Cannot say I know that song, Tazza,' I replied with some very firm shaking of the head, 'but if you think you would like to sing it for me, do not!'

The three of us walked down the wide, desolate streets towards the trolley-car station and Tazza did indeed did start singing 'Beautiful Women Are My Life'. Annie had been cold and distant for much of the day despite the goings-on of the night before. Now she threw her arm over my shoulder, though it seemed to be to say 'Help me walk, I have had one Guinness too many.'

I too felt very much on my alone.

There was a small note taped to the wall of the trolley-car shelter, hand-written in Czech. Tazza looked at it. 'The trolley bus is annulé*.' We would have to walk to our hotel. It was about forty minutes by foot, with me almost carrying Annie and Tazza singing what seemed like 900 verses of the same song as we trudged along the broken footpath beside the river.*

'Beautiful women are my life, my mornings, my noons, my starry starry nights . . .'

✣ ✣ ✣

TOO MANY HISTORY BOOKS, too many museums and probably too many letters to Craig Hercules as well. I lay in my bed and fell into a deep sleep to discover Maria and I – not Maria and Pete, but Maria and I – dressed in 1790s garb. My face was covered in powder and I was wearing green tights and a tall white wig and a huge silk cravat. Maria had an impossibly frilly dress with a pulled-in waist and a massive bustle pushing it out below the waist.

We were in a crowded courtroom and a man in a black hat read the sentence: *'Tête Tranchée'*. I didn't even know what it meant (I later looked it up), but I distinctly heard it said. And then almost immediately I was in the back of a horse-drawn carriage, sitting alongside this man who was supposed to be my confessor. He was telling me that I should join him in chanting psalms if I wanted the grace of God. But I didn't want the grace of God. I wanted to get out of the carriage.

The two men at the front of the carriage were gendarmes. And so were the two men at the rear and so were the men marching alongside. My fate was sealed. My confessor seemed to take the attitude that oh well, these things happen. I couldn't be as philosophical as that. It was my life, after all.

I was really there, it was all really happening. Every bump, every push, every hot flush. The droning of the confessor's voice. But I couldn't talk. There were too many things going through my mind: They can't really kill me, I haven't actually done anything, it won't really happen to me, they'll stop at the last minute. Maria won't let it happen!

But as I was forced through the crowd and up the steep stairs to a platform, I saw that a similar procession was passing through the crowd on the other side of the platform. It was her. Maria. Our last sights on this earth would be of each other being killed, or about to be killed. And the last impressions we would form of each other would be based on the qualities we displayed in the lead-up to that last action. Not the least of which was me pissing off overseas and leaving her high and dry. But there would be no time for disappointment or admiration or hatred or love.

I was thinking all this clearly and rationally, but all the time I was also kicking and trying to curl into a ball so that they couldn't carry me. And the guard on my right copped the back of my fist in the cheekbone, the one in front got a kick in the small of the back and, when he turned around, an even harder one straight in the cods. But none of this seemed to faze them or to slow them down. In a very short time I was at the top of the platform, where I saw Maria also surrounded by guards.

She was, by comparison, calm. Stooped and tearful and clearly terrified, but possessing a strength I lacked. Everything went silent. Surely the people in the crowd weren't going to stand around and allow this to happen. I looked at them, thousands of them, and for an instant could see all their faces individually. Every person I had ever known. Suddenly the drums started. A thousand sticks on a thousand stretched hides, providing the signal for the huge crowd to start cheering, and hissing and chanting, and singing and screaming. Those closest to the platform were yelling out 'finish him off, finish him off'. I punched and kicked and wriggled but eventually broke down in a howling mess when it was obvious I didn't have the physical strength to make even a tiny impression on the powerful men standing around me.

The executioner – maskless, all muscles and dressed in leather straps – for a brief moment emitted a small glimmer of understanding and said in a soft but firm voice: 'There is a chance, you know'. But he didn't explain himself further. The drums rolled again and I could see everything from above. The guards started marching the two little figures the few steps towards the two machines. There was the smell of blood in the air, and a browning gluggy mess underfoot. And terror. I was really there. I was really there and I knew I should have tried to say something like 'kill me, but spare her', but I had no voice and there wasn't a noble bone in my body. And I couldn't bear to look at Maria in case she was in fact saying just that.

They dragged me . . . or was it Pete, because at some point I woke up. That didn't stop me handing the dream across to Peter Franklin, continuing the story and writing it up as part of the book. So I, or Pete, was at the bottom of this machine and looked up to see two rails which almost disappeared into the clouds. At the top was a massive angled blade which sparkled like a suit of lights. I sensed they had dragged Maria to the similar machine beside it, but I was not game to look. I felt my head being pushed towards the indent in the wood beneath the glinting, malevolent blade so high above.

And instinctively I – or *he* because we certainly were in pure invention by this stage – screamed and threw his arm forward to stop them putting him in position. And in doing this Pete woke himself up and just about drilled a hole through the wall next to his bed. For a good ten minutes he thought he'd broken his right arm. But he was so hot and bothered by the dream that a broken arm seemed the least of his worries. He was, as he told Craig Hercules, still sweating an hour later.

It seemed so odd that my dreams were not about my

characters: they were my characters' dreams. And they fed back into the book, which fed back into my dreams. I spent many hours every day being someone else; the estranged husband of Maria, having peculiar thoughts about everything – and particularly French things – and relaying them back to the imaginary Herc in Sydney, interspersed with the modified story of a real person, deceased and much missed. And for the rest of each day I pretended to be a normal, sane person.

21

The Owl of Despair

Ronald explaining he had not received a Christmas card from Jane: 'It might have been lost in the post,' he said without emotion. 'Or maybe she was too busy.'

'You make a lot of excuses for her.'

He continued speaking before I had even finished. As if I had not spoken at all. I looked at his hands. They were shaking. And I noted again how thin and pale he had become.

'I am going to get a birthday card, though,' he said with a quiver in his voice. 'I have taken care of that.'

'How?'

'I sent the card to her, care of the school she is working at in Adelaide. I found her name on one of the electronic messageboards. I put in a self-addressed envelope, too. I wrote inside the card "Happy Birthday Ronald". All she needs to do is to sign it and drop it in a postbox.'

I looked at him and wondered whether he had gone completely stark raving mad.

✣✣✣

Ronald spent some of his last weeks sleeping on our couch. I should have felt guilty installing a manic depressive in the lounge-room when what Maria really wanted there was a set of built-in bookcases and one of those L-shaped chaise sofas. But I did not apologise. I did not even thank her for putting up with the difficulties Ronald caused her, like not being able to have her parents over. Quite the opposite, I took out my anger.

'Why do you keep complaining,' I bellowed at her. 'I would do exactly the same for one of your friends, if one of your friends was doing it so tough.'

But, Herc, the truth is that I, or the person I was back then, most certainly would not have done the same for one of her friends. And I knew it, and Maria knew it.

❖❖❖

IT WAS ONE OF Ronald's gifts that you could think you were in a conversation with him about something other than him. But you never really were. As time moved on, everything was ultimately about him, and at any moment he could seamlessly move into a diatribe.

Sure, the gods – single or plural – could decide to make it a little hard. To put a few barriers in the way. But what, Ronald would ask me, was in it for them to continually trip people up and to frustrate every avenue of endeavour? How could they get pleasure from this? What sort of sick mind would put a rat in a maze with no real path to the carrot and then enjoy watching it run around and around until all its energy was expended and it was stagnated by a combination of panic and exhaustion. At some point unfulfilled challenges cease to be good for the soul. They only saddened the soul and blackened it.

It was in a dream last night that Ronald came back to

me. He was in full flight. 'Why do those sadists up there choose to fill a street or a million streets with bright happy people wandering around in peace and what appears to be happiness and then choose to channel their misery only through certain people?'

He talked in phrases I had never heard him use, repeatedly saying 'the bluebird of happiness does not fly around here'. Yet he summed up his position – what he honestly believed to be his position – far more clearly than the wreckage of a human being that was Ronald in those final days.

'You know what the bluebird is?' he screamed. 'It is ignorance and contentment. The gift of stupidity is as good as the gift of all the intelligence and talent needed to fulfil every ambition. Damn that bluebird! If misery were a bird, he would be an owl. An owl who knew everything and sought to better his lot. But this owl – the Owl of Despair – would have clipped wings. It would not be able to fly. An Owl of Despair. What could be more amusing for the gods than that?'

AT THE START OF November Peter Franklin was still finding excuses not to give Maria an answer about returning home, and seven suspected *GIA* members were arrested after a canister bomb was found in Lille. There were further arrests by Scotland Yard and MI5 in London and suddenly there seemed to be scope for optimism. The bombing campaign might finally be over.

November also brought huge publicity for yet another significant French anniversary: twenty-five years since the death of Charles de Gaulle. Ceremonies were held on the Esplanade des Invalides, with ninety world leaders standing in the dark, and subtle lights and candles arranged to make a Cross of Lorraine. The General was Chirac's hero, a man who if still alive probably would have been asking why the French were not doing more nuclear tests. But de Gaulle had been an amazing man for his country. Not only did he successfully present France as a World War II victor, but he grabbed it a seat on the UN security council soon after and ensured that French was made one of the two official United Nations languages. And what timing: his twenty-fifth coincided with fifty years since the end of World War II – so he'd be in synch with big anniversaries forever.

Two days later, Armistice Day brought more tanks onto the Avenue des Champs Elysées. This time it was to celebrate the end of World War I at the eleventh hour of the eleventh day of the eleventh month. Chirac and others placed wreathes at the eternal flame burning for the unknown soldier – *le soldat inconnu* – under the Arc de Triomphe.

For the struggling writer at rue le Sueur, things were generally good though money remained low. Ross Farrington of Zentre Corporation may as well have slit Julia Thompson's pale and delicate throat and sprayed the blood all over his lovely Harbourside foyer, for all the folks at Mills & Boon cared. I had decided that the 'we are looking for new authors' caper was just a marketing trick to enable the company to keep its name in the media with an unchanging product. It's also a good way to sell books: I had bought two, enough to benefit Mr Mills *and* Mr Boon. I now had to concede that they really did have an aircraft hangar filled with retired army captains bashing away at typewriters.

Resigned to zero income, I wasn't going to stay beyond the expiry of my plane ticket in February. So I made a list of all the things I still wanted to do. They were all secondary to the book, of course, but I had usually run out of writing brain power by noon anyway. The tasks included re-visiting the Louvre, Musée d'Orsay and Musée Rodin, and also seeing Musée Carnavalet, the museum of Parisian history, completing my French classes, visiting Versailles and attending an authentic wine tasting.

On this last point, one Saturday I ended up with Sandrine in Marigny-Brizay, south-west of Paris, to attend a ceremony of ancient sacred oaths administered by a group of seven people in outrageously over-the-top red robes and gold hats.

Sandrine and I stood in a line with a few other civilians in a cellar built under a suitably elaborate chateau. A man passed us each an empty glass only slightly less capacious than a small swimming pool and spoke long sentences in archaic and – for me – completely incomprehensible French. Every so often he would pause, Sandrine would gently push me in the back, and I would join the others and say *oui*. If the push was harder, I would say *oui, bien sur* in order to sound even more definitive about my heartfelt commitment to whatever it was he was saying. When the first man finished, another started pouring what looked like several litres of white wine into my glass.

'Oh-la-la,' Sandrine said as the wine kept coming. I suspected I had been served a 'get the foreigner' special, as Sandrine's glass had an entirely normal portion in it.

'By the way, what did I just agree to, Sandrine?' I whispered between large gulps of wine that made little difference to the overall level.

'You have just sworn to forever promote the wines of the Poitou region.'

'Yep, no worries. Wasn't doing anything for the rest of my life anyway.'

'And when you have finished your wine,' she said cheerfully, 'you will be made a knight of the region. But only when you have finished every drop.'

When I finally struggled to the bottom of the glass, there was a large cheer and a man in an ornate red gown and gold hat took three steps forward. He was gently swaying from side to side (or was that me?). He raised a ceremonial pole and brought it down on each of my shoulders. This transformed an average citizen (albeit one who spent many hours every day writing but not sending letters to an imaginary taxi driver) into a *Sacré Chevalier d'Honneur* and a *Confrérir les Tire-Douzil de Marigny-Brizay en Poitou.*

Alas, the title wasn't going to make for an automatic front-row seat at any regal birth, wedding or funeral. A *tire-douzil* is, I was told, the bung that stops the hole in the side of a wooden wine barrel. Sandrine and I left with two cartons of the local red. It was nice, too, but I can't say I've done much to promote the region and its produce ever since.

❖❖❖

EVEN THOUGH IT WAS becoming horribly cold, I still managed to trace the canals that were once the supply routes of the city. It was supposed to be a walk for pleasure, and it would have been for more pleasure if (a) my breath wasn't imitating a dry ice machine at a second-rate rock concert and (b) I wasn't still so uptight about getting my manuscript finished before I left.

I still hadn't worked out how to bring the fictional Melanie out of seclusion, and I didn't have a clue what the Tazza character would do next. I worried that *Letters to Hercules* was becoming *Undermoon Bay* all over again. That I had used an entirely different brush technique to paint myself into the same corner. Or a different corner. But a corner nonetheless.

I walked alongside the northern arm of the stagnant, green Canal Saint-Martin, looking for the Hotel du Nord. It was a modest, whitewashed, almost featureless building that provided the setting for a novel and then, in 1938, a film about a young couple who check in to commit suicide. It was a theme light years away from anything being produced by UK or US films studios at the time. Sandrine told me that Arletty, the actress who starred in *Hôtel du Nord*, was later accused of horizontal collaboration with the occupying Germans. 'She turned to the men who were accusing her of sleeping with the enemy and said, "Well, it was your job to keep them out."'

Overnight temperatures dropped to minus four, and the peak during one day was no better than six degrees. It was a very small six at that; out on the street it felt like St Petersburg. It wasn't fully light until 8 a.m. I sat at my desk at the start of each day tapping away at my keyboard with the rain hitting the window, the outline of the trees and roofs outside silhouetted in the dull electric glow, and my beaten-up little heater doing an excellent impression of a two-stroke motorcycle with a tank of dirty fuel. This heater never warmed the room so much that I could take my jacket off. Sure, I didn't have to burn my laptop to stay warm, *La Bohème* style, or eat my manuscript as writers had to in the siege of Leningrad during World War II. But I should at least be allowed to mention it.

Anyway, I came closer than some to enduring the sort of hardship Henry Miller found in Paris of the early 1930s. After one French class I shared a *métro* with Anne. She of the Himalayan bustline was fuming about the teacher's reluctance to teach French entirely in English. In fact, to leave the French bits out altogether.

'I can't wait until we move back to England,' she said, somehow implying these nasty people were holding her against her will.

'So why are you here, why are you learning French?' I asked.

'Because René, my Swiss husband, is working such long hours that I scarcely see him. He is in the finance industry and can earn such loads of money at the moment that we have decided to stay a little longer. Then we shall move to Oxfordshire, where I will be able to have horses.'

I looked at her and then, well, looked at her again. But she wasn't finished.

'In the meantime, one amuses oneself shopping and learning a spot of French. It's a jammy little option.'

Anne of Cleavage clearly knew nothing of the hardships others faced. Such as having to drive back from Prague with a mad Pole and an imploding American novelist in a dilapidated 2CV which would soon be towed away and impounded by German authorities for being a long way short of roadworthy.

22

The Raid

Tadeusz went to find out about the car and we met back at the Europafair at midday. He brought two young women.

'I find the car and it is not un problème *but it will not be ready for us until late in the tonight,' Tazza explained. I was more concerned about how a fairly damn ordinary looking male could go to the police station or car compound, or whatever it was, in a strange city at 10.30 in the morning then arrive back less than ninety minutes later having not only done what he set out to do but having picked up two quite satisfactory-looking females along the way.*

'I have meeted some girls from Poland at the bus station,' he said with a lascivious smile. 'I present Lidia and Irena. They are from Warsaw but Lidia is born près de moi *in the south.'*

'Pleased to meet you,' I said, looking more at Tazza than either of the Polish girls, who were both seemingly absorbed in his extra-mysterious mystique.

'Do we have to pay to get the car?' I asked.

'It is all okay,' he replied. 'But we wait, bien sur*. Lidia says we can go with them to the swimming easily until then.'*

✣ ✣ ✣

THERE WAS A THUMPING *at the door in the blackness of night followed by Tazza's energetic voice.* 'Prosze! Prosze! Prosze! *We must go now!'*

It had already been a day of too many distractions for my brain to exercise the correct amount of suspicion, particularly after Annie had punched me mid-The Act for no apparent reason then stormed out and insisted she was never coming back. And it was only when we took the U-Bahn subway out to a large, barbed-wire-ringed compound that I realised the real reason we were going to pick up the car at such an unlikely hour. Tazza could sense I was packing shit.

'It is okay. I had a good look earlier. All you must do is parle *to the guard.'*

So, there I was, aiding grand larceny or whatever they call it in Berlin and shaking almost uncontrollably. But Tazza was as composed as always, offering a wry smile when he said, 'The risks are for me. They are not you.'

As instructed, I walked up to the little office next to the driveway, knocked on the glass and tried to speak to the guard who, thank God, did not have any German shepherds with him. He walked out of the office, past the barrier, to join me on the driveway, where I opened up my map. 'I am trying to find the bus to my hotel. I think I caught the wrong one and am now completely lost.'

The guard looked at me with a clinical expression that wordlessly said, 'I cannot understand the difficulty, the Berlin bus system is all so logical.'

'You are entirely on ze wrong side of town,' he explained in 'Hogan's Heroes' English as he took my map. 'Perhaps you have read ze wrong bus number. Ah, yes,

you have caught ze vun-oh-vun number bus instead of the vun-vun-vun number bus, so the best thing to do vould be to . . .'

I kept sneaking a look over his shoulder. Tazza was in the office scanning a board covered with car keys. Which was odd, because we had never lost the keys to Citroën, just the car to go with them.

The guard had a soft and helpful voice but shoulders like Mike Tyson and a huge baton strapped to his belt. I saw Tazza dart silently into the compound. The guard's voice went on and on. I wondered at what point I was meant to bail out, or whether I had to wait until Tazza made a charge at the barrier, which was probably going to write-off the Citroën and leave the barrier with no more than a mild headache. And, if Tazza was going to make a dash on his own, how was I supposed to get away?

As the guard commenced an excruciatingly complex explanation involving night buses and a walk – 'but not through zat park, zat is very dangerous' – a string of cars at the back of the compound had their lights and their horns suddenly come alive, one after the other. By the time the guard had grabbed his torch, said 'pardon' very calmly to me, and strode 100 metres or so to the other end of the compound, Tazza was back in the office hitting the button which caused the barrier to raise. He then disappeared again into the darkness.

The guard stayed at the other end of the compound a few seconds too long because soon one of the newly-lit cars started moving and nearly ran him over. He managed to smash one of the windows with his baton and was running closely behind it when it passed through the open barrier with a door swinging open for me to jump in.

Once we were safely out of the guard's reach, I sat among the beads of broken glass that had sprayed onto the front passenger seat, breathing heavily and wondering whether it was possible for my heart to beat any more forcefully. Tazza did little other than laugh and say: 'I told you it was pas de problème *in the late night'.*

But the road was a little wet and we seemed to be approaching an intersection far too quickly.

✣ ✣ ✣

NORMAN MAILER, THE AMERICAN writer, was presenting the French edition of his new book on Lee Harvey Oswald at the local FNAC, the huge book/music/electronics emporium. I organised to go with Isabelle. She had no idea who Lee Harvey Oswald was but had vaguely heard of Norman Mailer. She didn't know, however, what famous books he had written.

'Ah, well, he wrote . . . ah . . . ah. No, I think you've got me there.' I had failed another writer's test.

Mailer turned up but unfortunately and inexplicably he didn't say a word in any language. Just sat at a desk and signed books. Isabelle and I went downstairs to a café where, in the course of spending one hour in English then one hour in French, we sampled some freshly minted Beaujolais Nouveau. This light red wine, launched with great fanfare each year on the third Thursday of November, proved a little light and fruity for my taste. And for the rest of the world that year, it proved a little too French. International sales were at a record low.

Isabelle and I walked into the push of the Latin Quarter with its excitable crowds and outdoor restaurants below apartment blocks that are hundreds of years old. At a set of traffic lights we stood next to a man with a small triangular beard who was carrying a stretched canvas, blank and ready to be painted. Most of the people there, however, were New Zealanders. Some were probably local residents (I had met several Kiwis pretending to be Parisians), others had come in tour groups but all were rejoicing about a Rugby Test held earlier in the day at Parc des Princes, at the edge of the Bois de Boulogne.

'*Le rugby, c'est un religion dans la Nouvelle Zélande,*' I explained to Isabelle, clumsily, as we found a small bench next to what looked like a thousand-year-old wall.

'So I see,' she replied, without even asking the final score. There was a silence.

'I shouldn't say this, Anthony,' Isabelle suddenly announced in a low voice. 'But I feel like making love.'

It seemed the most unlikely thing for Isabelle to say. Maybe it was the Beaujolais. But one glass? 'Oh,' I said feebly, 'to anyone you know?'

Isabelle didn't answer. She sat there smiling, presumably (and hopefully) thinking of her new man. Or someone else. Perhaps the important thing was that she had smiled. She had actually smiled.

'I have started to read Orwell,' Isabelle suddenly announced, as if her previous comment had never been made. She reached for her bag and produced a paperback of *Inside the Whale and Other Essays*. 'You are right, he is a very clear writer. But it is not poetic, is it? It is journalism.'

And what was wrong with that?

Many of the Kiwis around us were wearing what was obviously the official tour sloppy joe: an All-Black jersey bearing the words: 'Chirac: You shat in our backyard, now it's our turn'. This was followed by something written in Maori that was not, I suspect, 'And furthermore, Jacques, I hope the wife and children are doing well'.

Chirac had his revenge a few days later at Mururoa Atoll with nuclear kaboom number four. The Australian government responded by forming the Canberra Commission on the Elimination of Nuclear Weapons. It was a commission fully empowered, no doubt, to write a stern letter to the *Sydney Morning Herald*.

✣✣✣

AS SANDRINE HAD PREDICTED, the industrial climate was heating up. The talk-tough Prime Minister, Alain Juppé, and the talk-even-tougher president, Jacques 'Boom Boom' Chirac, were trying to stamp out various long-standing work practices and social security arrangements they considered detrimental to France's modern economy. These included such things as the right of *les cheminots* (train drivers) to retire at fifty on a generous pension, an agreement dating back to the time when their smoke-filled lungs meant they were unlikely to live much longer than that anyway. Now, pointed out the government, they sat in air-conditioned glass booths and pushed buttons.

That might be true, agreed *les cheminots*. But Juppé's relatives – and those of various other politicians on both sides of the house – were living in ultra-luxurious Parisian apartments owned by the government and rented at bargain rates. In some cases they had been renovated to suit the tastes of the occupant, also at taxpayer's expense. This could possibly be described as a perk too but was not on the eradication list.

The result of the stand-off was strikes. And nobody does strikes quite like the French. On the last day of November only eight out of 500 regional trains were running. The drivers occupied their bosses' offices and there was not a single functioning *métro* line or bus within Paris. The mail sorters at La Poste were also *en grève* and the EDF and GDF (the power and gas companies) announced cuts because their own workers had walked off the job. Not to be outdone, university students stormed out, demanding more facilities and more teachers. At Benoit's university they were probably demanding more weapons of mass destruction too.

One morning it was estimated that the ring around Paris contained *bouchons*, or traffic jams, extending 500 kilometres (*bouchon* means cork; even the French word for traffic jam has a wine association). Hitchhikers, or *autostoppeurs*, were sometimes waving down cars that were travelling slower than walking pace. The smarter ones carried helmets so they could jump on the back of motorcycles. Soon the Eurotunnel was shut down, Channel ferries were redirected to Belgium and Holland, and the car plants *fermé*d their *portes* because they had no way of removing the finished cars from the factory compounds. Just for good measure, driving instructors decided it was the right moment to have their own protest by forming a parade of learner vehicles and driving it out into the car park that was now Parisian traffic. And what were the driving instructors protesting about? The driving test inspectors, who had been on strike for six weeks.

From here, the industrial situation deteriorated. Air

crews announced their strike would start on 7 December, but they looked set to be beaten to the punch because other staff at Charles de Gaulle and Orly airports had threatened to occupy the runways in the interim. Nuclear and hydro power stations were being turned off due to strikes within and without, and industrial action was being planned at pretty well every branch of the public service and every government department, as well as the Bank of France, prisons and hospitals.

Did the union of unaffiliated novel writers and students of the French language also go out? Not as such, though when the *métro* wasn't running, this member didn't go to his course. It would have been a ninety-minute walk each way for a 120-minute class, so I decided it was more profitable to study at home. To this end I was still working through French children's books and Brel's lyrics and such riveting texts as *501 French Verbs*. I was also trying to read Albert Camus in the original. Even though the book in question – *L'étranger* – was written in an unusually simple style, it took me several minutes per paragraph and even then I suspected I was not getting the full measure of his message. Indeed much of his message at all.

When I tried to catch up with Isabelle or Benoit for a conversation exchange it took well over an hour to walk to the centre of town. That wouldn't normally be a problem as there are few more interesting strolls anywhere in the world. Except, of course, when it is raining, sleeting or snowing – and it seemed to be doing one or the other each day. Or when every square metre of footpath is covered with the cars and motorcycles people have driven and ridden into the public transport-free city.

23

The Thought on the Stairs

*So, Herc, as we approached the set of red lights, Tazza yelled what sounded like '*Hamulse sa zepsute*' in a voice which was still unpanicked though a fair bit more urgent. I did not need to know any Polish to realise that he meant something very closely approximating 'the brakes are not working'. After mashing the pedal to the floor without any great effect, he snapped at the handbrake, causing the car to do a 360-degree spin across the intersection. We hit nothing, which was amazingly lucky.*

Tazza said, 'Perhaps I drive more slowly from here,' and he skilfully managed to keep it all straight and unbent for the fifteen minutes or so it took to get back to the hotel. When I finally woke, Tazza was already up and under the car, strapping up cables or tubing and taping a piece of plastic across the broken rear window.

'They are going to be looking for our number plate, aren't they,' I said with thinly veiled panic as we approached the border late that day.

'I am glad you tell me,' Tazza replied calmly before pulling over to the side of the road and attaching a set of plates he had liberated from the compound at the same time he had recovered the Citroën.

'I never do the stealing by *habitude*,' he explained as he turned our French-registered Citroën into a German one with the Swiss Army knife that he called a Polish Police knife. 'But they should never take away my car and break my brakes and hit my glass.'

It was just the two of us now. I suspected that Annie was already on her way back to Prague to again find happiness under some large, bearded Czech painter. And that I had just been fodder for her book.

As it turned out, Tazza and I were not even stopped at the *douanes* booth. We breezed across the border, despite the events of the night before, despite the fact our car was clearly still unroadworthy, and despite the fact France is supposed to be exercising special precautions because of the bombing campaign. The slackness had another benefit, though I was too nervous to even think about it at the time. I never had my dodgy paperwork checked.

The 2CV's brakes lasted right into Paris, failing only on a back-street near my apartment, when Tazza ran up the exhaust pipe of another car. The other driver never even stopped. But then in Paris, unless someone is killed, they usually do not. Tazza dropped me home.

'It has been a wonderful *voyage*,' he said, as if nothing out of the ordinary had happened, as if there was nothing remarkable about leaving as three and returning as two. 'It is so important to have the great *amis* like you, Peter.'

The monologue continued and at one stage I was worried he was going to tell me he loved me. Fortunately that did not come to pass.

✣ ✣ ✣

THE TADEUSZ CHARACTER WAS developing into the bloke for whom nothing was too difficult, who could always be optimistic about a situation while Peter Franklin could see only the worst, who could discover a solution when Pete could find only a problem. Notwithstanding a basis in fact, Tazza always did the thing his character dictated he should, rather than whatever it was the author was energetically trying to force upon him in order to make the rest of the plot work. Yes, after all these months of writing, I had characters – or at least a character – strong enough to take on a life of his or her own. More importantly, the fictional Tazza was becoming less the real Tadeusz and more what I had wanted my lost friend to be: someone who overcame his huge and obvious disadvantages and triumphed. Sure Tazza was frustrating and erratic, but he was charged with energy, he used all the talents he had, and many he didn't, and he was going somewhere. He was, to borrow Anaïs Nin's phrase, a man whom life made drunk.

As the Tadeusz character developed, I theorised – or perhaps simply realised – that we write for many reasons, noble and ignoble, but often we are doing one thing above all others. We are subconsciously trying to take control of things in a way that we can't in real life, and redress the things in our selves and our circumstances that we can't change. Even when we hide behind fictional characters and events, we are having a second go at the things we should have said, the things we wished we could have said, and the things we might have done that would have made it all turn out right.

The French have the expression *l'esprit d'escalier*, or 'the thought on the stairs'. It refers to the bright idea, the brilliant retort, the fabulous witty jibe, the conversation-killing, unanswerable debating point you think of after you've left the room and the moment has passed. *Letters to Hercules* included hundreds of pages of *l'esprit d'escalier*.

❖❖❖

ONE WEDNESDAY, FOR NO particular reason, I experienced what the French would call *un petit déclic*. The language suddenly started sounding like individual words rather than a mess of sounds with no clear start and finish. In the wake of this minor epiphany, did the city seem warmer, cleaner, friendlier, did the man on the street suddenly walk up and engage me in conversation, and the world around me fall into synch, as it would in the chorus of a musical comedy number? Er, no. The city was still a filthy, slushy, gridlocked mess. But I felt less like *I* was crammed with French words parked bumper-to-bumper and not likely to go anywhere. Sure, I was still a sentence behind when I heard anything and even then usually couldn't put all the pieces together quickly enough to get the meaning. But at least some of my efforts were paying off.

❖❖❖

THE COMBINATION OF THE cold weather and *la grève* was particularly hard on the homeless. They would normally try to make money in the *métro* during the day, and sleep there at night to escape the sub-zero temperatures. The doors to the rail system were now all locked, and there wasn't even the hot air coming through the *métro* street vents that might otherwise have provided a warm spot to sleep. A group of striking bus drivers agreed to pick up the homeless and take them to shelters. The government loaned the busses. Where my brown-paper man had gone, I had no idea.

On December 7, the fourteenth day of the strike, there was a combined demonstration of the aggrieved at the Carrefour de l'Odeon, on the Boulevard St Germain, and at about 200 other sites across France. Five days later we saw the biggest *manif* so far. Soon Bosnian, Croat and Serb delegates and other heads of state would gather in Paris to sign a treaty ending fighting in Bosnia-Herzegovina, where the first NATO peacekeepers had already arrived. This agreement hopefully meant the end of the fighting in the former Yugoslavia, which had gone on for four years, killed more than 200,000 people and made up to six million homeless. They had to bring the delegates in by helicopter, though, because Paris roads were at a standstill.

Public service unions called for a 'test of strength' and managed to gather somewhere between 300,000 protesters (police figure) and 560,000 (union figure), at Paris's Place Denfert-Rochereau. The next day doctors marched through the streets, along with art teachers. What the art teachers were demanding, I knew not. Perhaps more subdued colours and a fresh and innovative interpretation of the natural world.

The million or more cars coming into Paris each day were running over businessmen in suits and middle-aged women trying to make it to work on newly purchased rollerblades and bicycles, and the ambulances couldn't get anywhere near them. If that wasn't enough, youths in the suburbs were setting fire to things almost every night. The main streets of Paris were still patrolled by men with machine guns. The truckies were talking of blockading the city, so panic buyers had cleared the supermarket shelves. French language classes were cancelled until further notice.

Despite such chaos, it was business as usual for some. I walked through Place Vendôme as light snow fell and gusts of wind made it swirl and never quite hit the ground. While pulling the collar of my biggest jacket right up around my ears, I saw a new yellow Lotus sports car being unloaded from a truck outside the Ritz Hotel. The Lotus had a huge Christmas ribbon wrapped right around it and a bow on the roof.

24

AND IN CONFUSION

THE HEAT IN THE ROOM was becoming intense. I had already drunk half the duty-free Scotch – how I had put a full bottle in a cupboard and forgotten about it was a mystery – and was absolutely convinced that Ronald was here with me in the apartment.

I could swear, Herc, that he was really here. He was talking. Talking, talking, talking. The beads of sweat ran freely down my face and I distinctly remember standing up and screaming. 'Bullshit, Ronald. Bullshit! Bullshit! Bullshit! You never made an effort. You never ever tried. You loved being the victim. You did not use your abilities or your brilliant mind. You just soaked up everything you could get and did not contribute a bloody thing.

'If the government and your folks and the Department had had the sense to cut you free and push you out to sea years ago, you would have been better off, not worse off . . .'

I do not know what else I said, Herc, or indeed whether I really said anything. It was a mad, drunken exchange with no reference point as to where the real world started and ended. But whether I actually said it or not, I sensed it, I felt it, I articulated it with my entire being. At that moment I hated Ronald and everything he had done to himself. And to me. He had left me alone, yet he was talking only about himself and his woes and did not even care about the consequences of his selfish bloody departure.

The hate was so strong that I could not stand to be in the room with him for one more second. I needed fresh air and space around me. I thudded my glass down on the carpet, battled with the door and ran into the corridor, colliding with a short, thin woman dressed in a business suit.

'Are you all right?' she said in English with a soft French accent, and maybe just a hint of American. I am not sure whether I replied or not. I just slumped down to the ground and sat against the railing and nursed my head. I was breathing faster than I ever had before. This delicately built, dark-haired girl kneeled down beside me and put her hand on my shoulder in a clinical but entirely sympathetic way. When I looked up I saw that the door next to mine was open. The woman with her hand on my shoulder could be only one person.

✣✣✣

I KNEW I COULD finish a complete first draft of *Letters to Hercules* if I worked hard enough, and didn't stop to dwell on my first ever Christmas when the ice on the windows wasn't made of stick-on plastic. Benoit had other ideas. 'I want you to come to my house. My parents are away and the housekeeper has helped me prepare a pre-Christmas meal, with a course from each of the regions of France. Many friends want to meet my Australian author.'

Isabelle brought me a bottle of Champagne. 'You must open this, Anthony, on the day you finish your book.' Tazza scootered up with another bottle of red wine. 'Not Georgian this time, for my *bon ami* Tony. I bring *le vin Australien* – and a Polish honey cake.'

Sandrine's family invited me to their big meal on Christmas day. 'Every one of us is preparing a separate course,' she said, 'except you. You are the guest.'

I am ratting on all these people, I thought. Carlos the early morning chief of staff was right after all. I am a stupid prick. How could I face these people after *Letters to Hercules* hit the shelves?

Jacques Chirac didn't invite me to dinner. He celebrated his Yuletide with a 30-kiloton nuclear explosion. The bomb technicians were just about the only public employees who didn't walk out that time. At the start of that chilly January I wrote even more intensely, determined that I would not go home with more than one incomplete manuscript. Despite ratting-on-people reservations, I remained convinced the writing was back on track, that what I was producing was radical, exciting and refreshingly original. I was now thinking of *Letters to Hercules* less as an educational break from *Undermoon Bay* than as a fully-fledged novel in its own right.

Although the French had long since posted him notice to quit, Peter Franklin had by this time started to suspect, of his own volition, that there were good reasons to go back to Oz and return to at least some aspects of his old life. I guess he had to, as the nature of the book meant he couldn't easily stay in Paris longer than the author.

'There are only two things I am certain about,' Pete

wrote to Craig Hercules. 'That I would be mad to go back, and stupid not to.'

I resolved to finish *Letters to Hercules* then return to *Undermoon Bay* back in Australia and complete that as well before trying to get anything published. Of course I'd have to find some money to live on while doing this, but Sydney was cheaper than Paris. And such an approach would help me get around the usual dilemma of having all your life to write your first novel and twelve months to produce your second.

✣✣✣

THE GOVERNMENT BUCKLED OVER its industrial changes and no sooner had Paris started moving again, than the death of François Mitterrand brought it back to a standstill. Mitterrand was seventy-nine and his long-expected demise brought Parisians out in tens of thousands to place flowers (particularly roses, the symbol of the Socialiste party) at locations associated with the man. It wasn't hard to find them: Mitterand spent billions on architectural monuments, including the Opera Bastille and the underground extension to the Louvre Museum that incorporated the glass pyramid in the main square.

A Day of National Mourning was called, centred on the Place de la Bastille, where enormous photos of the former president had been erected. The cold and the rain didn't stop an army of admirers spilling out of the enormous square and into the surrounding streets, highlighting for me the extraordinary reverence with which the French hold their former leaders, and Australians don't. So many people gathering at night under huge black and white photos lit by spotlights, with rain drizzling onto tens of thousands of dark umbrellas looked curiously like a scene from an old film about a boldly imagined, slightly terrifying future.

World leaders gathered at Notre-Dame cathedral to celebrate a full Catholic mass for an avowed agnostic. There was also a more simple service in Mitterrand's hometown of Jarnac, where the former president's widow, Danielle, and their two sons stood beside Mitterrand's long-term mistress, Anne Pingeot, and his illegitimate daughter Mazarine. How French, I thought, imagining Benoit's booming voice: 'He wasn't just an administrator and nothing more. *Non, non, non.*'

As if to shut down the reverence-fest, Mitterrand's doctor Claude Gubler published a book called *Le Grand Secret*. It claimed Mitterrand had been diagnosed with prostate cancer back in 1981 and had falsified the health records he presented to the public each year since then. In his last eighteen months as president, Dr Gubler claimed, Mitterrand was totally unable to cope with the demands of office.

To Mitterrand-haters it was more proof that he was a power hungry liar. But to others, the disclosures were tantamount to violating a corpse, as well as a gross breach of patient confidentiality. The book was also a gross breach of normal practice in a country so zealous of guarding public figures' privacy. The family sued, the book was banned, the publisher fined a record amount and the author sentenced to a four-month prison term. However, *Le Grand Secret* sold 40,000 copies in the two days before it was removed from the shelves, and Dr Gubler's jail term was *avec sursis*, meaning suspended. I would have taken a full custodial sentence to have my book published and given so much publicity.

By late January the city was experiencing more snow than it had seen for ten years. I walked up the steps of the Eiffel Tower to look down on a completely white Paris.

It all ended with a bang – the biggest one yet. Chirac had already intimated the sixth test, of a 120-kiloton device at the Fangataufa Atoll, would be the last, even though the original program called for eight. So as not to appear to be backing down in the face of the global outcry, and dismal overseas sales of Beaujolais Nouveau, Chirac explained that the reduction was no more than a reflection of how clever the French technicians had been in extracting the vital information. Two days later Chirac announced that France had ended its nuclear testing 'once and for all' and would now sign the international test ban treaty.

25

Flight

With a clearer head, I may well have been terrified when Melanie sort of half-carried me back into my apartment. I may have feared I was going to be the subject of a medical experiment. But she spoke softly.

'We all have losses,' she said, 'and we all have different ways of dealing with them.'

I collapsed against the wall next to my desk, my knees drawn up to my chest. Melanie – I had to assume it was her – was now standing next to the sink, her back to me, making a cup of tea. She turned around and I could see her face clearly for the first time. I do not know why, but in my drunken state I was expecting to see Ronald's face framed by that long dark hair, as if it were just another way of him haunting me on this terrible night, as if this were not the surprisingly small girl next door but some enormous, unexplained manifestation of all my misery and confusion and self-disgust.

In Melanie's face I saw not Ronald's but that of a twenty-something professional . . . yet in that same face I could suddenly see Maria and my sister Louise, who did so much to try to reduce my grief but whom I could not even bring myself to hug during that horrible time. And whom I have not contacted once since I left Australia.

I looked at Melanie after I sipped the tea – with milk and one sugar, as if she had taken a precise order – and I am sure my mouth just fell open. Suddenly everything became clear. The living, the vital, the here and the now had been banging on my wall . . . not just that wall, but every wall, and I had been ignoring it in favour of wallowing in the past. I had failed to understand that what had happened at every point was what had to happen. No more and no less. It could not, and probably should not, have been any other way. The great NSW Jackpot Lottery of life. That was Ronald's own phrase.

'Many things have been put to rest this evening,' Melanie said. 'I will always be next door if you need me.'

The answer came out without me even thinking. 'I know that now.'

That was last week. I am still buzzing with the bizarre and unpleasant excitement of the encounter. Indeed, of the two encounters. I woke the next morning with a huge hangover, and still unsure how much of what I remembered of the night before was real. But I had thrown off a great weight. I had realised that the person for whom I was doing so much grieving was too self-obsessed to care. That his time had come simply because he could no longer see straight and was not interested in trying to. He was like one of those people in books and films who die not because something has happened to them, but because they simply no longer want to live. And I realised that I was well on the way to doing exactly the same thing.

I now know – or think I know – that the 'meeting' with Ronald and my reaction to it was an entirely positive thing. Like a piece of noble treason. An act of perfect lack-of-contrition. A 'sorry but you will never get the better of me' declaration. A hate letter for someone you love; one that needs to be delivered for the sake of life itself. If that all sounds very purple, Herc, it cannot be blamed on alcohol. I am stone cold sober and have been so for five whole days. And the above is exactly how I feel.

✣✣✣

I WAS LEAVING PARIS three days after my French course finished, two days before the lease ran out and one week before my yellowing plane ticket clocked up one year and expired. I was flying back to the great unknown. In the meantime, there was a written and oral French exam to sit, despite so much of my course having been wiped out by the strike. I was collared after the exam by Sarah, who wanted to do a post mortem. She asked how I went ('Horribly,' I said, concisely), and what I had done in the 'written expression' section ('I wrote as little as possible, because that reduced the chance of mistakes.').

'Well, I wrote as much as possible, lovey,' she replied, 'because that increased the chance of someone like me getting something right.'

It probably always works this way, but language-wise I was making the most dramatic progress at about the time I was leaving. There had been a snowballing effect; the more I learned the easier it was to learn more, and now I was going back to a country where all sorts of tongues were spoken, but almost never French. I was still finding it difficult in shops and banks, particularly with impatient servers or a queue behind. And people in shops still replied in English when I spoke to them in French. Even people working in bread shops and ticket offices spoke *la langue de Shakespeare* – seemingly unaware that they, as French people, were supposed to be famously vehement in their resistance to it. Eventually I decided I just didn't care and continued to talk in French no matter what language they answered in, and no matter how grumpy they were.

Leaving Paris involved handling the French bureaucracy in reverse. Having the gas and telephone cut off and deposits returned, taking care of other administrative things and freighting to Australia the huge number of books I'd collected along the way was no easier than expected. At the EDF office one day, trying to get my electricity deposit back, I saw all these people queuing and I rounded them up on the outside and went straight for one of the desks where a clerk was sitting. Hell, if those people weren't getting on with it, why should I wait for them?

There were farewells to attend to. I caught up with Tadeusz to say 'good *au revoir-derci*!' His final words to me were '*Milo z panem robic interesy*', which I know means something approximating 'It's a pleasure to have done business with you'. I know because his parting gift was a Polish phrasebook.

'This is for you,' he explained. 'Not just for this day but for all the next days and next years.' I think he meant I could keep it. I looked at his face – his darting black eyes, his blond fringe, his ridiculous little beard – for what I assumed would be the last time.

'Tazza,' I said during a rare pause at his end, 'I hope

someday I'll read in *Paris Match* that you've made a billion francs. Because Tazza – my good Polish mate Tazza – firstly it would mean that I could read French properly and secondly, I'd love to see you do well. I'd love to see you give a gentle finger to these Parisians, and I'd love to see you do it from a huge penthouse overlooking Parc Monceau. With your own private lift.'

I meant every word of it. I was the richer for having known him.

I completed one last on-screen read-through and tidy-up of *Letters to Hercules*. I would have preferred to do the tweaking on a print-out, but at 480 foolscap pages I feared the book would kill my little bubblejet printer. I invited Isabelle over.

'To friends and a complete first draft,' I said, pouring two glass tumblers of the Moët she had given me for Christmas. Another flurry of snow hit the apartment window.

'Cheers and *santé*,' she said, her demeanour just that little bit less straight-faced than in the past. 'But surely, Anthony, I can now read it.'

'No, not a word. Okay, three words,' I said, hitting a key on the laptop. 'I will show you the title on the screen, that is all.'

Isabelle put her glass tumbler on the desk and leaned forward. '*Letters to Hercules*. It sounds very classical.'

'I think you'll be surprised,' I said guardedly.

'I want to be surprised.'

She didn't want to be surprised, really.

'I have brought you a little parting gift,' Isabelle said as she passed me an elaborately wrapped stack of little French paperbacks, including works by Rimbaud, Pascal,

Montaigne, Rabelais, Proust and Maupassant, plus Paul Verlaine's *Femmes* and *Hombres*.

'That Verlaine one is a little special,' she added as I opened a sketch of, well, what you'd expect would illustrate poetry considered so obscene it was suppressed even in France until well after World War II.

Isabelle smiled. She even laughed a little. But it was an unsure smile and a slightly sad laugh. 'And whatever is in your mysterious manuscript, Anthony, I really, really should like you to have a great success with it.'

❖❖❖

I JUMPED ON MY suitcase and wondered how I could ever sneak so much bulk and weight onto an aeroplane. There was a knock on the door. It was my landlord, Alberto. He had brought his daughter, Anna, who had returned from her first stint of university in England. She did the talking. 'We have come to say goodbye, and to thank you for being such a good, ah, *locataire*.'

I could sense Alberto looking around the room to make sure I hadn't covered anything in graffiti or built an illegal extension.

'We have bought you a present,' said Anna.

'That's very generous of you,' I said, smiling a lot and hoping it was light and compact – or easily bin-able. Alberto passed something across.

'You use it for cooking, to rest the hot things on,' Anna explained as I pulled the tissue paper off a quite beautiful metal disc, with the outline of the Eiffel Tower in the centre. 'It is made of, 'owyousay, cast eye-ron.'

With that extra anchor in my bag, it was off to the airport. Sandrine's father had the car parked outside – triple-parked outside – with the engine running. Soon we were off.

'So was it all a success?' asked Sandrine as Gilbert sped through a red light and screeched down a ramp onto the Boulevard Périphérique.

'Sure, I've been in France, what, nine and a half months and I've certainly enjoyed myself. I have a complete manuscript of what I think could be a very, very good book, and another one that is maybe fifty per cent complete. And one day, I promise, I'll tell you what they are about.'

Sandrine offered a patient smile.

'Your French is good too,' she added generously. 'A lot of people have spent more time here and haven't learned any French and haven't written anything either. So you are ahead there.'

Others, I thought to myself, have become fluent, or have banged out *The Great Gatsby* or *Tropic of Cancer*. So I was behind there.

'I think of it like this,' I said to Sandrine above Gilbert's almost constant sounding of the horn. 'Even if nothing else ever comes of what I have done here, it has been a fascinating time and a wonderful opportunity to do a lot of thinking on a lot of subjects. A sort of mental spring cleaning, going through the attic and hurling out ideas and opinions that have been sitting around for ten or twenty years, and cleaning up and improving the ones that are worth hanging onto.

'And I'm truly sad to be leaving such a beautiful city, and people like you.'

Note the phrase 'even if nothing else ever comes of what I have done here'. People say things like that. They don't actually mean them. Something just *had* to come of it. I'd put so much work into it. I didn't want to think that it was even remotely possible that I'd blown my savings on a folly. That my dreams were just . . . dreams.

26

Dismissing You Already

In these past few *months I have run through the whole Ronald story, which was clearly what I needed to do as belated mourning. In the process I have successfully chiselled away my idealised past, that undefined feeling that things and people used to be better. It is as if my distorted memories were just so many possessions, that I am a character in Greek mythology that I read about in those illustrated oh-so-English children's books I was given when I was young. This character trimmed back his estate to just a cup with which to drink. That is, until one day when he was sitting on his mound of earth thinking deep non-material thoughts, and he saw a boy drink from the stream by scooping the water with his hands.*

At that point the man realised that he did not need a cup either. And he certainly did not need a Montblanc Meisterstück *149 fountain pen.*

⁂

Tazza rang yesterday. *I think it was to tell me that he was too busy to talk. Nonetheless I needed to see a familiar face, so I suggested we meet for a coffee. He squeezed it in between his various jobs and courses. Tazza drove me to a tiny café next to one of the old canals in the east of the city. The Citroën still had plastic over the rear window and canvas over the boot and even more bumps and scratches than before. There was a definite lean to one side. Tazza wore a shiny new leather jacket, which would not have looked out of place on a rock star, and was scrubbed and shaved and looked the most presentable I had ever seen him. And he parked in a bus zone, just like a real Parisian.*

'I am slowly coming around to the idea, Tazza,' I explained, 'that I should at least consider going home. Not just to my country, but to my city, my street and my house.'

Tazza looked at me, narrowed his eyes and stayed still for longer than at any time since I had met him. Then he said in the clearest English I had heard him use: 'So many times we do not get even one chance. Do not miss it, my good friend Peter, when we get two'.

That was enough to tip the balance. So yes, Herc, I am doing it in reverse. I have left no addresses or numbers with anyone here. I am making a clean break. Because I do not want to be the person I have been here, any more than I want to be the man who left Sydney almost a year ago. For me the past few days have been magic. Like one perfect, new, sunny beginning. Setting off afresh. A new calendar. Starting at day one, just like the French revolutionaries or the Khmer Rouge. But without the guillotine, or the plastic bag over the bonce.

The people I have met here have saved me life. With the good and bad things they have done (and I have done to them), each has changed me just that little bit. And

Maria: she has put up with so much but is still willing to have me back. There have to be some changes on both sides, but they will be so much easier to discuss when I am not filled with poison, when I am not somehow blaming every one alive for not living up to my mythologised standards of the departed. But it is also you, Herc, who helped save me. You heard me out – I would like to think – when no-one else in the world was listening.

You have no memory of what I look like, I'm sure, and our one-sided correspondence must end here. But if a bloke ever jumps into your cab with a plain plastic ballpoint in his top pocket, and the look of a man who has been dragged away from a public execution at the last possible moment and given a second chance to make something of his life, ask that bloke his name. It just might be Peter Franklin. All the very best for the future, whatever you want it to be. Your bon ami, *Pete.*

✣✣✣

THE GHASTLY GREEN CARPET in my inner-city terrace had come with the house and I had never got around to replacing it. When I arrived home it looked even greener than when I had last seen it, and the rising damp was even more elevated. Worse still, when I left Sydney it was a big and vibrant city yet I returned to a small and dull town choking in the sleepy heat of February. Everything was slow, quiet, bland. I felt out of place, out of sorts, and very, very low. Yet I was also overcome with huge urgency. I had to draw a line under something and say 'finished', if only because so many people were asking the question I least wanted to hear: 'How did you go with your book?' And so I was back to writing within days or, more specifically, printing out *Letters to Hercules* for the first time and furiously writing notes in the margins.

I clung to the idea of finishing two books before submitting anything. I was determined not to speak to a publisher until I had a knock-'em-dead, couldn't-be-turned-down work in hand, and another one in the other hand. That way I could avoid deadlines, expectations and all those things that would follow a publisher's advance based on some promising early chapters. Assuming I could obtain a publisher's advance based on some promising early chapters.

With my self-administered literary grant exhausted I had bills to pay and had to start earning again. I began writing corporate profiles and technical literature for manufacturing companies. I believed this would be less taxing on my time and mind than returning to journalism. Anyway, I'd sworn not to return to journalism. I remained negative about my life but positive about *Letters to Hercules* as I prepared to pass it to my first reader. She worked through it – all 130,000 words – and I was too nervous to do pretty well anything else while this happened. She was a harsh and forthright critic and the world might, just might, contain people better at handling criticism than me. I went for long walks, pretended to read magazines, looked at the telephone sitting there in its cradle.

The report finally came back: my reader said bits of it were excellent but there were too many other bits. I attributed the comment to malice, spite and any other vile impulse that came to mind. Nothing makes an author's blood boil more than a negative critique from someone to whom the author has been generous enough to show his or her work. My house and my city were already bringing me down and now, after all the work I had put into this book, how dare she tell me it was anything less than the work of brilliance we both always knew I was capable of.

'Well, I'll get back to work and make it better,' I said, as I picked up her heavily marked-up print-out. What I thought though was: 'You are wrong. And won't you feel like a goose when it's a huge success.'

It didn't help that I had just turned thirty-five, the age at which Henry Miller declared himself a complete failure as a writer and man. Sure, his story eventually turned out well, but so many people we've never heard of must have also declared themselves complete failures at the same age – and been entirely correct. I realised I didn't have the energy in my disheartened and dispirited state to look at *Letters to Hercules* objectively. Instead I returned to early Australia, in an artistic sense at least. I had to start back at the very start. I had to completely rethink the style of *Undermoon Bay* and look at the characters from a completely different perspective, to delete things I had spent excruciating hours, days and weeks producing, in order to spend even more excruciating hours, days and weeks finding a new way to tell the same story. And that is what I started to do.

Gradually Sydney and Australia's charms again made themselves known. Many afternoons I played the tourist and walked across the Harbour Bridge or through the lush greenness of the Royal Botanic Gardens, dealing with the usual plot-point and characterisation nightmares as the cool, salty sea breezes swept across from the east. Work progressed feverishly on *Undermoon Bay*, version two, and when I finally felt I was making serious progress with it, I returned for a fresh encounter with Peter, Tadeusz, Maria, Annie and Herc.

Many Great Works have been written in the manner of *Letters to Hercules*. All the pointers were there: an intense, almost fanatical push of energy, the stimulation of strange environs, the inspiration of dramatic circumstances and the complete artistic isolation of the author from normal influences. However, it became apparent this time through that although *Letters to Hercules* had been produced in the same way as many masterpieces, there were few other similarities.

Sure, when I reread some parts of the manuscript they still seemed vibrant and original and funny and sad and personal and engaging. There was tension, action and movement and how dare she criticise my efforts. But when I read other parts I scratched my head and thought 'My God, how did that seem good at the time?' and 'Why the hell did I write that . . . how did it even seem acceptable?' I realised at that moment there *is* something more devastating than a negative critique. It is the realisation that the critique makes a lot of sense and confirms what the author may have already secretly suspected but was fighting with every ounce of self-delusion he could call on. Yes, my 130,000 words included many of the wrong words, and where I had used the right ones, they were often in the wrong order.

Worse still, I couldn't run away from the fact that *Letters to Hercules* betrayed what I had set out to do – to write real fiction. Yes, I could tell myself that I was trying to come to terms with events and that, at any rate, I was changing places, times, names and dialogue. I could also half-convince myself that real life was a starting point and nothing more; that the structure was a technique to break through the impasse, and as the fictitious story developed, the connection between my story and that of Peter Franklin, or Ronald's story and that of my friend, had been thoroughly severed.

But no matter what I said to myself, and no matter how hard I tried to believe it, the reality was that my original intention was adulterated beyond recognition. With *Letters to Hercules* I broke my original rules almost point-for-point. I was revisiting my childhood, I was scrawling in the first person, I was setting the thing in my own world. I was taking real events and fictionalising them, I was getting back at enemies by incorporating characters in my story who were obviously based on real people, I was ratting on my friends and colleagues by appropriating their foibles, peccadilloes and failed relationships for my own literary ends.

I had always resolved that my friend and our friendship would never be reduced to an after-dinner story. Yet here I was using those events and worse still, those feelings, as the basis of a novel for the whole world to see. And that wasn't the end of it. Much that I didn't like about my own personality had made its way into that of Peter Franklin, while what had started as a sympathetic portrayal of the Ronald character had ended up a harangue. The screwy parenting he had, the chemical imbalances in his system, the constant need for attention that was almost certainly the result of a lack of it at some crucial point in his early life . . . all this somehow accounted for nothing. I just ended up angry with the waste and, in some sections, I reduced his problems to nothing more than an assault on me. It seemed as if he was behaving like he was solely to cause injury. I was the victim, not him.

I didn't like the person I had become in those pages. It wasn't me, or it wasn't the me I wanted to be. And when looking over the manuscript with fresh eyes, I realised the supposedly big questions it set out to ask looked remarkably compact. Funny what happens in a vacuum, isn't it.

I still didn't discuss the details of my work with the wider world. But as we sat in an inner-city pub, my mate Greg could sense something was amiss.

'I don't know,' I finally responded. 'Well, I do know. It's the book, of course. It always is. I've wanted to write fiction almost since I was born. I finally got the chance . . . and in Paris I thought I had actually finished a novel that was worthwhile. Now I'm realising that I've stuffed it up.'

'You don't need to get so upset,' Greg replied, as he took a musician-sized swig from his schooner of Toohey's New. 'It's not like you are the only hopeless failure. Most people come well short of achieving their ambitions.'

The bastard.

'Seriously,' he continued. 'You're not without talent, and you're certainly putting in the hours. I refuse to believe your book isn't good.'

'I'd love to think you were right,' I sighed. 'But at the moment my supposedly finished book is unreliable fact and equally unreliable fiction.'

'Don't be so hard on yourself,' Greg said. But then friends are meant to say things like that.

'If I don't mark myself harshly,' I replied, recalling a voice from long ago, 'I'll never improve.'

✣✣✣

MY LIFE AND MY novel-writing had converged on the streets of Paris, much as they had for Henry Miller. Though also nothing like they had for Henry Miller. Now in my mind they had to be separated and the experience written off as part of an apprenticeship. In a more romantic period of history I would have torn *Letters to Hercules* into little pieces, or sat throwing it page by page into the fire, watching my writing being consumed by the flames, my failure burned from the annals of history and sent skywards.

Joyce threw an early version of *Portrait of the Artist as a Young Man* into a fire in disgust, reputedly because he believed others didn't recognise his genius. I was about to do something similar because I couldn't recognise a smidgeon of genius in myself. But in the modern age you don't do anything as poetic or filmic as burn or tear up your manuscript. Sure you can scorch or rip up the print-out, and I did the latter with enormous thoroughness. But the real act is in deleting the file, and the back-up. And the back-ups of the back-ups you made and sealed and mailed to various secure houses with the instructions 'not to be opened under any circumstances'.

When you think everything is gone, you then try to forget that it ever existed. But of course you deliberately forget to wipe one disc, just in case. Because a novel represents so much work and to lose a complete work, even a thoroughly unsatisfactory work, would always be regretted.

By the time I had hit the delete button on *Letters* and resolved to work exclusively on *Undermoon Bay*, I was nervous. I had been writing fiction for twelve months straight, and still had nothing presentable. I couldn't have imagined just how much more time was to pass with me having still nothing finished to my satisfaction.

It took another year of intense work to produce the first complete manuscript of *Undermoon Bay*. It was a 150,000-word tome telling the complete story of the independent city-state from the time half of Australia's First Fleet formed the colony at Foundation Point, Undermoon Bay. The writing style was beautiful, delicate and precise, if I may say so myself. Which, under the circumstances, I may. But, alas, those qualities alone don't make for a good book, any more than a catchy title or a delightful typeface does.

'Bits of it are excellent,' explained my trusted, long-suffering reader, whom I was now talking to again. 'But again there are too many other bits.'

This time I could see her logic. The condition wasn't terminal but radical surgery was required. It seemed the contents fell into two categories: things that should be cut out and things that should be in earlier. *Undermoon Bay* contained too many words, too many events and not nearly enough continuity. There were too many characters, and too few of them passed my tiger test. Which is to say, if a tiger appeared out of nowhere and mauled a character to death, would anyone care? Just when I felt sick of trying to find a way of remoulding the mountain of words, events and people, a chance comment revealed a way of simplifying it. Reinvigorated, I completely re-wrote and restructured the manuscript, hacking out yet more chapters, characters and subplots.

After six more months of intense toil, I had a much better, brighter, tighter manuscript. The first eighty years was told in just a page or two of reminiscing, and the story stopped with the sound of gunshots on the eve of World War I. The printer Kingsley M. Baker didn't make the cut, nor Elvii the Pelvii, nor the First Undermann Regiment, which had had achieved singular – and peculiar – distinction under enemy fire in Africa. The new material was nothing like those early pieces I had written in Paris. It was smarter, wiser, richer, everythinger.

And by this time I'd managed to overcome my disgust with *Letters to Hercules*. It was not a mistake to write it; I needed to write it, though for myself and not for anyone else. I needed the practice in form and structure and, perhaps more importantly, I had to clarify certain things in my mind. I had to walk a few devils around the block to exorcise them.

My reader returned to *Undermoon Bay*, version two, and unfortunately still didn't think it read like a bought one. I produced a third version, completely revamped with new scenes and revised plotlines, and gave it to a neighbour, who was fortuitously also a retired book editor. She was an equally harsh critic, but the comments were improving. She even went to far as to say, in a Boston accent that twenty-five years in Australia hadn't softened, 'I think you have a special gift.'

I hope she believed it. I needed to believe somebody believed it, because the idea of a fourth bout of cutting, culling, tightening and improving was starting to scare me.

When I'd set out to reinvent *Undermoon Bay* in Sydney, I was working in a tiny attic overlooking a building site where a Bi-Lo supermarket complex was growing taller each day. While awaiting the verdict on *Undermoon Bay*, version three, I had started work on a new novel with the working title of *New Novel.* I saw it as a way of clearing the brain before going back to what I was sure would be my final, definitive, couldn't-be-turned down version of *Undermoon Bay*. And I started giving into requests for journalism, sadly facing the reality that even if my novel was launched and was a moderate success by Australian fiction standards it was going to earn me less than a few weeks' solid journalism.

✣✣✣

I PICKED UP THE phone to hear Benoit's voice as clear as if he were in the same room as me, as if he were again making my coffee saucer rattle. Benoit – the most French person in the world – had decided to move to Sydney to improve his English and study common law, as opposed to France's Napoleonic Law.

'October, eh?' I said. The concept of moving Down Under to improve your English was unusual enough, and I worried further that Australia was a lot less like France than France was. He'd be unhappy, I figured. 'You can stay in the spare room until you set yourself up.'

'No, I will book an 'otel for the first few days – I must be independent,' he said. 'But tell me, are you published yet?'

At least I was no longer betraying anyone, so I could open up a little. 'I have almost finished a radically different fourth version of the book I started in France. It is a historical novel called *Undermoon Bay*.'

'It is taking a long time, no?'

'I always knew it was going to take a while.'

The Bi-Lo was long since finished, along with an adjoining Kmart and Coles. Yet I was still sitting in that same small attic for twelve or more hours a day, surrounded by manuscripts. I had completed two-and-a-quarter literary novels (though only one and a quarter remained), plus a couple of children's books. But I'd never gone back to the Mills & Boon.

A lesser man would have screamed at the ceiling regularly, whereas I did it only every so often. And for every bad week, there were a few hours of joy unlike anything to be found in the business world. When something went right, when I looked at a phrase or a sentence or a paragraph and said to myself 'that has nailed it exactly', there was a private elation that seemed to make it all worthwhile.

More than three years had passed since I had written the first lines of *Undermoon Bay* in Sandrine's apartment in Paris. For most of those three years it was never far from the top of my mind, even when working on other things. It had made me deliriously happy and at times the prospect of failure had made me as miserable as I had ever felt. But now I had made it to a self-declared finish line. I had distilled thousands of hours of work into 400 pages, every single sentence as good as I could make it. I was sure *Undermoon Bay* was everything that *Letters to Hercules* wasn't and, importantly, it had none of my life in it. Yet because of what I had learned with *Letters to Hercules*, I had managed, I thought, to finally give *Undermoon Bay* a heart.

In mid-1998, I sent the first three chapters to Penguin Books, which I saw as the only company capable of eventually releasing *The Complete Penguin Tony Davis*.

I quickly received an enthusiastic reply. Send us the rest poste haste, they said. And I posted it very hastily indeed.

'Never a moment's doubt,' I lied to myself.

Epilogue

A Qualified Success

The dream start was followed by the long nervous wait. The author picked at the edges of New Novel. *He took the chance to earn some money. He was going to need it for the long haul, what with his forthcoming three-book deal with Penguin and everything. He waited a week, then another week. Then a month, then another month. Should he phone? He was unsure, but then he never felt as small and powerless as when dealing with the faceless organisations that held something as important as his literary future in their hands.*

What if they thought he was harassing them? What if he blew his chance because they thought he was pushy. But then, what if he blew it because the manuscript never arrived and he never phoned to check? He was staying awake at night worrying.

✣✣✣

'Hello,' I said obsequiously. 'I sent in a manuscript to Robyn. Called *Undermoon Bay*. She asked me to send it.'

'Robyn is not really working here at the moment,' said a cold, disinterested voice. 'Well, actually, she's on very extended leave.'

How could that happen, how could my sole fan within Penguin, within the entire fiction publishing industry, have left straight after requesting the manuscript?

'Davis, hmm,' said the woman. 'No, definitely no record of your manuscript.'

'Should I send another one in?'

'You could do that,' she replied with no discernible enthusiasm. I dispatched it immediately.

A week later, on an impossibly warm and clear Sydney October day, Benoit rang the bell. Backlit in the doorway by the brightness outside, he looked twice his normal size. When my eyes adjusted, it was obvious he was laden with packages.

'I have brought things to remind you of your time in Paris,' this one-man tourist board boomed effusively, with sweat running down his temples. Beneath the cargo, he looked much thinner than when I had last seen him, with a new, short-cropped haircut.

'Look what military service has done to you,' I said.

'Yes, I am smoking now too,' he replied.

Benoit walked through the door, plunked his plastic bags and packages down and pulled out three small tins of paté, a bottle of red wine and a small stack of French CDs. He also produced a packet of Gauloises and a lighter from his top pocket.

'Thanks for bringing these things, Benoit. And sorry about the weather.'

'No, no, no. The weather is good, it is fine.' He lit his cigarette, then held his finger up and smiled as if he had just understood my comment about the weather. 'And Tony, this was on the doorstep.'

Benoit rifled among his things and produced a large, white, oblong package. The Penguin logo was clearly visible on the top left-hand corner. From that point everything happened in slow motion. Benoit must have noticed me lose colour, he must have sensed all life falling from my voice. Penguin wasn't likely to send back the manuscript to tell me it had been accepted. Benoit took his cigarette out of his mouth and passed the envelope across. It came to me smoothly, slowly, silently. I could see the little orange flightless bastard bird winking malevolently at me, as if to say, 'stiff shit, son'. Benoit said something, then something else. Even a voice like his wasn't going to cut through my panicked contemplation. It could be a mistake, of course. The envelope could contain an edited, marked-up copy. Or there could be a contract within the envelope, a contract that ran to 400 one-sided pages – the precise same bulk as the book – because there were so many countries and territories requiring rights.

'Thanks,' I whispered to Benoit as I slowly tightened my grip on the package. I felt like my insides had been hoovered out. 'I'll be back in a minute.'

I walked out to the small rear courtyard and ran my shaking thumb along the edge of the envelope. Out fell the complete bound and jacketed manuscript I had prepared for Penguin, and a form letter. The first word of the second sentence was 'Unfortunately'. I put it all down on a bench, took a deep breath, walked back to Benoit in the front room, looked at him straight in the eye and mustered the best imitation of a smile I could manage. 'So, coffee?'

✣ ✣ ✣

It took weeks to come to terms with the fact that my final, definitive, couldn't-be-turned down version of *Undermoon Bay* had been turned down. But at least Penguin said they wished me well. Elsewhere. And I could hope that other publishers could see the book's merits.

Alas, they couldn't.

I had rewritten and massaged *Undermoon Bay* to within an inch of *my* life, yet the rejection letters came in so quickly I suspected those publishers had also eliminated the time-consuming step of reading the book. As I read yet another form letter from someone who had 'carefully considered the manuscript', or was filled with 'regret that such a work cannot be fitted into our publishing program at this time', I blackly contemplated using these declarations of failure to wallpaper the attic office. And I laughed a small, sad laugh when I thought of how I had carefully torn up my print-out of *Letters to Hercules* a few pages at a time, making sure that the rip went straight through the centre of the text. Such was my thoroughness, I made separate piles of the left and the right halves and threw them out in different bins, just in case someone tried to reassemble and read so much as a single page. How stupidly optimistic was that?

Then I read in the newspaper that a student without a single prior published word to her name was soon to receive an international, multilingual launch for her first novel. The publisher insisted it was on merit alone and had nothing to do with who she was. Which happened to be Mazarine Pingeot, the illegitimate daughter of François Mitterrand, spectacularly outed by *Paris Match* just before the president's death.

Had she put as much work into her book as I had into

Undermoon Bay? Had she, at twenty-three years of age, spent as much time refining her craft? Had she produced other novels and written them off as nothing but practice? I wanted to doubt it, but there was a more depressing possibility. Maybe she had the raw talent to effortlessly knock out what I could produce, or fail to produce, only through years of sheer hard work.

Maybe her book was good enough and mine wasn't.

Either way, the growing realisation that my supposed *tour de force*, my *pièce de résistance*, my Great Work, wasn't going to be published in even one country and one language made it harder to motivate myself on new projects, or to even continue with *New Novel*.

It hurts to be rejected. It can hurt for years afterwards. And in the here and now I couldn't evade the fact that I was thirty-seven years old and turning down paying work to produce manuscripts that nobody wanted. The world was becoming wired and webbed, and I was sitting in my attic office, alone, stalled, dispirited. And so I did it. I sold out. Took a real job.

After years working in shorts and bare feet, I put on a suit and walked out into the real world. That didn't stop me getting up earlier and earlier each morning to write yet more. Or publishers continuing to reject it. I'd regularly turn up to the office having already completed three hours of writing at home – and having added to that huge, unread pile of words.

Without warning, the calendar declared it was ten years since I had awarded myself that original literary grant. Reflection was needed. Serious reflection. In that decade I had written hundreds of thousands of words of fiction.

I had mapped out novels, plays and short stories. I had invented characters, painted immense scenes, instinctively grabbed my pen or dictation machine in the middle of a walk, a business meeting or a conversation to note yet another gem or germ of an idea for a play, novelette or weighty literary opus, or to record a snippet of dialogue that I thought could simply, starkly reveal something about a character.

I had pulled apart and remade thousands of pages in the hope I could make each of them just that tiny bit better. I had worked away mornings and nights with the heartfelt belief that if I tried hard enough I could achieve something special. Yet, as a writer of fiction, I remained every bit as unpublished, every bit as unpaid, every bit as unread. I had given everything to soar above that row of parked cars but had misjudged the speed, the angle and the distance and had thudded like a rag-doll from roof to roof.

Wasn't it time to grow up, to move on, to accept that humans shouldn't try to fly without wings? Couldn't I console myself by saying that like Rick and Elsa from *Casablanca*, or indeed F. Scott, Ernest and James Augustine Aloysius Joyce, I'd always have Paris?

No, no, *non!* Only in movies and Mills & Boon novels is that ever enough. I may never win the Nobel Prize for Literature and – this following thought really does make me shudder – I may never even have a novel published. But to never have a serious work of fiction on the bookshop and library shelves wouldn't be nearly as big a failure as to never write one. Or two or three.

And that is not all I have learned along the way. A life seen from the inside doesn't need to be an endless series of defeats. You can, for example, lie to yourself. Or more seriously, you can finally begin to understand that success or failure in the marketplace is not a referendum on your worth as a human being. You can even start to appreciate that The Great Work may not be the book itself. The Great Work just might be the act of getting up each morning and striving to do what you most want to do better than you have ever done it before. And then one day – perhaps, just perhaps – better than anyone has ever done it.

It's a more than *Letters-to-Herculean* task but this writer, for one, will keep trying. Yes I will I said yes I Will yes

Acknowledgements

Thanks to: Carolyn Walsh for her unlimited support and wise advice, Jude McGee, who commissioned the project and guided its early stages, Jessica Dettmann, who so skilfully produced the final edit, Fiona Henderson and John O'Brien, who showed so much faith, and the late Anne Sahlin for her encouragement, expertise and friendship. Huge gratitude too to those who read the manuscript along the way and gave invaluable feedback: Glenn Morrison, Alexa Moses, Dave Mason-Cox, Steve McLaren, Michael Stahl, my parents Pedr and Dolores and my brothers Damian and Glyn. Lastly, to the wonderful Ludis – my family away from home.

Tony Davis lives in Sydney, Australia, with his wife, Carolyn, and their three young sons: William, James and Daniel.